The Michigan Historical Reprint Series

Reprints from the collection of the University of Michigan University Library

This volume is produced from digital images created through the University of Michigan University Library's preservation reformatting program. The Library seeks to preserve the intellectual content of items in a manner that facilitates and promotes a variety of uses. The digital reformatting process results in an electronic version of the text that can both be accessed online and used to create new print copies. This book and thousands of others can be found in the digital collections of the University of Michigan Library. The University Library also understands and values the utility of print, and makes reprints available through its Scholarly Publishing Office.

For access to the University of Michigan Library's digital collections, please see http://www.lib.umich.edu.

The Scholarly Publishing Office seeks to disseminate high-quality, cost-effective scholarly content through both print and electronic publishing. Information about the Scholarly Publishing Office can be found at http://spo.umdl.umich.edu.

The Scholarly Publishing Office
the University of Michigan
University Library

HISTORICAL SKETCH

OF THE

UNITED STATES NAVAL ACADEMY.

PREPARED BY DIRECTION OF

REAR-ADMIRAL C. R. P. RODGERS, U. S. N.,

SUPERINTENDENT U. S. NAVAL ACADEMY,

FOR THE

DEPARTMENT OF EDUCATION AT THE
INTERNATIONAL EXHIBITION, 1876.

BY

PROFESSOR JAMES RUSSELL SOLEY, A. B.,
U. S. NAVY,
HEAD OF THE DEPARTMENT OF ENGLISH STUDIES, HISTORY, AND LAW, AT
THE U. S. NAVAL ACADEMY.

WASHINGTON:
GOVERNMENT PRINTING OFFICE.
1876.

CONTENTS.

PART I.—HISTORICAL SKETCH.

PART II.—THE NAVAL ACADEMY IN 1876.

APPENDIX.

PART I.

HISTORICAL SKETCH.

CHAPTER I.

THE EDUCATION OF THE OLD NAVY.

1795–1845.

Before the Navy Department was established by the act of 1798, the Navy could hardly be said to have any independent existence. The acts of Congress had provided for a small armament, and a body of officers proportioned to the number of ships. The officers were selected from the merchant service, the upper grades being filled by those who had served with distinction during the Revolution. The Navy thus got a few commanders of tried ability and courage; and most of the junior officers proved themselves brave men and good seamen. As a beginning of the future organization, eight midshipmen were placed on board each ship.* These were appointed by the President from civil life, under no limitations as to age, education, or fitness, except what the appointing authority saw fit to impose on itself. Most of them had never been at sea before, and very few knew anything of either the theory or practice of navigation. Some of them, like Decatur,† got help and instruction by attending schools of navigation; but such cases were rare, and in gen-

* Act approved March 27, 1794; act approved July 1, 1797.

† Mackenzie's Life of Decatur, p. 25, (in Sparks's Am. Biog.)

eral they had to pick up the necessary knowledge by noticing what went on about them and by asking questions. They became the pupils of the older officers, when the latter were willing to teach them; but whatever education they got was fragmentary and technical, and depended chiefly upon their own efforts.

The Naval Regulations issued in 1802 assigned no particular duties to the midshipmen,* but directed the commanding officers to consider them as meriting in an especial degree the fostering care of the Government. Commanders were to see that the "schoolmasters" performed their duty toward the midshipmen by "diligently and faithfully instructing them in those sciences appertaining to their department;" while the midshipmen, on their part, were to consider it a duty they owed to their country "to employ a due portion of their time in the study of naval tactics, and in acquiring a thorough and extensive knowledge of all the various duties to be performed on board of a ship of war."

The schoolmaster had for many years been a part of the English naval organization; but as yet he did not exist in our service. No provision had been made for schoolmasters in the acts of Congress, and the reference here must be to the chaplains, who at that time supplied their place. The same regulations say elsewhere of the chaplain:† "He shall perform the duty of a schoolmaster; and to that end he shall instruct the midshipmen and volunteers in writing, arithmetic, and navigation, and in whatsoever may contribute to render them proficients. He is likewise to teach the other youths of the ship, according to such orders as he shall receive from the captain. He is to be diligent in his office, and such as are

* Naval Regulations issued by command of the President, January 25, 1802, p. 23.

† Page 18—*Of the Duties of a Chaplain.*

idle must be represented to the captain, who shall take due notice thereof."*

The system of giving instruction on board of cruising-ships, imperfect at the best, was barren of results where the chaplains were the teachers. The duty had no necessary connection with their profession, and the subjects they were compelled to teach were wholly foreign to their training and studies. They were appointed without any reference to their fitness for this work, and their qualifications for the place of teacher of navigation were not submitted to any test; they had no

* Taken, with modifications, from the English regulations, as will be seen by the following extract from the "Regulations and Instructions relating to His Majesty's Service at Sea," London, 1734, p. 136:

"*The Schoolmaster.*

"ARTICLE I.

"No Person shall be warranted to serve as a Schoolmaster in any of His Majesty's Ships, who has not been first examined before the Master, Wardens, and Assistants of the *Trinity-House* of *Debtford-Strond*, and produced a Certificate, under their Hands, of his being well skilled in the Theory and Practice of the Art of Navigation, and qualified to teach Youth therein; and another, under the Hands of Persons of known Credit, testifying the Sobriety of his Life and Conversation.

"II.

"He is to employ his Time on board in instructing the Voluntiers in Writing, Arithmetic, and the Study of Navigation, and in whatsoever may contribute to render them Artists in that Science.

"III.

"He is likewise to teach the other Youths of the Ship according to such Orders as he shall receive from the Captain, and with Regard to their several Capacities, whether in Reading, Writing, or otherwise.

"IV.

"He is to be early every Morning at the Place of Teaching, and to represent the Names of such as are idle, or averse to Learning, to the Commander, in order to his taking Course for their Correction."

examination before appointment like that which the schoolmasters of the old English navy had to pass before the master and wardens of the Trinity House. It was only in cases of fortunate accident that they knew anything about the subject before they were called upon to teach it. Except as far as their calling presupposed a liberal education, they were no better fitted for the work than any other officer of the ship. They might help out what was wanting in the rudimentary training of the midshipmen, but they were in no way qualified to make them "artists," or even "proficients," in their profession.

Notwithstanding the faults of this system, it continued in force for many years with only slight modifications. The act of January 2, 1813,* authorizing the construction of four seventy-four-gun ships, provided that each of them should carry a schoolmaster, appointed by the captain, with a pay of $25 per month. Each ship had twenty midshipmen, who were under the instruction of the schoolmaster. In 1816, again, ten seventy-fours were authorized,† and the provision of the act of 1813, in regard to the number and grade of officers, applied to them, in the absence of special legislation.

This change, slight as it was, was a change rather for the worse. In the first place, the professional teachers were limited to the line-of-battle ships, and the midshipmen who went to sea in a vessel of any smaller class had to get what they might from the chaplain; the old regulation in regard to the duties of that officer continuing still in force with very slight changes.‡ Moreover, the compensation was so small that

* Statutes at Large, 2, 789.

† Act of April 29, 1816. Statutes at Large, 3, 321.

‡ See Naval Regulations of 1818, American State Papers, Naval Affairs, 1, 532.

only an inferior class of men could be obtained for the service. The schoolmasters held a very subordinate position on board the ship, being quartered either with the warrant-officers, or with their pupils, the midshipmen; and their pay ceased when the cruise was finished. Under such circumstances no teacher of ability would be found who would give up higher compensation on shore, and submit to the confinement of the ship, the restraints of military discipline, and the discomforts of a sea-voyage.

The Hon. William Jones, who was Secretary of the Navy during President Madison's administration, saw the necessity of some improvement in the system of instruction, and made a recommendation accordingly, in a communication addressed to the Senate, in regard to the re-organization of the Navy.* He said: "I would suggest the expediency of providing by law for the establishment of a naval academy, with suitable professors, for the instruction of the officers of the Navy in those branches of the mathematics and experimental philosophy, and in the science and practice of gunnery, theory of naval architecture, and art of mechanical drawing, which are necessary to the accomplishment of the naval officer."

This recommendation evidently had in view a school or college which should do for the Navy what the West Point Academy had already begun to do for the Army. The Military Academy, founded in 1802, was then in full operation. There was no good reason why a naval academy should not have been established at the same time, and the plan was certainly proposed. In a report† made by the Secretary of War, James McHenry, in 1800, submitting a plan for a military academy, he mentioned four schools—a fundamental school, a school of engineers and artillerists, a school

* November 15, 1814. American State Papers, Naval Affairs, I, 320.

† American State Papers, Military Affairs, I, 133.

of cavalry and infantry, and a school of the Navy. The last was to have a director, a professor of mathematics, a professor of geography and natural philosophy, an architect, and a drawing master. It was to teach those appointed to or destined for the Navy "the application of the knowledge acquired in the fundamental school in arithmetic, algebra, geometry, statics, and navigation. To this end, after having passed examination, (*sic*) they shall make voyages or cruises, under skillful officers, for certain periods, during which time they ought to be exercised in the maneuvers and observations most useful in service, and be instructed in whatever respects rigging of vessels of war, pilotage, and the management of cannon."

The main defect of this plan, otherwise a good one, was the union of the schools for two dissimilar branches of the service, necessarily controlled by different departments of the Government, upon one foundation—a sort of military university, where all branches of the art of war might be taught in the various schools. It is a question whether this would not have seriously interfered with the efficiency of the institution. At any rate, it was not adopted. In the academy which grew out of the plan, as is well known, there was no provision for the training of naval officers, and the Army from that time enjoyed an incalculable advantage in the systematic training of its cadets,—an advantage which, for more than forty years, was denied to the Navy.

If the friends of the Navy who were in high official positions in the early part of this century had understood the wants of the service, and had pressed them upon the attention of Congress with the earnestness shown by the advocates of a military academy, the Naval School would perhaps have been founded at the same time; or, on the other hand, greater demands might have been thought extravagant, and might have killed the whole project. The Navy, at that time, had had no opportunity of fighting its way into popularity, and any step looking to its increase or improvement was bitterly opposed by the anti-federalists, then and long afterward the party in power. When the nation, rather than expend a reasonable sum for the building of frigates, was willing to give away a far greater amount in the shape of a disgraceful tribute to the Barbary Powers, to secure exemption from piratical depredations, it is not extraordinary that no movement was made toward the foundation of a school solely for the benefit of naval officers. At that time many men doubtless thought and hoped that the prosperity of the United States was in no way dependent upon a Navy, and that the existing establishment might presently be abolished. They had not yet learned the fact that a nation with a large commerce is bound to do its part in maintaining the police of the ocean; and they made the fatal mistake of supposing that, upon the outbreak of a war, a navy could be built to order, and an efficient maritime force organized, with the ease and rapidity with which a militia is transformed into a body of combatants. Hence, in 1802, the Navy was not generally looked upon as a permanent organization.

After the war with Tripoli, popular and official prejudices gave way to some extent. In 1808, Col. Jonathan Williams, the senior officer of the Corps of Engineers, made a report of the progress of the Military Academy,* in which he suggested its removal to Washington, and advised the appointment of a professor of mathematics, with assistants, who should teach, among other things, nautical astronomy, geography, and navigation. In this he clearly had in view the education of naval officers, some of whom were afterwards taken from the graduates of West Point. The President

* American State Papers, Military Affairs, I, 228.

transmitted Colonel Williams's report to Congress, with a message, in which he said: "The idea of removing the institution to this place is worthy of attention. Besides the advantage of placing it under the immediate eye of the Government, it may render its benefits common to the Naval Department."

The message was referred to a committee in the Senate, and ten days later a bill was reported; but, after being twice considered and postponed, it was finally laid aside for other business.*

In a plan for a peace establishment of the Navy, prepared in compliance with a resolution of the House of Representatives by Secretary Thompson, he said:† "Although perhaps not falling strictly within the scope of the resolution, yet the present affords a fit opportunity of suggesting the importance of establishing a naval academy for the instruction of our young officers in the sciences connected with their profession. As this is intended as a mere suggestion of a measure deserving consideration, I have not thought proper to present any plan for carrying it into effect. This may be done hereafter should the measure meet with a favorable reception; nor is it deemed fit for me, at this time, to urge the many considerations which will readily occur to all liberal and enlightened minds in favor of such an institution."

Mr. Southard, who succeeded Mr. Thompson at the head of the Navy Department, and who filled the office for six years with great ability, never ceased to urge upon Congress the importance of the step proposed by his predecessor. He pointed out clearly the defects of the existing system. In

* Annals of Congress, Tenth Congress, first session, 1, pp. 171, 176, 361.

† American State Papers, Naval Affairs, 1, 816. Communicated to the House of Representatives, December 10, 1822.

his report on the plan for a peace establishment, made January 24, 1824,* he said: "A great portion of the science of naval commanders can be acquired only on the ocean, and by years of labor and discipline. It is vain to hope for a triumphant defence of our national interests and character there without we thoroughly train, educate, and discipline those who have to fight our battles. To insure such a defence beyond hazard, it is confidently believed that the nation will cheerfully meet the requisite expense. Connected with this point it is not improper to suggest that the early education of most of our officers is very unequal to the character they have subsequently to sustain, and that an effectual remedy can be found only in the establishment of a naval school." In another place in the same report he said: "Schoolmasters are proposed for the two highest rates of vessels, and, as we have yet no school for the instruction of young officers, and as the duties of the chaplains, both as clergymen and teachers, demand purity of character, enlargement of mind, and *scientific attainments*, a higher salary would be useful to secure the services of those who are worthy of the station."

In his annual report on the condition of the Navy, made December 1, 1824,† he said: "Several laws seem necessary to render the establishment economical and efficient; but especially some provision should be made for the education and instruction of the younger officers. We have now the light of experience on this point in the Army, and its salutary effects are very manifest. *Instruction is not less necessary to the Navy than to the Army.*"

One month later, in a special report‡ to the President in regard to alterations in the organization of the Navy, Secre-

* American State Papers, Naval Affairs, 1, 907.

† American State Papers, Naval Affairs, 1, 1003.

‡ January 1, 1825. American State Papers, Naval Affairs, 2, 44.

tary Southard pressed yet more earnestly upon the attention of Congress the want of a naval school: "There is still another alteration which, in my opinion, ought to be made, and which is even more important than those already mentioned, to promote discipline, efficiency, and economy, and to prevent the recurrence of courts-martial in the service—the establishment of an academy, or providing in some effectual mode for the instruction of the young officers. These are taken from the poor, who have not the means of a good education, as well as the rich, who have. They enter, from the nature of the duties, at so early an age that they cannot be accomplished, or even moderately accurate, scholars. They are constantly employed on shipboard or in our navy-yards, where much advancement in learning cannot be expected. Their pay will afford them a support, but no means of literary improvement. The consequence necessarily is, and such is well known to be the fact, that very many advance in age and rise in grade much less cultivated and informed than their own reputation and that of the country require. For this evil there is but one remedy, and that is to be found in the wisdom and beneficence of the Government, from which they receive their offices, and to whose honor and interest they are devoted. It is the formation of a school which shall combine literary with professional instruction; a competent portion of common learning with a profound knowledge of everything connected with military science, seamanship, and navigation; the theory with the practice of their profession. The considerations which urge respect for this recommendation are connected with everything which the nation has to hope from the naval establishment. They may be glanced at, but cannot be suitably discussed, in this report. The situation of our country, the nature of its territory and its coasts, the extent of its commerce, the character of its institutions and its political connections, all point unerringly to that establishment as the security for its peace and honor. It no longer remains a debatable question whether we shall look to the Navy as one of the means by which our interests are to be most cheaply and most securely protected. It has been settled by a course of events which have carried the nation forward to a point where, on this subject, it has scarcely the liberty to choose. It has interests to protect and duties to discharge which it cannot, if it would, disregard.

"The problem now to be solved by it is in what mode our naval means may be commanded most surely, and with the least possible burden, combining most efficiency with the smallest expense.

"The answer is believed to be plain. By giving to our officers the greatest amount of science and skill, by fitting all to command the vessels we may choose to build and the seamen we may be enabled to enlist. By these means, and these only, may we, in times of quiet, keep in employment as small a number of vessels as our commerce may absolutely require; and yet, at the moment of trouble, swell it to the full extent which our protection may demand and the number of our seamen will permit; the latter being the only limit which can be placed to our naval power. It is not, however, in this circumstance alone that well-instructed officers will induce economy. The better instructed and more intelligent an officer is, the more skillfully and precisely, and, of course, the more economically, will he perform the duties assigned him. *Ignorance is always, skill never, prodigal.* There is no business, profession, or occupation in the circle of society to which this principle applies with more energy than to our naval establishment. Discipline and efficiency, also, necessarily result from the same cause. Educated in such a school as it becomes the Government to establish, moral principles are secured, good habits formed, subordination learned, honorable feelings encouraged and confirmed, skill acquired, science and discipline necessarily combined.

"The illustration of these truths is before us in another branch of our national defence, to which the favor of the Government has been extended; and the suggestion will be pardoned that no sound argument can be urged in its favor which does not receive additional force from the situation in which the Navy is placed, and the interests and hopes which are connected with it.

"Our future national conflicts are to rest principally on it, come when they may. It is also the bearer of our honor and our fame to every foreign shore. The American naval officer is, in fact, the representative of his country in every port to which he goes, and by him is that country in a greater or less degree estimated. With a well-regulated national pride, this consideration alone should insure him ample means of instruction and improvement.

"A school, to be useful to the Navy, must combine theory with practice. It must, therefore, be located where the attention may be directed to the construction, equipment, armament, and sailing of vessels. Governor's Island, in the harbor of New York, seems to be well fitted for all these objects. The buildings and improvements already upon it, with slight alterations and repairs, would probably be sufficient for present accommodation; and if the public interests would permit its transfer for a time from the War to the Navy Department, and an appropriation were made of $10,000 for the support of instructors, the school might be put into operation with very little delay, and its permanent location be hereafter determined."

In response to these recommendations, a resolution was introduced in the House early in the session* by Mr. Liv-

* January 3, 1825. Gales & Seaton's Register of Debates, i, pp. 112, 113, 127.

ingston, of Louisiana, calling for a committee to consider the expediency of establishing a naval academy. It was briefly discussed, and excited little interest. The next day it was called up again, and meeting with a slight opposition and only a feeble support, the question was put and lost.

Notwithstanding this failure, the Secretary returned to the attack again at the beginning of the next session. In his report* of December 2, 1825, he said: "Without an organization of some kind, without a revision of our penal code and of our rules and regulations, and without a *naval school*, tardy amendments may be made in the naval service and in its administration, but it is in vain to hope for speedy, useful, and very practical changes. The power of the Department is unequal to such objects."

This report was sent to Congress among the executive documents accompanying the first annual message of President John Quincy Adams, who had come into office in the preceding March. He had held consultations with the Secretary on the subject,† and was firmly convinced of the importance of the measure and of the benefits that would result to the naval service. He made special reference to it in the message, and urged the necessity of immediate action. Alluding to the early organization of the Navy, he showed very clearly how the service had been left to develop of itself, and how little systematic attention had been paid to its growing wants. He said:‡

"Our Navy commenced at an early period of our political organization, upon a scale commensurate with the incipient energies, the scanty resources, and the comparative indigence of our infancy, and was then found adequate to cope with

* American State Papers, Naval Affairs, 2, 98.

† Memoirs of J. Q. Adams, by C. F. Adams, 7, pp. 57, 90.

‡ Gales & Seaton's Register of Debates, ii, part 2, p. 6 of Appendix.

all the powers of Barbary, save the first, and with one of the principal maritime powers of Europe. But it is only since the close of the late war that, by the number and force of the ships of which it is composed, it could deserve the name of a Navy. Yet it retains nearly the same organization as when it consisted only of five frigates. The rules and regulations by which it is governed earnestly call for revision, and the want of a naval school of instruction, corresponding with the Military Academy at West Point, for the formation of scientific and accomplished officers, is felt with daily increasing aggravation."

About two months after the opening of the session,* Mr. Storrs, of the Naval Committee of the House, reported a bill for the establishment of a naval school. It proposed that the President should fix the location of the school on any of the lands held by the United States for military or naval purposes; that he should appoint one professor of natural and experimental philosophy, one professor of mathematics and navigation, one teacher of geography and history, and one of French and Spanish, and one fencing-master; for all of which an appropriation was made, the amount of which was to be fixed. Later in the session the same or a similar bill was introduced in the Senate,† but neither of them came to anything. Congress showed itself still apathetic in regard to the whole subject.

About the time when these bills were under consideration, in January, 1826, a resolution was adopted by the Maryland House of Delegates, in session at Annapolis, which is of curious interest in connection with the history of the Academy. It was as follows:

"*Resolved by the general assembly of Maryland*, That our

*January 20, 1826. In Gales & Seaton's Register of Debates, ii, p. 1055, the text of the bill is given in full.

†May 8, 1826. Gales & Seaton, ii, 696.

Senators and Representatives in Congress be, and they are hereby, requested to call the attention of their respective houses to the superior advantages which the city of Annapolis and its neighborhood possesses as a situation for a naval academy, and that they use their best exertions in favor of the establishment of such an institution."

This resolution was communicated to the Senate February 7, 1826, and would doubtless have had some effect in fixing the locality had the school been established; though the decision in favor of Annapolis in 1845 had no connection with it.

In the second annual message, December 5, 1826, the President again suggested the expediency of establishing a school, together with other improvements in the naval organization. By this time the attention of Congress, or at least of the Naval Committees, had become aroused, and a bill for the gradual improvement of the Navy was introduced in the Senate,* embracing several measures, and especially the foundation of an academy. It was wider in its scope than the bill of the last session, and less specific in its details, giving ampler powers to the President, and leaving more to his discretion. It met with warm opposition, and led to many spirited debates, in which the proposed academy was advocated with great eloquence and ability by Robert Y. Hayne, of South Carolina, the projector of the bill, and by others, especially General William H. Harrison, Asher Robbins, of Rhode Island, and Samuel Smith, of Maryland. It passed the Senate, but the House made several amendments, one of which, to strike out the clauses relating to the academy, was carried by a vote of 86 to 78. The Senate refused to agree to any of the amendments, except the one mentioned, which was carried by a vote of 22 to 21. The House finally yielded the other

* February 15, 1827. Gales & Seaton, iii, 348, 379, 501, 506–524, 1363, 1500.

points, and the bill in its modified form became a law. But for this majority of one in the Senate, the academy might now be in its fiftieth instead of its thirtieth year of existence.

At the opening of the next Congress, Secretary Southard again "respectfully but earnestly" presented the subject of a naval school to the consideration of the Government. He said:* "The reason for the preference of the Army over the Navy in this respect is not perceived;" a statement which no one could controvert. The President in his message reiterated with still greater emphasis the old arguments:†

"The establishment of a naval academy, furnishing the means of theoretic instruction to the youths who devote their lives to the service of their country upon the ocean, still solicits the sanction of the Legislature. Practical seamanship and the art of navigation may be acquired upon the cruises of the squadrons which, from time to time, are dispatched to different seas; but a competent knowledge even of the art of ship-building, the higher mathematics, and astronomy; the literature which can place our officers on a level of polished education with the officers of other maritime nations; the knowledge of the laws, municipal and national, which, in their intercourse with foreign states and their governments, are continually called into operation; and, above all, that acquaintance with the principles of honor and justice, with the higher obligations of morals, and of general laws, human and divine, which constitute the great distinction between the warrior-patriot and the licensed robber and pirate; these can be systematically taught and eminently acquired only in a permanent school, stationed upon the shore, and provided with the teachers, the instruments, and the books adapted to

*American State Papers, Naval Affairs, 3, p. 54.

† Third Annual Message, December 4, 1827. Gales & Seaton, ii, p. 2784.

the communication of the principles of these respective sciences to the youthful and inquiring mind."

No action followed the message, and the Navy remained without a school. In 1829, when Jackson became President, John Branch succeeded Southard as Secretary of the Navy. In two successive reports he called attention to the want of a school, but without success. In the first annual report on the condition of the Navy,* December 1, 1829, he brought forward some new arguments in its favor. "The establishment of schools for the junior officers of the Navy, in the various branches of science appertaining to their profession has so often been recommended to the favorable consideration of Congress, and has so uniformly been passed by without obtaining their sanction, that it is with reluctance that the subject is again introduced to their notice. A firm belief, however, that its tendency would be to qualify them for a better discharge of the high trust, which may, at some future day, devolve upon them in their capacities as commanders, forms a sufficient motive for renewing the recommendation. It has been remarked by a naval officer of much experience and observation that no inconvenience in the Navy is more sensibly felt than the general ignorance of the officers of foreign languages, in addition to which there is often great difficulty in procuring competent and proper persons to act in their ships of war as interpreters and linguists; nor has any allowance ever been made by Congress for the pay and subsistence of such persons. The perplexities and disadvantages under which our officers are placed by these circumstances may readily be conceived. They are brought into contact during their cruises with nations speaking different languages; subject to be drawn into correspondence with the authorities of different places; under the necessity often to board vessels

* American State Papers, Naval Affairs, 3, p. 350.

of other nations for the purpose of examining their papers and documents; and often without the ability to understand their import and tendency. In time of war valuable prizes are lost from an inability to translate their papers and to detect covered property and simulated documents; unnecessary and illegal detentions of vessels are made, and consequent damages obtained from the Government.

"The schools which have been employed at New York* and Norfolk in the instruction of midshipmen in the elementary branches of mathematics have been mere temporary arrangements made by the Department, and have never been fostered or recognized by law. Their introduction into use has not been effected by means very regular or direct, but they have been tolerated by Government, having been found useful, notwithstanding the very limited range of instruction afforded by them. It is respectfully proposed that, until some better system can be matured, these schools be authorized by law, and that such appropriation be made for their extension and support as will enable young officers to acquire a knowledge of such foreign languages as may be important for them to possess in the future pursuit of their profession."

In his next annual report† Secretary Branch used the same strong arguments, dwelling specially upon the necessity of giving naval officers a thorough training in international law and in the law of courts-martial; and he contrasted forcibly the elaborate school which had been given to the Army, with the pitiful provision of twenty-five dollars per month allowed to the schoolmasters on board the larger ships of war; but all to no purpose.

* The Naval Register for the years 1827 and 1828 mentions nine chaplains in the service, and one of them is specified as being on duty at the "naval school, New York."

† See Appendix A, where the extract is given in full.

Three years afterwards, when Secretary Woodbury was at the head of the Navy Department, "A bill relative to naval schools" was introduced in the House by the Naval Committee.* The object of the bill was not to establish any new system of instruction, but to make the existing system more efficient. It appears from the report of the committee that there were at this time three "naval schools,"† as they were called, in existence, connected with the navy-yards at Boston, New York, and Norfolk. Attached to each were one or two instructors and a few pupils. The Department had lately issued an order (so called in the report, but more properly a suggestion) to all midshipmen not otherwise employed to repair to one of these schools to receive instruction; but as there was no provision for allowing them traveling expenses, few had taken advantage of it. This difficulty the new bill proposed to remove,

* See Appendix B for report of committee and draught of bill.

† See American State Papers, Naval Affairs, 4, 486.

Statement of the actual condition of the naval schools as at present organized, the number and character of the professors employed, of youths instructed, and the annual expenditures to maintain them, December, 1833.

Number and character of professors.	Number of youths instructed.	Annual expenses.		General remarks.
		Pay, &c.	Contingencies.	
BOSTON.				
One teacher of mathematics and languages.	6	$981 75	Small amount for books, instruments, and stationery. Quarters or rooms are furnished in receiving-ships.	Since the late order the numbers will, at the end of this quarter, probably be more than doubled.
NEW YORK.				
One teacher of mathematics.	15	981 75		
One teacher of languages.		662 50		
NORFOLK.				
One teacher of mathematics	31	981 75		

as well as that which arose from the want of competent teachers and from the low rate of compensation. It provided that the chaplains and schoolmasters should receive $1,200 a year, and that the former should be required, in addition to the duties now imposed upon them, to instruct the junior officers in mathematics, in natural and moral philosophy, in history, and in such other branches of science as might be deemed by the Secretary best calculated to advance the interests of the service.

The tendency of this measure was to increase the faults of the old system, by giving the chaplain more work that was foreign to his profession, about which even the best chaplain could not be presumed to know much. Teaching was still to be given largely at sea; and the shore-schools were to be carried on without any uniform system or careful supervision. The bill failed to meet with hearty support, even from the Secretary, and it led to nothing.

Next year, however, one feature of it was adopted—that relating to the pay of instructors. In the act to regulate the pay of the Navy,* the compensation of professors of mathematics, when attached to vessels for sea-service, or in a yard, was fixed at $1,200; and from this period dates the first connection of some of the more eminent men of that corps with the service. Secretary Dickerson, in his report† on the condition of the Navy in the following December, spoke of the importance of the change, and of the regulations which had been adopted with a view to getting the best men for the vacant professorships. He pointed to the need of an institution, and suggested sending a class of 100 midshipmen to West Point to receive scientific instruction. This suggestion was never acted upon; the schools were continued

*Approved March 3, 1835, Statutes at Large, 4.

†See Appendix C for extract in full.

at the navy-yards, and schoolmasters (or professors, as they were usually called) were ordered to sea. The number of teachers was not fixed by law, and it varied according to the wants of the service and the balance of the contingent fund of the naval appropriation.*

The inducements of higher pay secured the services of good men as teachers, but they had no better opportunities than their predecessors. They continued to be the companions of their pupils, until by a special act of Congress,† passed solely for this purpose in 1842, it was provided that professors of mathematics in the Navy should be entitled to live and mess with the lieutenants of sea-going and receiving vessels.

Before this time the officers of the Navy had themselves set on foot a movement to bring the wants of the service to the notice of Congress. A meeting of officers was held on board the U. S. S. Constitution, and an earnest protest was sent to the Secretary of the Navy. The resolutions were signed by fifty-five officers, several of whom are still in the service, and among them the present Vice-Admiral of the Navy. The report of the proceedings, transmitted to the Senate April 23, 1836, is given in full: ‡

"At a meeting of the commissioned and warrant officers of the United States Ship Constitution, held on board for the purpose of concerting measures to effect the establishment of a naval academy, the following preamble and resolutions were unanimously agreed to:

"Whereas, having ever felt the most ardent desire to prosecute successfully the profession to which we are devoted, to advance the interests of the Navy, and to perpetuate the commercial prosperity of our common country, consigned in

* The table given on page — will show the extent of this variation.

† Approved August 31, 1842.

‡ From the copy in American State Papers, Naval Affairs, 4, 884.

part to our safe-keeping; and taught by the experience of the past that neither industry nor talent can spare the advantages offered by early education, earnestly desirous of the means of securing it, and deploring the inadequacy of the existing system to accomplish either the object of the Government or to meet our heartfelt wishes for professional instruction, and believing, as we do, that a respectful representation of the anxious hopes which the entire Navy have ventured to indulge for so many years, and to the consummation of which they look with the deepest interest, will receive the consideration to which so excellent an object is entitled, and find from liberal authorities that indulgence which is ever acceded to generous aspirations and laudable exertions; we have, therefore,

"1. *Resolved*, That we deem education to be of peculiar importance to the sea-officer, and that amid the progressive improvements in the arts and sciences which distinguish the present age the military marine would be most conspicuous if guided in its advance by the lights of education.

"2. *Resolved*, That we look to the establishment of a naval school as the only means of imparting to the officers of the Navy that elementary instruction in scientific knowledge which at the present day has become almost indispensable to the military seaman.

"3. *Resolved*, That from circumstances arising in part from professional causes, the ship's schoolmaster can rarely, if ever, impart such elementary or scientific knowledge, or advance the education of the naval officer, and that were the office absolutely abolished (of so little utility is it) that no evil would arise therefrom.

"4. *Resolved*, That believing the expense incurred by Government in providing ships' schoolmasters and professors of mathematics for the benefit of the junior officers of the Navy (and from which little or no advantage is derived) would liberally sustain a scientific institution, we should see with pleasure said funds directed to the establishment and support of a naval school.

"5. *Resolved,* That copies of these proceedings be furnished to the Secretary of the Navy, with a request that he will lend his countenance and support to our undertaking.

"6. *Resolved,* That we will severally and collectively use our most strenuous exertions to effect an object so dear to us, and which promises to confer so much dignity upon the Navy, so much honor on our beloved country.

"7. *Resolved,* That a committee of ten be appointed to take charge of the subject, and conduct it to its final disposition.

"8. *Resolved,* That the Secretary of the Navy be requested to lay a copy of the foregoing resolutions before the President of the United States, and that a copy of them be sent to the chairman of the Committee on Naval Affairs in the Senate and in the House of Representatives.

"J. B. MONTGOMERY, *Lieutenant.*
"F. ELLERY, *Lieutenant.*
"ISAAC BRINCKERHOFF, *Assistant Surgeon.*
"EDW. C. RUTLEDGE, *Lieutenant.*
"G. F. PEARSON, *Lieutenant.*
"JAMES FERGUSON, *Master.*
"THOMAS THEO. SLOAN, *Lieutenant Marines.*
"*LEVIN MYNN POWELL, *Lieutenant,* (*now Rear-Admiral.*)
"THOMAS I. BOYD, *Surgeon.*
"JAMES EVERETT, *Chaplain.*
"HENRY ETTING, *Purser.*
"JOS. L. C. HARDY, *Lieutenant U. S. M. C.*
"MONTGOMERY LEWIS, *Passed Midshipman.*
"J. W. REVERE, *Passed Midshipman.*
"CHAS. CRILLON BARTON, *Passed Midshipman.*

* The names starred are those of officers still in the service.

"JAMES B. LEWIS, *Midshipman.*

"R. LLOYD TILGHMAN, *Midshipman.*

"JNO. N. MAFFIT, *Midshipman.*

"GEO. T. SINCLAIR, *Midshipman.*

"GEO. W. RANDOLPH, *Midshipman.*

"JOHN F. MERCER, *Passed Midshipman.*

"*FRANCIS S. HAGGERTY, *Midshipman, (now Captain.)*

"B. F. SHATTUCK, *Midshipman.*

"*JOHN M. BERRIEN, *Passed Midshipman, (now Commodore.)*

"JAMES L. HENDERSON, *Passed Midshipman.*

"JAMES W. COOKE, *Passed Midshipman.*

"*WILLIAM RONCKENDORFF, *Midshipman, (now Commodore.)*

"E. E. ROGERS, *Midshipman.*

"*STEPHEN D. TRENCHARD, *Midshipman, (now Rear-Admiral.)*

"A. HUBLEY JENKINS, *Midshipman.*

"W. T. MUSE, *Passed Midshipman.*

"JAMES F. DUNCAN, *Passed Midshipman.*

"FREDERICK OAKES, JR., *Passed Midshipman.*

"W. C. NICHOLSON, *Lieutenant.*

"F. A. NEVILLE, *Lieutenant.*

"*CHARLES STEEDMAN, *Passed Midshipman, (now Rear-Admiral.)*

"FRANCIS P. HOBAN, *Midshipman.*

"*WILLIAM RADFORD, *Passed Midshipman, (now Rear-Admiral.)*

"ROBERT WOODWORTH, *Assistant Surgeon.*

"The undersigned, officers of the United States ship Vandalia, concur entirely in the above preamble and resolutions.

"THOMAS T. WEBB, *Master, Commandant.*

"ISAAC N. BROWN. *Midshipman.*

"EDWIN A. DRAKE, *Midshipman.*

"*R. N. STEMBEL, *Midshipman, (now Rear-Admiral.)*

"FAYETTE MEYNARD, *Midshipman.*

"*S. C. ROWAN, *Acting Master, (now Vice-Admiral of the Navy.)*

"WILLIAM M. WALKER, *Passed Midshipman.*

"C. A. HASSLER, *Assistant Surgeon.*

"E. T. DOUGHTY, *Lieutenant.*

"THOS. W. CUMMING, *Midshipman.*
"WILLIAM PLUMSTEAD, *Surgeon.*
"E. MUSSON, *Midshipman.*
"FRANCIS ALEXANDER, *Midshipman.*
"M. C. WATKINS, *Midshipman.*
"WILLIAM SMITH, *Lieutenant.*
"JAMES BROOKS, *Purser.*"

The resolutions were transmitted by the Secretary of the Navy to Congress, and the Naval Committee of the Senate, of which Ex-Secretary Southard was a prominent member, made a favorable report.* The report was similar in argument and expression to many of the reports made by Southard on the same subject when Secretary; but, like so many earlier efforts at legislation, it failed to produce any result, partly from party opposition, and partly from a dread of the expense it might possibly entail upon the Government.

In 1838 the Secretary of the Navy, J. K. Paulding, in his annual report, dated November 30, again mentioned the subject:

"The subject of a naval academy has been more than once presented for consideration. Such an institution is earnestly desired by the officers of the Navy, and it is believed would greatly conduce to the benefit of the service generally. The propriety of affording young midshipmen the means and opportunities for the acquisition of that knowledge and those sciences which are either absolutely necessary or highly useful to their profession, would seem to have been recognized by Congress in the liberal provision for teachers and professors of mathematics on board our ships of war and at the principal navy-yards. Those, however, who have had the best opportunities for observing the practical operation of this system are of opinion that it does not answer the pur-

* May 16, 1836. See Appendix D.

poses for which it was intended, and that other and more effectual means are required."

In March, 1839, the first appropriation was made for building three steam-vessels for the Navy.* This was the beginning of a change in the motive-power of vessels that was destined to revolutionize the methods of naval warfare and the character of the naval profession. The skillful handling of a ship under sail was the chief accomplishment of the old sea-captain, and could be learned nowhere so well as on the deck of the vessel itself; and a certain period of sea-training early in life was necessary to make a successful officer. By the introduction of steam, though practical seamanship was still an essential, other things were superadded with which a naval officer must be familiar if he would assist instead of retarding the development of his profession. The progress of science was to have a new interest and a new importance for him. Hence, if the school was a want of the service before, it now became a necessity. Though schoolmasters might have been able to teach young officers something of the theory of navigation at sea, and chaplains to supply in some measure the defects in the early education of midshipmen, when stationed for a few months at a navy-yard, it was not to be supposed that either of these classes of teachers, situated as they were, could give even an empirical knowledge of the laws of physics or the workings of marine engines. Accordingly, the Secretary of the Navy, Abel P. Upshur, in 1841, called attention once more to the urgent need of a naval school: †

"The propriety of establishing naval schools has frequently been submitted to the consideration of Congress. I again

*Approved March 3, 1839.

† Executive Documents, Twenty-seventh Congress, second session, No. 2, p. 364.

respectfully bring it to your notice, as a subject of increasing interest to the Navy. The use of steam-vessels in war will render necessary a different order of scientific knowledge from that which has heretofore been required. This important object can be best attained by the establishment of naval schools, provided with the necessary means of uniting practice with theory. The advantages which the Army has derived from the Academy at West Point afford a sufficient proof that a similar institution for the Navy would produce like results.

"The professors of mathematics have no permanent connection with the Navy, but are called in only as their services are needed, and are not paid except when on actual duty. The consequence is that they cannot rely on this employment for support, and are often reluctantly driven to other pursuits. It is to be presumed that men whose talents and attainments qualify them to be teachers in the Navy are equally qualified to be teachers on land; and as this latter is the less precarious position, the best qualified will be the most apt to seek it. Hence the Department cannot rely with any assurance on being able to command suitable professors at all times when their services may be required. It is, I think, of great importance, that some provision should be made on this subject. I also recommend that a certain rank or position be given to the professors, which will relieve them from the necessity of messing and sleeping with their pupils.* This close and constant association is well calculated to weaken the respect and influence which their relation to the young officers ought to inspire, and which is necessary to give due effect to their instructions. I doubt whether their services upon the present system are worth the money which

* This objection to the position of professor was removed, as has been already stated, in the following summer.

they cost, although they would be highly valuable under proper regulations."

In the following August * a bill was introduced in the Senate to establish five naval schools, at unoccupied fortifications to be transferred from the War Department to the Navy. After a short discussion, the bill was amended so as to provide for only one school, at some fortification near Fortress Monroe. In this form it passed easily by a large majority, only five Senators voting in the negative. † Congress, however, adjourned soon afterwards, and the bill was never reached in the House.

In his annual report of December, 1842, Secretary Upshur called attention to the need of statutory enactments providing for the selection and appointment of midshipmen: "The Department has been left free to appoint whom it pleased, and as many as it pleased, without any law whatever to guide or regulate its judgment."

As a remedy for the existing evils, he proposed:

"1. The naval establishment shall be fixed by law, ascertaining the number of officers to be allowed in each grade. * *

"2. There should be established proper naval schools on shore. Little or no attention has hitherto been paid to the proper education of naval officers. Through a long course of years the young midshipmen were left to educate themselves and one another; and it is creditable to them that they lost few opportunities of doing so. Suitable teachers are now provided for them; but their schools are kept in receiving-ships and cruising-vessels, in the midst of a thousand interruptions and impediments, which render the whole system of little or

* Debated August 8 and 9, 1842. See Benton's Abridgment of Debates, xiv, p. 478.

† Executive Document, Twenty-seventh Congress, third session, No. 2, p. 539 *et seq.*

no value. Under such circumstances, the foundation of a solid education can rarely be laid. This subject was brought to the attention of Congress at its last session; I again earnestly recommend it. The schools shall be established at such of the old military fortifications on the seaboard as may afford suitable accommodations, and as may not be required by the War Department. The officers and teachers shall be supplied from those actually in the naval service, and all nautical instruments, boats for practice, &c., shall be furnished from the Navy."

In continuation, he dwelt upon the fact that the West Point cadets were furnished with an education which naval officers lacked, though the latter "need it much more, and have fewer opportunities."

The evil alluded to in regard to the selection of midshipmen had long existed, and steps had been taken to remove it. By an act approved August 4, 1842, the appointment of midshipmen had been limited to the number in the service on the 1st of January, 1841,* beyond which they were not to be increased till the further order of Congress; but no provision was made for their distribution. As a consequence, certain sections of the country were far more highly favored than others.† This was corrected by a clause in the appropriation bill approved March 3, 1845, providing that midshipmen should be appointed from each State and Territory in proportion to the number of Representatives and Delegates, the appointee being an actual resident of the State from which he was appointed. As it was impossible for the Secretary

* Modified by act 3d August, 1848, so as to extend to 464 midshipmen.

† According to a statement of Mr. Everett, in a debate on the naval appropriation bill in the House of Representatives, May 13, 1842, out of 158 midshipmen appointed in the past year, 31 were from Virginia, 20 from the District of Columbia, and 19 from Maryland. See Army and Navy Chronicle for May 31, 1842.

of the Navy to know much about the inhabitants of each congressional district, he naturally came to rely somewhat upon the testimony of the member representing the district in regard to the fitness of an applicant for appointment. From this it was an easy step to the present system, legalized by the act of August 31, 1852, by which no one can be appointed a midshipman except on the recommendation of the member of Congress representing the district in which the applicant resides. This system had already been adopted in making appointments of cadets at West Point.

Between 1842 and 1845 the subject of improved instruction for the Navy came constantly before the public, in the shape of bills introduced in Congress, petitions, reports of the Secretary of the Navy, and articles in the newspapers.* The existing system of schools at the navy-yards and on shipboard was the object of much unfavorable criticism, as well as the corps of professors itself.

Early in 1844,† Senator Bayard introduced a bill providing for the establishment of schools of instruction in the naval service, and two weeks later‡ the same Senator presented a memorial from the officers of the United States Ship Vincennes, praying that the office of professor of mathematics be abolished and that naval schools of instruction be established in its stead. About the same time a report§ on the organization of the Navy, prepared by Commodore Charles Stewart, was transmitted to Congress by the Secretary of the Navy. Commodore Stewart advocated a school with a limited course of instruction, with special reference to

*See files of the Madisonian, the Southern Literary Messenger, and Army and Navy Chronicle, for these years.

†January 23. See Army and Navy Chronicle February 1, 1844.

‡February 3. Army and Navy Chronicle February 8, 1844.

§February 1, 1844. Army and Navy Chronicle April 4, 1844.

mathematics, languages, international law, and the principles and mechanism of the steam-engine.

The position of the professors was still in many respects unfortunate. They had no rank, and only within two years had they been quartered apart from their pupils; and their pay was intermitted when they were not actually performing duty.* This point is of importance, as it had a direct bearing upon the foundation of the Naval Academy, and was in this way a fortunate thing for the service; but it made a serious reduction in the compensation of professors, and compelled them to take short and infrequent vacations.

In 1842 Mr. Fessenden had introduced a bill in the House to give professors commissions with rank and continuous pay, thus placing them on the same footing as the pursers, surgeons, and other staff-officers; but the attempt failed at that time. For six years the professors kept up their efforts to improve their position; and finally, in 1848, an act was passed limiting their number to twelve, and giving them the privileges they had asked for.†

In the mean time other changes had taken place which had a direct influence upon the reform. In 1840, the professors on duty at the four great naval stations were employed at

* See a letter of "A Veteran Professor" on this subject in the Army and Navy Chronicle December 9, 1841.

† "An act making appropriations for the naval service," approved August 3, 1848, § 12, Statutes at Large, 9, p. 272, provides:

"That the number of professors of mathematics in the Navy shall not exceed twelve; that they shall be appointed and commissioned by the President of the United States, by and with the advice and consent of the Senate, and shall perform such duties as may be assigned them by order of the Secretary of the Navy, at the naval school, the Observatory, and on board ships of war, in instructing the midshipmen of the Navy or otherwise; that when on duty, the pay of a professor of mathematics shall be at the rate of $1,500 per annum, with a ration, and when on leave or waiting orders, $800."

the receiving-ships in giving midshipmen their final preparation before the examination for promotion, which was held every summer. This examination was chiefly in seamanship and navigation, and was conducted by a board of naval officers of high rank. One of the professors, Mr. McClure, was at the Naval Asylum in Philadelphia. In 1841,* McClure dying, William Chauvenet, who had just been appointed a professor, was ordered to succeed him. Chauvenet showed so much ability and met with such marked success, that it was decided to close the other schools gradually and to discontinue all shore instruction elsewhere. A French instructor† was already attached to the Philadelphia school, and in 1844 Lieut. J. H. Ward and Prof. Henry H. Lockwood were ordered there, to instruct in gunnery and kindred branches.

The midshipmen preparing for examination were now sent, as far as possible, to Philadelphia, but the attendance was voluntary, and there was little or no discipline. The instructors were able men, but the school had no organization. Professor Chauvenet had charge of the instruction in mathematics and navigation, and Lieutenant Ward of that in gunnery, while Professor Lockwood, a graduate of West Point, and previously an Army officer, occasionally relieved both the other instructors. Gunnery was not required at the examination for promotion, so that Lieutenant Ward could only depend upon the interest he might arouse and the desire of his pupils to learn as an incentive to exertion. His first lecture, delivered early in 1844, was full of earnest advice to the midshipmen, and pointed out with great force and clearness the importance of scientific study to the young naval officer. It is well worth reading, as showing the spirit

* Perhaps early in 1842, as his name appears in the Register of that year.

† Called in the Register a professor of mathematics.

which prompted the movement for a higher education in the service.*

At this time (1844), there were in the service fourteen professors at sea, one at Boston, one at Norfolk, three at Philadelphia, and three on special service. There were also three teachers of languages, employed respectively at Boston, New York, and Norfolk.

The yearly cost of maintaining this force was as follows:

22 professors, at $1,200	$26,400
3 teachers of languages, at $624	1,872
Total	28,272

This money was not appropriated by Congress specifically for this purpose, but was considered in the estimates for the yearly appropriation bill; and it was the custom of the Department to take this amount from the pay of the Navy and from the allowance for contingent expenses, putting its expenditure in a separate item of "Instruction." Owing to the fact that professors received no pay when off duty, the amount expended in any year might be reduced or increased by placing a greater or less number of professors on waiting orders. Thus in 1845, when two professors were waiting orders, the sum allowed for instruction remained the same as in 1844, while the amount spent was reduced.

The following tables show the number and assignment of professors and teachers from 1835 to 1850, inclusive, being made up from data furnished by the Navy Registers for sixteen successive years:

* See Army and Navy Chronicle, May 30, 1844, where the lecture is given in full.

TABLE 1.—1835–1842.

PROFESSORS OF MATHEMATICS.

	1835.	1836.	1837.	1838.	1839.	1840.	1841.	1842.
Boston	1	1	1	1	1	1	1	1
New York	1	1	1	1	1	1	1	1
Norfolk	1	1	1	1	2	2	1	1
Naval School, Philadelphia	......	......	......	......	......	1	1	1
Naval Asylum, Philadelphia	......	......	......	......	......	......	1	1
At sea	......	2	6	6	9	9	8	13
Waiting orders	......	1	......	2	1	1	3	4
Total	3	6	9	11	14	15	16	22

TEACHERS OF LANGUAGES.

	1835.	1836.	1837.	1838.	1839.	1840.	1841.	1842.
Boston	......	......	......	......	1	......	......	......
New York	......	1	1	1	1	1	......	1
Norfolk	1	1	1	1	......	1	1	2
Total	1	2	2	2	2	2	1	3

NOTE.

1837. John H. C. Coffin appointed January 23, 1836.
1838. J. C. Fremont appointed April 4, 1837.
1840. D. McClure appointed June 17, 1839.
1841. M. Yarnall appointed February 1, 1839.
1841. J. Meiere appointed November 9, 1840.
1842. M. H. Beecher appointed June 14, 1841.
1842. H. H. Lockwood appointed November 4, 1841.
1842. W. Chauvenet appointed December 30, 1841.

McClure appears last in Register for 1842. The first date indicates the Register in which the name first appears.

TABLE 2.—1843–1850.

PROFESSORS OF MATHEMATICS.

	1843.	1844.	1845.	1846.	1847.	1848.	1849.	1850.
Boston	1	1	1	......	......	......	......	......
New York	1	......	1	......	......	......	......	......
Norfolk	1	1	1	......	......	......	......	......
Naval School, Philadelphia	2	3	4	......	1	1	......	......
Naval Asylum, Philadelphia	......	......	......	......	......	......	......	......
Special service	......	3	2	1	......	......	......	......
Depot of charts	......	......	1	......	......	......	......	......
Coast Survey	......	......	1	......	......	......	1	1
Observatory	......	......	......	3	4	5	7	7
Naval School, Annapolis	......	......	......	2	2	2	3	3
At sea	14	14	9	5	2	1	......	1
Waiting orders	4	......	2	11	13	12	1	......
Total	23	22	22	22	22	21	12	12

TEACHERS OF LANGUAGES.

	1843.	1844.	1845.	1846.	1847.	1848.	1849.	1850.
Boston	1	1	1	......	......	......	......	......
New York	1	1	1	......	......	......	......	......
Norfolk	......	1	1	......	......	......	......	......
At sea	1	......	......	......	......	......	......	......
Waiting orders	......	......	......	3	2	2	2	......
Total	3	3	3	3	2	2	2	......

The provision for instruction in the Navy for the ten years before the foundation of the Naval School may be clearly seen from these tables. They illustrate all the faults of the system. Instead of concentrating the force, and thereby giving it strength and unity and the basis of an efficient organization, it was spread out in fragments at navy-yards, and, worse still, in cruising-ships. The increase of the force had led to no corresponding improvement of results. The intermission of pay prevented stability in the corps, and the professors designated as being on waiting orders might as well have been omitted from the Register, as far as their connection with the service was concerned.

Such was the state of affairs in 1845, when George Bancroft became Secretary of the Navy. His own profound scholarship, his rich and varied culture, and his personal familiarity with educational methods, enabled him to appreciate the want of the service and to devise a way in which it might be supplied. To him the Navy owes the foundation of the Naval Academy. He saw, as his predecessors had also seen, that a dozen separate schools without organization or intelligent supervision, constituted as appendages to navy-yards and sea-going men-of-war, could produce no satisfactory results. He had seen, moreover, the failure of many efforts at legislation with a view to reforming the system. But he discovered what those before him had failed to see, that with him lay the authority to remedy the evils, and that the means were already provided. By placing a large number of the professors upon waiting orders—that is, by dispensing with their services—a large part of the annual outlay* for instruction might be saved; and by concentrating a few of the best men of the corps of instructors at a suitable place, a school might be formed with an independent organization.

On the 2d of June, 1845, a board of officers convened at the Philadelphia Naval Asylum for the examination of midshipmen entitled to promotion.† This board was composed of Commodores George C. Read, Thomas Ap Catesby Jones, and Matthew C. Perry, and Captains E. A. F. Lavallette and Isaac Mayo.

In addition to the examination of midshipmen, the Secretary gave them certain duties as an advisory board to make

* $28,200. See page 39.

† Niles's Register, 68, p. 276.

suggestions in regard to a naval school. His instructions were given in the letter which follows:

*Secretary Bancroft to the Board of Examiners.**

"NAVY DEPARTMENT,
"*Washington, June* 13, 1845.

"SIR: I desire the assistance of your board in maturing a more efficient system of instruction for the young naval officers. The opportunity which your present arduous and responsible duties as examiners of the school afford you of giving practical and useful advice leads me to solicit your co-operation by as full a communication of your opinion as is consistent with your convenience.

"Fort Severn has been recommended to me as a more suitable place for such a school than the Naval Asylum, especially as a vessel could be stationed there to serve as a school in gunnery.

"The present term of instruction is too short. Might it not be well to have permanent instruction, and to send all midshipmen on shore to the school? What plan of studies is most advisable? I hope your board will find time and will be disposed to aid me by their suggestions.

"I wish, also, that they would nominate for my consideration a board of three experienced officers, whose qualifications incline them to give long-continued attention to this subject, and who could have the permanency necessary to assist me, until a plan can be matured. If from your own number you would select such a board, or would take a wider scope in your selection, it would be acceptable to me.

"I am, respectfully, yours,
"GEORGE BANCROFT.

"Commodore GEO. C. READ,
"*President Board of Examiners, &c., Philadelphia, Pa.*"

* From the copy in the Navy Department.

In compliance with these directions, the board gave the subject a fuller and more exact discussion than it had ever had before from any official body. In the course of their deliberations they called on the professors at the Asylum for advice, and the conclusions reached were drawn up in an elaborate report.

REPORT OF THE BOARD OF EXAMINERS.*

"U. S. NAVAL ASYLUM,
"*Philadelphia, June* 25, 1845.

"SIR: Your communication of the 13th instant, addressed to Commodore Geo. C. Read, calling on the Board of Examiners of Midshipmen for the present year to render the assistance of its members 'in maturing a more efficient system of instruction for the young naval officers,' has been received and respectfully considered, and, after due consultation and mutual interchange of opinion, the undersigned beg leave to make the following report:

"Three of the undersigned are ignorant of the precise situation of Fort Severn and of its fitness for a naval school in regard to accommodations, healthiness of location, and conveniences of the vicinity for gun-practice, but they are told by their associates, Commodore Jones and Captain Mayo, that the fort embraces sufficient space and the harbor and neighboring shores offer all the requisite advantages for gun-practice and evolutions of steamers and boats. Supposing, then, that Fort Severn is selected, and there is ample accommodation within its walls for the officers and students of the establishment, it may be remarked that the Government already possesses all the necessary means for *commencing* at once a naval school, which may be enlarged and perfected at some future time. It would be very desirable that a grade of

* From the copy on file at the Navy Department.

naval cadets inferior to that of midshipmen should be created by law, who should compose the primary classes of the naval school, and from which all appointments of midshipmen should be made after the candidate for such appointment should have passed through a stated course of elementary professional education, and acquitted himself to the entire satisfaction of the authorities of the school, and a board authorized to determine with rigid scrutiny his fitness for an ultimate career in the Navy. These cadets should be appointed in the same manner as those at West Point, and their pay, over which they should have no control, should be only sufficient to clothe and feed them. Twenty dollars per month would be adequate. By making this grade the source from which all others shall spring, and by imposing upon it acquirements of a comparatively high character, most of the delinquencies now so common in the Navy would be unknown when the proposed system shall have been thoroughly incorporated into the service. But, whether a grade of naval cadets may or may not be created, a naval school such as it is proposed to recommend would operate equally to the advantage of acting midshipmen as now appointed; the difference would lie only in the designation and pay of the existing and proposed grades. It having been assumed that the school shall be established at Fort Severn, and the necessary accommodations having been prepared, it is recommended that the following be a part of its regulations:

"OFFICERS OF THE ESTABLISHMENT.

"One captain, to command in chief ashore and afloat.

"One commander, as executive officer.

"Three lieutenants.

"One surgeon.

"One assistant surgeon.

"One purser.

"One chaplain.

"One secretary to senior captain and superintendent-in-chief.

"One clerk to commander.

"One purser's clerk.

"One purser's steward.

"An officers' guard of marines, the commanding officer of which, assisted by competent drill-sergeants, to give instruction in infantry tactics and the sword exercise. A sufficient number of servants, cooks, &c.

"BOARD OF INSTRUCTION.

"One professor of the English language, to embrace instruction in constitutional and international law.

"One assistant professor of the English language.

"One professor of the French language.

"One professor of mathematics, to embrace instruction in marine surveying.

"One assistant professor of mathematics.

"One professor of natural philosophy and chemistry.

"One instructor of drawing and mapping.

"In connection with the primary school there should be stationed at some suitable anchorage in the vicinity a practice-frigate and a small steamer, for the purpose of facilitating instruction in naval-gunnery tactics and the operation of the steam-engine. These vessels should have full appointments of commissioned and warrant officers, with the exception of midshipmen, of which class there should be, of those who have passed their examination, six for the frigate and four for the steamer. The practice-frigate would necessarily be stationary, but the steamer might be advantageously employed in transporting munitions, provisions, &c., to the naval school, during which employment practical instruction in the use of the steam-engine might be imparted.

"Having thus given a plan of the entire establishment of the school both ashore and afloat, and supposing it to be authorized and ready for operation, the undersigned would recommend that all persons who may from the time of its commencement be appointed to the Navy, whether designated as acting midshipmen or cadets, shall be required to enter the primary class, through which and the succeeding steps they should only reach a permanent position in the service; and to make them eligible for their final examination for promotion to the rank of lieutenant they should accomplish the following course of studies and sea-service: First, after appointment to the Navy, they should be required to remain two years attached to the primary school, at the expiration of which period they may receive their warrants as midshipmen, provided their conduct and scholastic advancement has been satisfactory. From the primary school they should proceed, as warranted midshipmen, to a sea-going ship to remain constantly at sea three years. On returning from their first sea-service a leave of absence, not exceeding three months, is to be granted to them to visit their friends, with orders to join, on its termination, the practice-frigate, in which vessel and in the steamer they are to pursue a course of practical studies, to which the information previously acquired at the primary school and at sea will be applied. To the practice-ship they are to remain attached at least one year, when they will be entitled to their second and final examination; and it is recommended that no greater number be examined and passed than may be actually required for the immediate exigencies of the service. It now remains to point out more particularly the course of studies to be pursued at the primary school. As experience has shown that the system of instruction established at the Military Academy at West Point has operated most happily, it is recommended that the laws for the government of that institution be adopted in the organization of the naval school, so far as it can be done compatibly with the genius of the two services and the ulterior professional pursuits of the naval student. To this end, it is proposed that the requirements enforced at West Point in regard to the physical and mental qualifications of applicants for admission be rigidly exacted at the naval school. That the students at the naval school be divided into two classes, corresponding with the third and fourth class of the Military Academy, and the course of studies and exercises to be almost identically the same; the only difference should be in omitting in the mathematical department the abstruse study of the Calculus, and occupying the time thus saved in more practical branches. That there take place at the naval school semi-annual examinations, to be conducted by the academic board under the supervision of the captain or superintendent-in-chief, of the results of which full reports be transmitted to the Navy Department, setting forth the conduct of the student and recommending the dismissal of all who may be found delinquent, either in reference to their studies or personal deportment. That annual examinations (the first to be held at the end of two years from the commencement of the school) be conducted by the academic board, assisted by three persons to be appointed by the Secretary of the Navy, the whole to be under the direction of the superintendent-in-chief. Before this board all the students shall be brought who may have been attached to the primary school the whole period of two years, and in case of passing their examination, they will receive their appointments as midshipmen and be ordered immediately to sea. Those who may fail to pass should be invariably dropped from the rolls. By making the final examinations of the primary students extremely strict, both in regard to moral conduct and academic improvement, none but the meritorious will find their way into the Navy. It is suggested that the primary school be of a strictly probationary character; that the age of admission of the students should not be less than thirteen nor more than fifteen years, and for the reason that, in case of failure to pass the final examination, they will be of suitable age to enter upon some other profession. The undersigned might go further into details, but as it is the intention of the Department to institute a board to assist in forming a code of regulations for the government of the proposed school, they refrain from extending their report.

"In regard to that part of your letter in which you express a wish that the undersigned should nominate three of their number, or some other suitable officers, to compose the contemplated board, they beg to remark that a feeling of delicacy impels them to prefer that the nomination should rest with the Department. If called upon, the whole or any three of them will most cheerfully contribute their best services in perfecting a work which promises so much good to the country, and to the Navy in particular.

"We have the honor to be, sir, respectfully, your obedient servants,

"GEO. C. READ,
"THOS. AP C. JONES,
"M. C. PERRY,
"E. A. F. LAVALLETTE,
"I. MAYO,

"*Board of Examiners of Midshipmen for the Year* 1845."

From this correspondence it appears that the Secretary had decided to establish the school, and that Annapolis was the place regarded most favorably for its location. Previous measures had looked to the transfer of one of the old Army posts in the neighborhood of Washington to the Navy Department for this purpose; and Fort Severn seemed to be in every way the best adapted. The Secretary of War was willing to give it up, but Mr. Bancroft undertook first to satisfy himself by personal inspection of its fitness. Accordingly, soon after the report was made, the following paragraph appeared in an Annapolis newspaper: *

"OFFICIAL VISIT to ANNAPOLIS.—Secretary Bancroft, Governor Marcy, Secretary of War, and Com. Warrington † arrived in this city last evening from Washington, and took quarters at the City Hotel. We understand the object of their visit to be to examine the condition of Fort Severn and the improvements commenced last fall, and now being completed. There is a rumor afloat that it is the intention of Government to remove the Naval School from Philadelphia to Fort Severn, which may be one of the reasons of this visit."

A short time after this visit of inspection, the Secretary directed a board, composed of Commanders McKean, Buchanan, and Du Pont, to consider the subject, and to recommend place and persons. This board decided upon Annapolis as the place, and Ward, Chauvenet, and Lockwood as the professors.

Commander Franklin Buchanan had already been selected by the Secretary to be at the head of the new institution. Born in Baltimore in 1800, this officer had entered the service at the age of fifteen, and had risen to the grade of commander, with a high reputation for ability in his profession, as a skillful, energetic, and systematic organizer. He had had several commands at sea before he was called to the new duty; and

* Copied in Niles's Register, July 19, 1845.

† At this time Chief of the Bureau of Navy-yards and Docks.

his selection by the Secretary was itself an evidence of his fitness for the position. Mr. Bancroft was no ordinary authority on matters of education. He had taken his degree at Harvard University in 1817, and at Göttingen in 1820, and had since that time had personal experience in teaching. He had taken a prominent part in literature and in public affairs, and he was therefore eminently qualified to devise a system of education and to choose fit men to fill positions of authority at the newly-established school. His directions to Commander Buchanan were full and explicit, as will be seen from the following letter which accompanied his orders:

*Secretary Bancroft to Commander Buchanan.**

"NAVY DEPARTMENT,
"*August* 7, 1845.

"SIR: The Secretary of War, with the assent of the President, is prepared to transfer Fort Severn to the Navy Department for the purpose of establishing there a school for midshipmen.

"In carrying this design into effect, it is my desire to avoid all unnecessary expense; to create no places of easy service, no commands that are not strictly necessary; to incur no charge that may demand new annual appropriations, but by a more wise application of moneys already appropriated and offices already authorized, to provide for the better education of the young officers of the Navy. It is my design not to create new offices, but by economy of administration to give vigor of action to those which at present are available; not to invoke new legislation, but to execute more effectually existing laws. Placed by their profession in connection with the world, visiting in their career of service every climate and every leading people, the officers of the American Navy, if

* From the original document on file at the Naval Academy.

they gain but opportunity for scientific instruction, may make themselves as distinguished for culture as they have been for gallant conduct.

"To this end it is proposed to collect the midshipmen who from time to time are on shore, and give them occupation, during their stay on land, in the study of mathematics, nautical astronomy, theory of morals, international law, gunnery, use of steam, the Spanish and the French languages, and other branches essential in the present day to the accomplishment of a naval officer.

"The effect of such an employment of the midshipmen cannot but be favorable to them and to the service. At present they are left, when waiting orders on shore, masters of their own motions, without steady occupation, young, and exulting in the relief from the restraints of discipline on shipboard. In collecting them at Annapolis for purposes of instruction, you will begin with the principle that a warrant in the Navy, far from being an excuse for licentious freedom, is to be held a pledge for subordination, industry, and regularity, for sobriety and assiduous attention to duty. Far from consenting that the tone of discipline and morality should be less than at universities or colleges of our country, the President expects such supervision and arrangement as shall make of them an exemplary body of which the country may be proud.

"To this end you have all the powers for discipline conferred by the laws of the United States, and the certainty that the Department will recommend no one for promotion who is proved unworthy of it from idleness, or ill conduct, or continuing ignorance, and who cannot bear the test of a rigid examination.

"For the purposes of instruction the Department can select from among twenty-two professors and three teachers of languages. This force, which is now almost wasted by the manner in which it is applied, may be concentrated in such a manner as to produce the most satisfactory results. Besides, the list of chaplains is so great that they cannot all be employed at sea; and the range of selection of teachers may be enlarged by taking from their number some who would prefer giving instruction at the school to serving afloat. The object of the Department being to make the simplest and most effective arrangement for a school, you will be the highest officer in the establishment, and will be intrusted with its government. It is my wish, if it be possible, to send no other naval officer to the school except such as may be able and willing to give instruction. Among the officers junior to yourself there are many whose acquisitions and tastes may lead them to desire such situations. For this end the Department would cheerfully detach three or four of the lieutenants and passed midshipmen, who, while they would give instruction, would be ready to aid you in affairs of discipline and government.

"Thus the means for a good naval school are abundant, though they have not yet been collected together and applied. One great difficulty remains to be considered. At our colleges and at West Point young men are trained in a series of consecutive years. The laws of the United States do not sanction a preliminary school for the Navy; they only provide for the instruction of officers who already are in the Navy. The pupils of the Naval School being, therefore, officers in the public service, will be liable at all times to be called from their studies and sent on public duty. Midshipmen, too, on their return from sea, at whatever season of the year, will be sent to the school. Under these circumstances, you will be obliged to arrange your classes in such a manner as will leave opportunity for those who arrive to be attached to classes suited to the stage of their progress in their studies.

It will be difficult to arrange a system of studies which will meet this emergency, but with the fixed resolve which you will bring to the work and with perseverance you will succeed.

"Having thus expressed to you some general views, I leave you, with such assistance as you may require, to prepare and lay before this Department, for its approbation, a plan for the organization of the Naval School at Fort Severn, Annapolis.

"The posts to which you and those associated with you will be called are intended to be posts of labor, but they will also be posts of the highest usefulness and consideration. To yourself, to whose diligence and care the organization of the school is intrusted, will belong, in a good degree, the responsibility of a wise arrangement. Do not be discouraged by the many inconveniences and difficulties which you will certainly encounter, and rely implicitly on this Department as disposed to second and sustain you under the law in every effort to improve the character of the younger branch of the service.

"I am, respectfully, your obedient servant,

"GEORGE BANCROFT.

"Commander FRANKLIN BUCHANAN,

"*United States Navy, Washington.*"

Commander Buchanan had already given much thought to the subject, so that his answer was ready very shortly.

Commander Buchanan to Secretary Bancroft.

"WASHINGTON, *August* 14, 1845.

"SIR: I have the honor to acknowledge the receipt of your communication of the 7th instant, directing me to lay before the Department for its approbation a plan for the organization of a naval school about to be established at Fort Severn,

Annapolis, the government of which you have been pleased to honor me with.

"Feeling sensibly the importance of the trust confided to me, after mature reflection, a close examination of the reports in relation to this subject from officers of high rank in the Navy, professors, and others, placed in my hands by the Department, and with the aid of Commanders McKean and Du Pont, the former of whom was so successful in his government of the Naval Asylum while the school was there held, I respectfully present for your consideration the inclosed plan, embracing, I believe, generally, the views expressed in your letter of the 7th instant.

"According to your instructions, the plan submitted is kept strictly, so far as my knowledge extends, within the means now at the disposal of the Department. As the Navy increases, and the country becomes alive to the advantages of a more extended education to those who are intrusted with the maintenance of its honor abroad, and who are so frequently called upon to perform intricate diplomatic services, an enlarged system will doubtless be provided for. Most of the reports made to you on this subject recommend a preliminary school and a more extended academic term. For the first no authority exists. Should the extension of the term of instruction be in accordance with your own views, it can be so arranged. But for the midshipmen now in the service I recommend that the present probation of five years be adhered to, and the proposed division of that period is based upon this view.

"All of which is respectfully submitted, by

"Your obedient servant,

"FRANKLIN BUCHANAN,

"*Commander.*

"HON. GEORGE BANCROFT,

"*Secretary of the Navy.*"

Accompanying this letter was the "plan" devised by Commander Buchanan, with the aid of Commanders McKean and Dupont. This plan was afterwards revised by the Secretary and by Commander Buchanan, and approved by the Department.*

PLAN OF THE NAVAL SCHOOL AT FORT SEVERN, ANNAPOLIS, MD.

"1. The Superintendent of the school will be appointed by the Secretary of the Navy from the list of officers not higher in rank than commander.

"2. The board of examination annually appointed will comprise at least two captains in the Navy; but except on that board no officer of higher rank than that of commander shall be ordered on duty at the Naval School.

"3. The Superintendent will have the immediate government of the institution, will be responsible for its management, direct all academic duties, and command all professors and others connected with the school. He will frame a code of rules and regulations for the internal government of the school, to be submitted to the Secretary of the Navy for his approval.

"4. Professors and instructors will be selected, so far as practicable, from officers of the Navy.

"5. Professors, under the orders of the Superintendent, will constitute a board for the transaction of business, will conduct the examinations during the course, decide on the merits of the midshipmen, report on the system of instruction, and suggest any improvements or alterations which their experience may dictate."

* The original plan is given in Note G of the Appendix of this volume. The approved plan went into operation, and, supplemented by Buchanan's regulations, governed the workings of the school until 1850. Both documents are copied from the originals in the Navy Department.

"6. Every applicant for admission to the school must be of good moral character, not less than thirteen nor more than sixteen years of age, and must be examined by the surgeon of the institution to ascertain if he be free from all deformity, deafness, nearness or other defect of sight, or disease or infirmity of any kind which would disqualify him from performing the active and arduous duties of a sea life. He must be able to read and write well, and be familiar with geography and arithmetic. The Academic Board will examine him on these branches, and certify to his capacity for admission into the school.

"7. When an acting midshipman receives his appointment, he is to be attached to the Naval School, subject to the exigencies of the service. Semi-annual examinations will be held at the school. Those who shall be found deficient at any examination will be dropped from the lists and returned to their friends. Those whose conduct and proficiency meet with the approbation of the Superintendent and Academic Board will be retained in the service and ordered to sea. After performing sea-duty for six months, and receiving a favorable report of his conduct during that time from his commander, he will be entitled to a warrant bearing the date of his acting appointment. Otherwise he will be dropped from the lists and restored to his friends.

"8. All midshipmen on shore, not on leave of absence, will be ordered to the Naval School.

"9. A midshipman, after serving three years at sea as now required, and having received a short leave of absence, at the discretion of the Department, to visit his friends, will report at its expiration to the Naval School to pursue his course of studies preparatory to his final examination.

"10. The course of studies will include English grammar and composition; arithmetic, geography, and history; navigation, gunnery, and the use of steam; the Spanish and French languages; and such other branches desirable to the accomplishment of a naval officer as circumstances may render practicable.

"11. The professors will be required to keep records of all the recitations, and report weekly to the Superintendent the progress and relative merit of the students. From these weekly reports the Superintendent will make quarterly reports to the Secretary of the Navy.

"12. Classes will be arranged according to the acquirements and capacity of the midshipmen.

"13. The final examination for promotion will embrace all the branches taught at the school.

"14. All midshipmen at the Naval School must provide themselves with such books as are necessary to pursue their studies, a quadrant, their uniform, and bedding.

"15. A sloop of war, or brig, may be connected with the institution as a school of practice in seamanship, evolutions, and gunnery.

"16. The board annually appointed under the Regulations of the Navy for the examination of midshipmen for promotion are to inspect generally the management of the institution, and report to the Secretary of the Navy on its condition and the means of improving it.

"GEORGE BANCROFT.

"Approved.

"NAVY DEPARTMENT, *August* 28, 1846."

The transfer of Fort Severn from the War Department was made at once in accordance with the following orders:

"General Orders No. 40.

"WAR DEPARTMENT, ADJUTANT-GENERAL'S OFFICE,
" *Washington, August* 15, 1845.

"1. Pursuant to the orders of the President, Fort Severn and the military site and jurisdiction near Annapolis, Md., is hereby transferred to the Navy Department, and will be placed in charge of Commander Franklin Buchanan, who has been designated by the Secretary of the Navy to receive the same.

"2. The public stores appertaining to the Quartermaster, Subsistence, and Ordnance Departments will be disposed of in such manner as may be directed by the chiefs of those Departments.

"3. Having seen that due precautions are taken for the security of the public property, the commanding officer (Bvt. Maj. J. L. Gardner, Fourth Artillery) will then proceed with his company to join the headquarters of his regiment at Fort Monroe.

"By order:

"R. JONES,
"*Adjutant-General.*"

Secretary Bancroft to Commander Buchanan.

"NAVY DEPARTMENT, *August* 15, 1845.

"SIR: The Secretary of War has issued an order for the transfer of Fort Severn and the whole military site near Annapolis to such officer of this Department as may be authorized to take charge of the same.

"You are authorized to make the necessary arrangements and to receive possession of the station.

"Respectfully, yours,

"G. BANCROFT.

"Commander F. BUCHANAN,
"*United States Navy, Washington.*"

It was subsequently agreed upon between the two Departments that the armament, as it stood, and everything belonging to the battery, should remain at the fort in charge of the ordnance sergeant, the whole to be under the control of the naval officer in command.*

Fort Severn was an old Army post, the site of which had been bought by the Government in 1808, at a time when Annapolis was considered a point of military importance. The grounds comprised about ten acres, nearly square in shape, inclosed on two sides by a brick wall, the other sides being open to the water. At the angle of the water-front stood the battery, a small circular rampart, mounting *en barbette* ten heavy guns, with a magazine in the centre. The point upon which it stood projected into the water, with the Severn River on one side and an arm of Chesapeake Bay forming the harbor of Annapolis on the other. The buildings consisted of officers' quarters and barracks, and were sufficient for the immediate wants of the new institution.

It was generally supposed at the time that the change was merely a removal of the Asylum school, and that, substituting Annapolis for Philadelphia, the details and general scope of the two would be the same. But such was clearly not the aim of the founder; and it soon became apparent that a new era was beginning in naval education. For the time being, the change showed itself more in an improved discipline than in an extended course of study. As the school was not recognized by law as an institution to fit candidates for the naval service, but only to educate those who had already become officers, it was only in the intervals of leisure from sea-duty that midshipmen could be taught. They might be compelled by the needs of the service to break off suddenly at any point in their studies; and they might be ordered to

* R. Jones, Adjutant-General, to Lieut. Col. G. Talcott, Ordnance Department, August 21, 1845. Lieut. Col. Talcott to Commander Buchanan, August 22, 1845. The Secretary of the Navy to Commander Buchanan, August 22, 1845.

join the school in the middle of the academic year. Hence, the greatest irregularity prevailed in the periods of study of different midshipmen, and in their coming and going, during the first five or six years, and it is difficult to give with exactness the number in attendance at any one time. The effect of this system was to render courses of study broken and instruction fragmentary.

In matters of discipline, however, the change was more apparent. Commander Buchanan was a man of inflexible will, and a stern disciplinarian, and his hands were strengthened by the prompt and cordial support of the Navy Department. He had, moreover, an able executive in Lieutenant Ward. The composition of the school made it a hard one to manage. The older midshipmen ranged from the age of eighteen to twenty-seven. They had no strong incentive to work, their opportunities for mental training had been few and slight since they had entered the service, and their sea-life of three or more years was followed by the improvidence and recklessness incidental to the sudden removal of restraint. For such a class of students an old provincial capital was a much better place than a commercial metropolis; and under Buchanan's management the institution prospered accordingly.

On the 7th of August the directions of the Navy Department were issued to Commander Buchanan. On the 14th, the "plan for a naval school" was submitted to the Department; and on the 10th of October the school was formally opened.

CHAPTER II.

THE NAVAL SCHOOL.

OCTOBER, 1845, TO JULY, 1850.

The academic staff of the school at its organization was as follows:

Commander Franklin Buchanan, Superintendent.

Lieut. James H. Ward, executive officer, and instructor in gunnery and steam.

Surgeon John A. Lockwood, instructor in chemistry.

Chaplain George Jones, instructor in English branches.

Prof. Henry H. Lockwood, instructor in natural philosophy.

Prof. William Chauvenet, instructor in mathematics and navigation.

Prof. Arsène N. Girault, instructor in French.

Passed Midshipman S. Marcy, assistant instructor in mathematics.

Lieutenant Ward* was president of the Academic Board,

---

*James Harman Ward was a son of Col. James Ward, of Hartford, Conn., and was born at that place in 1806. He graduated at the Vermont Military Academy, at Norwich, Vt., and entered Trinity College, Hartford. March 4, 1823, he was appointed a midshipman on board the United States ship Constitution, then under the command of Captain McDonough. March 3, 1831, he was promoted to the rank of lieutenant, which he held at the time of his appointment to the Naval School. Previously to his connection with the school he had been attached to the Mediterranean squadron, and had been for several years on the

the Superintendent taking no part in its proceedings. Passed Midshipman Marcy acted as secretary.

The formal opening of the school took place on Friday, October 10. At 11 o'clock on the morning of that day, the Superintendent assembled the officers of the school and the midshipmen who had reported, in one of the recitation-halls, and read to them the Secretary's letter, showing the views and purposes of the Department in regard to the organization of the school. He also read them the rules and regulations which he had established for the government of the students,* and addressed them "impressively and feelingly," says the National Intelligencer, in regard to their duties. His address was as follows:

"GENTLEMEN: In preparing the rules and regulations for the internal government of the Naval School, I have endeavored to confine myself to those points so absolutely necessary to the preservation of good discipline and harmony at an institution yet in its infancy, which we all, I am well assured, feel a pride should rank high in the estimation of our countrymen. Those among you who have served several years in the Navy know the value of wholesome laws and regulations; and to you I look with confidence for assistance in impress-

---

coast of Africa. Here he wrote his Manual of Naval Tactics, published in 1858, and still used as a text-book at the Naval Academy. In 1842 he delivered popular lectures on gunnery in Philadelphia, and later he published his Instructions on Naval Ordnance and Gunnery, a work which has accomplished much in the improvement of naval science. He also published a popular work called "Steam for the Million." He was detached from the Naval School in 1847. In 1853 he became a commander. At the outbreak of the war, in 1861, he was employed in defending the water-approach to Washington. He organized the Potomac flotilla, and was doing most efficient service, when he was killed in a gallant attempt to destroy a rebel battery on Matthias Point, June 27, 1861.

* See Appendix, note E.

ing upon the minds of those youths who have lately entered the service the absolute necessity of obedience.

"The Government, in affording you an opportunity of acquiring an education, so important to the accomplishment of a naval officer, has bestowed upon you all an incalculable benefit. But few, if any, now in the service have had the advantage that you are about to receive.

"The Regulations of the Navy require you to pass through a severe ordeal before you can be promoted; you must undergo an examination on all the branches taught at the Naval School before you are eligible to a lieutenancy; your morals and general character are strictly inquired into. It is therefore expected that you will improve every leisure moment in the acquirement of a knowledge of your profession; and you will recollect that a good moral character is essential to your promotion and high standing in the Navy.

"By carefully avoiding the first step toward intemperance, shunning the society of the dissolute and idle, and by cherishing the wish to deserve and the hope of receiving the approbation of your country, you can alone render yourselves able to occupy with honor the high standing in the Navy to which many of you are destined.

"I feel confident that all of you attached to this institution will endeavor to hold a high rank in the service by your application, zeal, intelligence, and correct deportment; and I shall deeply regret to hear that any individual among you has brought disgrace upon himself or upon his associates.

"Every indulgence, consistent with the rules and regulations of the institution, will be granted to those who merit it. The laws of the Navy point out the punishment of those who violate orders; and no commander is justified in overlooking offences against those laws, however painful it may be to him to enforce them. There is no discretionary power granted to him, although that power is sometimes exercised from necessity; the responsibility resting with the commander, from which he can only be relieved by the Secretary of the Navy or the President of the United States.

"It is at all times an unpleasant duty to a commander to be compelled to punish the misconduct of his juniors; but as an omission on his part to do his duty makes him as culpable as the offender himself, no officer who feels a proper respect for the service or himself will subject himself to so unpleasant a situation. We have no right as individuals to do that which may involve others in our misfortunes; and when we, as naval men, intentionally violate the laws that govern us, we cannot without dishonor to ourselves expect to escape punishment by making others responsible for our crimes.

"Having thus briefly given you my views on the subject of discipline, and the importance I attach to a strict compliance with all laws, orders, and regulations, I submit them to you all with the hope that you may be benefited by them."

The character of Commander Buchanan's administration is shadowed forth in his opening address. The first lesson of the young naval officer is subordination; and it was of paramount importance that the first administration of the school should exact this if nothing else. Two years of lax discipline at the start, in the period when the tone of a school is set and school traditions are fixed for all time, would have been a lasting element of weakness, from which the Academy was saved by the strong government of Buchanan.

The opening of the school was noticed in the papers of the day with favorable comments. The National Intelligencer said:*

"We understand the object of Mr. Secretary Bancroft,

* Quoted in Niles's Register, October 18, 1845.

in removing this school from Philadelphia to Annapolis, to be: 1st. To avoid the temptations and distractions that necessarily connect with a large and populous city to the detriment of young officers; 2d. To concentrate the services of excellent teachers, already in the employ of the Government, which have been hitherto in a great degree lost; 3d. To insure moral discipline and mental culture, by organizing and maturing an academy where the professors and students may be habitually kept together when on land, under the wholesome restraints of laws. To these purposes the Government property at Annapolis is admirably adapted. The situation is healthy and secluded, and yet of easy access. It is situated at the mouth of the Severn River, a beautiful tributary to the noble Chesapeake, affording ample opportunity to the young officers to apply their professional acquirements practically by being from time to time afloat. We conceive that Mr. Bancroft has discovered a most commendable sagacity, as well in selecting this admirable location, as in making it one of the leading features of his administration of the Navy Department to mature an institution indispensable to the welfare of this favorite branch of the public service."

The Maryland Republican, an Annapolis paper, a few days later, said:*

"The school is being organized with all the rapidity consistent with methodical arrangement. The various buildings have been repaired and surprisingly improved, considering the small expenditures and the brief time allowed, especially the quarters allotted to the midshipmen; and the professors are busily employed in classifying the sailor-students agreeably to grade, merit, and the nature of the prescribed studies. About forty young gentlemen have already

* See Niles's Register, October 18, 1845.

reported themselves, whose handsome appearance and gentlemanly deportment give a cheerful aspect to the streets of our quiet city."

As the Republican said, the classification of the "sailor-students" had already been undertaken. On the 4th of October, the Superintendent directed the professors to convene as a board and arrange the classes of midshipmen, lay out the course of instruction, and fix the hours of recitation. In his letter to the board he named as subjects of the course mathematics, natural philosophy, chemistry, gunnery and the use of steam, geography, English grammar, arithmetic, history, the French and Spanish languages, "and such other branches desirable to the accomplishment of a naval officer as your judgment may dictate."

Lieutenant Ward, as president of the board, called the professors together, and after two days' deliberations submitted a report, which was approved by the Superintendent. On the 11th, the day after the opening of the school, the professors met their pupils and gave them the first directions in regard to studies and hours of recitation; and on Monday, the 13th of October, the school was fairly in operation.

The report of the board of professors, prepared in accordance with the Superintendent's instructions, is given below.*

"REPORT.

"The board assumes that the academic year will extend at least until the last week in June, thus allowing nine months for the course of study.

"I. *Course of instruction.*—The instruction in this school to be comprised under the following six professorships:

"1. Mathematics.

"2. Natural philosophy.

* Journal Academic Board, 1.

"3. Chemistry.

"4. Ordnance and gunnery, and the use of steam.

"5. History, geography, English grammar, &c.

"6. French and Spanish languages.

"The board would suggest that instruction be given in fencing. It is presumed that a competent person, to be rated as gunner's mate, may be procured, who will be otherwise useful in the institution. This instruction to be given in the hours of recreation, and not to be obligatory upon the midshipmen.

"The board would also suggest that the manual exercise, or infantry-drill, be introduced. It would occupy not more than a half-hour daily, would be a healthy exercise, and would tend to elevate the military character of the school. Professor Lockwood offers his services as instructor in this branch for the present.

"The board is also of the opinion that, in the present arrangement of the studies, regard should be had to the eventual introduction of drawing.

"II. *Classification of midshipmen.*—It is proposed to call the two principal classes in this school the junior and senior classes.

"Midshipmen who have just been admitted into the service and have not yet been at sea, to be members of the junior class.

"Midshipmen entitled to examination for the grade of passed midshipman at the end of the academic year to be members of the senior class.

"Midshipmen who have been at sea, but are not entitled to said examination, to be assigned to either the junior or senior class, or to such sections of these classes as they may be best fitted to join.

"III. *Division of studies.*—The studies of the junior class to be arithmetic, elements of algebra and geometry, navigation as far as the sailings and the use of the quadrant, geography, English grammar and composition, and the French or Spanish language. The junior class to attend, also, the lectures in natural philosophy, ordnance, and chemistry, which are delivered to the senior class.

"The studies of the senior class to be algebra, geometry, plane and spherical trigonometry, nautical astronomy, navigation, descriptive astronomy, mechanics, optics, magnetism, electricity, ordnance, gunnery, the use of steam, history, composition, the French or Spanish language.

"Both classes to be exercised in the infantry-drill and fencing, in case these branches are introduced.

"IV. *Division of time.*—(Provisional.)*

"1. *General programme for the whole school.*

"School from 8 a. m. to 12 m.

"Recreation and dinner from 12 m. to 1.30 p. m.

"School from 1.30 to 4.30 p. m., except on Saturday.

"Recreation and supper from 4.30 to 6 p. m.

"Study from 6 to 10 p. m.

"2. *Programme of recitations and study of the senior class.*

"In mathematics and natural philosophy, the class to be divided for the present into two sections:

"Mathematics, daily, first section from 8 to 9 a. m.; second section from 9 to 10 a. m.

"Natural philosophy, daily, first section from 8 to 9 a. m.; second section from 9 to 10 a. m.

"Study from 10 to 11.

"Ordnance, gunnery, and steam on Tuesday and Saturday, from 11 a. m. to 12 m.

* Altered October 29, 1845. Rec. Academic Board, 1, p. 6.

"Chemistry on Thursday, from 11 a. m. to 12 m.

"History and composition on Monday, Wednesday, and Friday, from 11 a. m. to 12 m.

"French or Spanish, daily, except Saturday, from 1.30 to 4.30 p. m.

"Study from 6 to 10 p. m.

"The sections to be exercised in the use of the sextant and other astronomical instruments at any hour favorable to observations, provided such exercise does not in any way interfere with recitations in other branches, or with the preparation for the same.

"3. *Programme of recitation and study of the junior class.*

"Lecture on natural philosophy, daily, from 8 to 9 a. m.

"Study from 9 to 10 a. m.

"Mathematics, daily, from 10 to 11 a. m.

"Lectures on gunnery, &c., and chemistry, from 11 a. m. to 12 m.

"French or Spanish, excepting on Saturday, from 1.30 to 2.30 p. m.

"Geography, English grammar, and composition, daily, excepting Saturday, (study and recitation,) from 2.30 to 4.30 p. m.

"Study from 6 to 10 p. m.

"The class to be exercised at suitable times in the use of the quadrant.

"V. *Merit and demerit rolls.*—The merit of all recitations to be registered upon a scale ranging from *ten* downwards; the demerit roll ranging from *one* upwards,—the demerit of unexcused absence from recitation being 10, of unexcused tardiness 5, and all other delinquencies according to the decision of the Superintendent in the particular case.

"At the end of the academic year the average merit of the midshipmen to be made out from the merit and demerit marks made during the year, and this relative rank, at the final examination, to be determined by combining their marks for the studies pursued in the school with those given by the board of examination for proficiency in seamanship.

"The relative weight to be allowed to the different branches studied in the school, (in combining them for rank): mathematics 3, and all other branches 2; in other words, that 10 in mathematics be reckoned 30; in all other branches as 20.*

"VI. *Reports.*—The professors to make weekly reports to the Superintendent, stating the merit of each recitation and the average merit for the week, the absences and other delinquencies of the midshipman in his class or section. The form of these reports to be according to the model herewith submitted.

"VII. *Meetings of the Academic Board.*—The Academic Board to hold weekly meetings to deliberate on the transfer of midshipmen from one class or section to another, and upon such other matters as may arise for their consideration.

"No transfer of any midshipman from one class or section to another to be made until it shall have been approved by the Superintendent.

"VIII. *Roll-calls.*—The rolls to be called at each recitation, within five minutes after the ringing of the bell. All midshipmen entering after that time to be marked and reported to the Superintendent as tardy."

The report was approved, and on the 13th the work of instruction began. On the same day Commander Buchanan wrote to the Secretary: "I am highly gratified at the disposition shown by the young gentlemen to apply themselves with energy and zeal to their studies."

This first arrangement, crude and hasty as it was, is to be noticed as forming the groundwork, together with the plan

* Modified by resolution of Academic Board, February 14, 1846.

and regulations, of the school organization for the next five years. It will be observed that the senior class was made up of midshipmen who had been three or more years at sea, and who were preparing for their examination for promotion. The junior class was composed of acting midshipmen, newly appointed, who had never been at sea, and who were sent to the school to wait their turn. The accessions to either class might take place at any time during the year, and midshipmen of either class were liable to be detached at any time, as the exigencies of the service demanded, and as actually happened many times during the first years. It is therefore difficult to determine with exactness from the records how many of either class were at the school during the year, the arrivals and departures being so frequent, and the numbers in consequence constantly changing. At the end of January, 1846, four months after the opening of the school, there appear to have been 36 midshipmen of the date of 1840,† who were preparing for examination, 13 of the date of 1841, who were to remain pursuing studies and attending lectures until drafted for service at sea, and 7 acting midshipmen, appointed since September of the previous year. The last joined the school under a conditional letter of appointment from the Secretary of the Navy. "If approved by the surgeon and found respectable in intellect and acquirement," they were enrolled as acting midshipmen and received warrants, which were given them conditionally, and which contained this proviso: "After a course of attendance at the Naval School, if the Superintendent shall report favorably of your merits, but not otherwise, you will be retained in the service." By regulation, they were to remain at the school one year, and at the end of it to pass a satisfactory examination and be ordered to sea. At the end of a probationary term at sea, they

† Date of entry into the service.

were to receive, as had previously been the case, a midshipman's warrant; and after three years of sea-service, they were to return and spend another year at the school preparatory to examination for promotion. This programme was not regularly carried out, though it served in a general way to govern the practice of the institution. The midshipmen of the date of 1840—that is, who had entered the service during that year—were the first to graduate at Annapolis, finishing their course in July, 1846, and they were followed in succession by the subsequent dates until the re-organization of the school in 1851. The number of midshipmen of the date of 1841 being 186, too large to be examined at one time, and that of 1842 very small, the former were divided into three classes, who came in successive years, the last division graduating in 1849. The date of 1842 graduated with them, but were classed separately. There were no appointments in 1843 or 1844, in consequence of the act of 1842 limiting the number of midshipmen, and the date of 1845 followed the last division of the '41's and '42's.*

The examination for promotion of midshipmen of six years' standing continued to be held every summer, as heretofore, by a board of naval officers of high rank. Formerly, the examination had been confined to seamanship and navigation; now, according to article 13 of the "plan," it was to embrace all the branches taught at the school, and seamanship in addition. The examiners were to act as a board of visitors, to inspect the workings of the school and to suggest improvements.

An article in the Nautical Magazine,† published near the close of the year 1845, speaks in terms of high praise of the new school and its Superintendent. "The appearance, order,

* Circular of Navy Department February 26, 1846. Lull, p. 10.

† Quoted in Niles's Register, January 31, 1846.

and studious habits of the midshipmen generally reflect the highest credit upon them, upon the institution, and upon the service of which they are members. The police and discipline are conducted by the Superintendent in person, with the tone, system, and energy for which he is distinguished. Aided by the zealous efforts of those having charge of the various branches of instruction, he has already given to the institution a consolidated character which would render it difficult for an observer to detect traces of its recent origin. Under his administration of affairs its friends may look with confidence for such development of usefulness from year to year as eventually to produce results which will equal the wants and expectations of the Navy, and will stand as a monument of honor to the Secretary by whose patriotic, zealous, and judicious efforts it has been founded."

Thus it was that in four months after the first inception of the plan, and less than eight months after assuming the duties of his office, Secretary Bancroft was enabled to present to the country a fully-organized academy, in efficient working order, which was destined to do for the Navy what West Point had so long done for the Army. He had accomplished during a single recess of Congress what his predecessors had for thirty years in vain attempted to secure by legislation; and it had been done simply by a more judicious application of the means which Congress had already provided. In his annual report* of December 1, 1845, he stated briefly the steps he had taken:

"Congress, in its great desire to improve the Navy, had permitted the Department to employ professors and instructors at an annual cost of $28,200; and it had been used, besides the few employed at the receiving-ships and the Naval

* Executive Documents, Twenty-ninth Congress, first session, No. 2, p. 647.

Asylum, to send professors with the midshipmen to every ocean and every clime. But the ship is not friendly to study, and the office of professsor rapidly declined into a sinecure; often not so much was done as the elder officers would cheerfully do for their juniors. The teachers on board of the receiving-ships gave little instruction, or none whatever; so that the expenditure was fruitless of great results. Many of the professors were able and willing, but the system was a bad one. The idea naturally suggested itself of seizing the time when the midshipmen are on shore and appropriating it to their culture. Instead of sending migratory professors to sea with each handful of midshipmen, the midshipmen themselves, in the intervals between sea-duty, might be collected in a body and devote their time to suitable instruction. For the pay of the instructors Congress has provided. In looking out for a modest shelter for the pupils, I was encouraged to ask for Fort Severn, at Annapolis. The transfer was readily made by order of the Secretary of War, and a school was immediately organized on an unostentatious and frugal plan. This institution, by giving some preliminary instruction to the midshipmen before their first cruise; by extending an affectionate but firm supervision over them as they return from sea; by providing them suitable culture before they pass to a higher grade; by rejecting from the service all who fail in capacity or in good disposition to use their time well, will go far to renovate and improve the American Navy.

"The plan pursued has been unpretending, but it is hoped will prove efficient. A few professors give more and better instruction than four-and-twenty at sea. No supernumerary officer has been ordered to Annapolis; no idle man is attached to the establishment. Commander Buchanan, to whom the organization of the school was intrusted, has carried his instructions into effect with precision and sound judgment, and with a wise adaptation of simple and moderate means to a great and noble end."

The progress of the school during the year 1845–'46 was such as to satisfy its authorities and justify the expectations of its friends. Such breaches of discipline as occurred were followed by prompt punishment, and in some cases by dismissal. A vacation of a fortnight was given the students at Christmas. This practice continued till 1849, when the time was reduced to two days.* In January, 1846, it was ordered that examinations of acting midshipmen should be held in the April and October following.† In February a regulation ‡ was adopted depriving midshipmen whose weekly average was below 40 per cent., of liberty to leave the grounds of the institution—a rule which still exists in a modified form. At this time the liberty-hours, according to article 23 of the regulations, were from 4 to 10 p. m. A few days later, a scale of numbers was adopted § fixing the relative weights of different branches of study in computing the final marks. These numbers were used as co-efficients, the final mark in each branch being multiplied by the co-efficient of the branch, and the aggregate of the products making the final mark of the midshipman. The scale was as follows:

Mathematics and navigation, 3.
Gunnery, 2.
French, 2.
Natural philosophy, 2.
English, 1.
Chemistry, 1.

* Rules, Regulations, and Orders, 36, 46, 56, 82.

† Rules, Regulations, and Orders, 37.

‡ Rules, Regulations, and Orders, 38. Revoked October, 1846.

§ Report of Academic Board and letter of Secretary Bancroft, February 14, 1846, in letters of the Secretary of the Navy on file in the Superintendent's office, United States Naval Academy.

The scale is stated in the report to be based upon—1. Professional importance of each branch; 2. Time or ability required to obtain a competent knowledge of the branch, in connection with time actually assigned it at the school; and, 3. Known disposition of students to reject certain branches.

The first annual examination was held in June, 1846. The Board of Examiners, which assembled on the 20th of that month, was composed of Commodores Lawrence Kearney and M. C. Perry, and Captains McKeever, McCauley, and Mayo. During the examination the school was visited by the Secretary of the Navy. According to the instructions of the Secretary, all the midshipmen were examined in the branches they had studied, the professors questioning the students in the presence of the board. In addition, the senior class had the usual examination in seamanship. The order upon the navy-list of the midshipmen examined for promotion was determined by these examinations. The final mark was found by the same method as that used by the professors in determining academic standing; 5 was assigned as a factor in seamanship, and the table of relative weights remained otherwise the same.*

At this examination there were examined fifty-two midshipmen of the date of 1840, or earlier. Of these, eighteen had joined the school later than December 1, 1845, and had consequently had but six months at their studies. Some of these had even had less than three months. The irregularity of attendance stood very much in the way of successful instruction, and could only be justified by the necessities of the service. The attendance at the school during the first year may be seen approximately from the following table: †

* Record of Examining Board, 127.

† Obtained by a collation of the Navy Register for 1846 with the journal of the officer of the day and the record of the Examining Board.

Members of the senior class present throughout the year	34
Members of the senior class arriving after December 1, 1845, and remaining till end of year	18
Seniors present, June examination	52
Seniors detached before June	39
Total connected with senior class at any time	91
Junior class, or acting midshipmen, (periods wholly uncertain)	10
Total at school	101

Except for the unavoidable irregularities in the periods of study, the career of a midshipman from his first appointment to his promotion would have comprised one year at the school, three years at sea, and a fifth year at the school, followed by the final examination. The examination was conducted according to the following rules, prescribed by the Secretary ot the Navy:

"RULES TO GOVERN EXAMINATIONS AT THE NAVAL SCHOOL AT FORT SEVERN, ANNAPOLIS, MD.*

"The Board of Examiners will meet at the Naval School, Annapolis, Md., on the 15th of July annually, and examine all the midshipmen attached to the school. The midshipmen whose warrants bear date prior to [date left blank] are to be examined in all the branches taught at the school, in conformity with the plan for a naval school.

* These rules are found in a pamphlet issued by the Navy Department, entitled, "Plan and Regulations of the Naval School at Annapolis. Washington: C. Alexander, Printer. 1846." They agree substantially with the copy of the orders of the Department to Commodore Lawrence Kearney, president of the Board of Examiners of 1846, bearing date June 19, 1846, and preserved in the record of the board of 1846, page 10.

"The professors are to examine the midshipmen in the several branches of their studies in the presence of the board. The board is to judge of the merits of the candidates in these branches; but in giving numbers, the general average on the professors' reports, which will be submitted to the board by the Superintendent after the academic examination, must be considered the basis. These reports will contain the academic standing, deduced from all the branches, and give the aggregate for each candidate, or sum of the products obtained by multiplying the average in each branch by its proper factor. To this aggregate the board will add the product obtained by multiplying the averages in seamanship by its factor in order to obtain the aggregate representing the relative merit in all the academic branches and seamanship combined. The list thus obtained will be modified by the board on the ground of the officer-like qualities of the candidates, their moral and general character, the correctness of their journals, and the character of their letters from the commanders with whom they have served. When the board deems it necessary to modify the list referred to, its reasons must be specifically given in the final report to the Department, and the proposed modification will be subject to the revision of the Department. The list, as approved, will establish rank.

"As it is important that the Department should be fully informed as to the respective merits of the candidates, the board will make separate reports of their qualifications in the several branches upon which they shall be examined, and also a general report showing the relative rank to which they should be entitled.

"The board will adopt the scale of merit from one to ten in seamanship, as in the other branches; and in making up their general average for the assignment of rank, the multiplier of five will be used in this branch. As a much higher value is thus placed on seamanship than on the other branches, the board is directed to exercise a sound judgment in deciding upon the numbers to be given to the candidate before them, previous to the examination of another.

"A failure to pass in any branch other than seamanship and navigation is not absolutely to *reject* an officer, provided he passes high in those branches. An officer who shall be *rejected* will be dropped from the navy-list and restored to his friends. An officer who shall fail to pass in any of the branches taught at the school, and yet displays character and talents that will render his services valuable to the Navy, may, if the board is satisfied that there is a good excuse for the failure, have his case suspended upon its recommendation till the next examination, when, if he pass, he is to be assigned his proper rank among those with whom he may be examined. A failure to pass a second time can admit of no excuse, and must remove him from the service. Sickness, which may have prevented an officer from studying, may be considered a good reason for a second examination, provided his general deportment be correct. The time spent at the school by each midshipman will be considered by the board, and a due allowance made for any deficiencies resulting from the want of time to acquire a knowledge of the various academic studies.

"In regard to the junior classes of midshipmen, the same rules in general must apply to them which are hereby directed to be observed in the examination of the class for promotion. The examination of the juniors may be more cursory, and seamanship will be omitted. The board will inform the Department if they have severally made good use of their time at the Naval School; and if any show a clear incapacity for the naval service, they must be reported, and their names will then be dropped from the list, and they will be restored to their friends.

"The board will, in conformity with the sixteenth article of the 'Plan for a Naval School,' inspect generally the management of the institution, and report to the Department on its condition and means of improving it.

"All the proceedings of the board will be recorded in the 'Examination Record-Book,' and deposited with the Superintendent of the school.

"Approved:

"GEORGE BANCROFT.

"NAVY DEPARTMENT, *August* 28, 1846."

In addition to these instructions, before the examination of 1845, a special order had been given by Secretary Bancroft that the Examining Board should make a preliminary inquiry of each midshipman whether he had incurred any debts at the Academy which remained unpaid; and if his answer was not satisfactory, he should be considered as having failed to pass. The letter of the Secretary* containing these instructions said: "The Department is determined to do all in its power to encourage habits of frugality and strict honor in pecuniary transactions, and consequently to discourage a disposition to incur debts beyond the means of punctual payment." Secretary Mason, Mr. Bancroft's successor at the head of the Navy Department, wrote, later,† to Commander Buchanan in the same spirit. He spoke of the importance of guarding "the young gentlemen against pecuniary indebtedness, which, without means of payment, leads to swindling," and ordered that "no acting midshipman shall visit a tavern, hotel, or eating-house without permission."

These regulations, more or less modified, have continued in force to the present time.

† May 4, 1846.

* December 17, 1846. The shore-pay of a midshipman at this time was $350 per annum.

Towards the end of the first academic year the want of additional buildings began to be felt. The Board of Examiners of 1846, in their report on the condition of the school, remarked upon the crowded state of the midshipmen's quarters, and upon the need of new buildings and apparatus. Commander Buchanan stated that want of space had compelled him to put from three to ten midshipmen in a room.

The Secretary had already foreseen these difficulties, and had made an appeal to Congress in behalf of the school. The expenditure, under the last appropriation, for instruction had now been reduced one-half, by placing eleven professors, out of twenty-two, on waiting orders. (See table.) Further reductions were contemplated, and were rapidly being carried out. The Secretary was, therefore, in a position to put the matter before Congress in these terms: "It has been your custom to appropriate a certain sum for instruction in the Navy, to pay the persons employed for this purpose. Within the past year the number of these persons has been diminished, while the benefit to the service has been vastly increased. All that is now asked is that you will continue to appropriate the same amount as formerly, but that it may be devoted specifically to this new system of instruction." To this Congress made a ready response in the appropriation bill of that year.* "Of the money appropriated in this act for pay of the Navy and contingent expenses, enumerated, an amount not exceeding $28,200 may be expended, under the direction of the Secretary of the Navy, for *repairs, improvements, and instruction* at Fort Severn, Annapolis, Md." This, it will be noticed, was exactly the amount of the former appropriations.

No time was lost in setting about the work. Three days after the bill became a law the Secretary informed Commander

* Act approved August 10, 1846, § 4.

Buchanan* that a certain sum was to be expended "in such additions and alterations as will enable the Department to attach to the school 100 midshipmen, to be well accommodated." The work, begun at once, consisted in the enlargement and refitting of the quarters, and the erection of a building to be used for a dining-hall, athenæum, and kitchen. The foundation of a hospital was laid, the chaplain's quarters were enlarged, and other changes and improvements were carried out.

After the June examination the school had a vacation from the 10th of July to the 10th of October. At the latter date the students again assembled, and on the 12th the school was re-opened by the Superintendent, who met the professors and students, and read out to them the plan and regulations, as had been done the year before. This custom was kept up by Buchanan's successor.

Meanwhile Secretary Bancroft had been appointed minister to Great Britain, and he was succeeded at the head of the Navy Department by the Hon. John Y. Mason, of Virginia. Mr. Mason continued the policy of his predecessor in fostering and developing the school. In a letter to Buchanan, of December 17, 1846, he spoke of the great interest which he felt in the Naval School, and of "an anxious desire that the favor of Congress may not be withdrawn." He closed his letter by saying: "I have read with satisfaction and a hearty approval your remarks to the midshipmen at the opening of the school. No branch of the military service can be maintained without the observance of discipline and subordination. If officers do not set the example of obedience to the laws and regulations of the service, they cannot require or expect it of the men under their command, and the consequence must be inefficiency of the Navy, mutiny, and disgrace to the

* The Secretary of the Navy to Commander Buchanan, August 13, 1846.

flag, which every officer ought to be ready to lay down his life to honor and defend."

In his annual report,* December 5, 1846, the Secretary gave a statement of the progress of the school and renewed the appeal to Congress. "The Naval School during the past year has been continued under the judicious superintendence of Commander Franklin Buchanan, and gives renewed promise of usefulness to the service. At the last session of Congress it was made the subject of no special appropriation, but permission was given to apply a limited sum ($28,200) from the existing appropriations. This moderate provision has enabled the Department to make some necessary additions to the accommodations of the school, and has been found sufficient for its economical support. It is hoped a similar provision will be adopted for the ensuing year."

Accordingly, the appropriation bill for 1847† repeated exactly the provision of the year before, with this addition: "And for the purchase of land for the use of the Naval School at that place, not exceeding twelve acres." The purchase alluded to was made in the following summer. It comprised land lying northwest of the fort territory, and was the first addition to the original site made under the Navy Department. The details of the purchase will be found in the chapter on 'Grounds.'

At the beginning of the second academic year slight changes had been made in the programme of study. Examinations of acting midshipmen were held in March and June. The class numbered twelve at the first examination, and nine at the second. These examinations were oral, and the president and professors of Saint John's College were invited to

* Executive Documents, Twenty-ninth Congress, second session, No. 4, p. 385.

†Approved March 3, 1847.

be present.* Most of the midshipmen examined were ordered immediately to sea.

The war with Mexico was now in progress, and Commander Buchanan had applied for active service soon after the first outbreak of hostilities.† The important work in which he was engaged at the time led the Department to postpone action upon his request, and early the next year he renewed it. The school being now fairly under way, the application was granted, and on the 16th of March, 1847, he left Annapolis to take command of the United States ship Germantown. He took an active part in the later operations of the war, being present at the capture of Vera Cruz, and at several other engagements.‡ He was succeeded at the school by Commander George P. Upshur, lately promoted from the grade of lieutenant. The corps of instructors remaining much the same, the school routine was not affected by the change of Superintendents.

At this time, according to the Navy Register of 1847, there were fifty-seven midshipmen at the school, besides the acting midshipmen. The examination for promotion took place in July, Commodore Thomas Ap Catesby Jones being president of the board; and during the examination the school received an official visit from the Secretary of the Navy.

* Record Academic Board, I, pp. 11, 12.

† Commander Buchanan to the Secretary of the Navy, May 14, 1846.

‡ After the close of the war Captain Buchanan returned home, having fully sustained his reputation as an able officer. In 1852 he commanded the Susquehanna in Commodore Perry's expedition to Japan, which resulted in the opening of that country to foreigners. In 1861 he took the side of the South, and, his resignation not being accepted, he was dismissed the service. He took a prominent part in the war, being in command of the Merrimac in her engagement with the Monitor, and of the ram Tennessee in the Mobile fight in August, 1864, on both of which occasions he was wounded, and on the second taken prisoner. After the war he was for a time president of the Maryland Agricultural College. He died May 12, 1874.

Before the beginning of the new academic year, in September, 1847, Lieutenant Ward was ordered to sea. He went as executive officer of the Cumberland, then flag-ship of the Gulf squadron, under Commodore Perry. Professor Chauvenet was elected to succeed him as president of the Academic Board, and Lieut. John A. Dahlgren took his place as instructor in gunnery.* During the year Dr. Lockwood gave lectures on international law, and the course in general was revised and improved.

There were, however, defects in the system which the board had no power to remove, and they now began to be seriously felt. The chief difficulty arose from the irregularity in regard to admission, attendance, and graduation. During the academic year 1847–'48 thirty-one acting midshipmen attended the school, of whom more than half reported after January 1, 1848.† They were admitted one at a time at intervals of a few days; and hence the class under instruction contained students in every stage of progress, but no two alike. The professors were at a loss how to classify them, or, indeed, how to conduct their studies at all, without having as many classes as there were pupils. At short intervals, also, came orders detaching them, sometimes singly, sometimes in bodies of three or four. At such times notice was given to the professors, an examination was held, and the party of midshipmen discharged, to renew their studies at any time in the distant future when it might be convenient for the Department to order them home. With regard to the senior midshipmen, the case was nearly as bad.

* On temporary service. Journal of officer of the day, October 23, 1847. He was soon afterward detached.

† Thirty-seven candidates for admission presented themselves during the year, and for the examination of these thirty-seven, the committee of the Academic Board convened thirty-one times, between November and June.

They were ordered to and from the school at irregular intervals, only a portion remaining through the year.

In spite of these obstacles, the school was doing a good work. The examinations in the several branches served to give point and direction to the studies of young officers, and, if they accomplished nothing else, they at least had some effect in excluding unworthy candidates for appointment. Secretary Mason said in his report of 1847, in speaking of the Naval School:* "The examinations before an applicant can enter the service, and those which determine his qualification for promotion, after five or six years of service, exert the most beneficial influence in retaining only those who have the mental endowments essential to a skillful and accomplished naval officer."

With the limited force of instructors at the command of the Department, it was impossible to have accomplished teachers in each branch, and it was necessary to shape the course according to the abilities and attainments of the officers whom the school was fortunate enough to get. After Ward and Dahlgren left, their places could not be exactly filled, and Professor Lockwood, whose range of scientific study was very wide, took charge of gunnery and other subjects, while steam was joined with chemistry. In October, 1848, the academic faculty was as follows:†

Commander G. P. Upshur, Superintendent.

Lieut. Sidney S. Lee, executive officer.

Dr. John A. Lockwood, instructor in chemistry and steam.

Prof. W. Chauvenet, instructor in mathematics.

Prof. H. H. Lockwood, instructor in astronomy, mechanics, and gunnery.

Professor Girault, instructor in French.

Chaplain Jones, instructor in English.

* Executive Documents, Thirtieth Congress, first session, No. 8, p. 957.

† Journal Academic Board, 1, p. 36.

William M. Chauvenet, assistant in French.

Passed Midshipman William N. Jeffers,* assistant in mathematics.

Changes meanwhile were suggested, and it was even proposed to apply to Congress for legislation. But, in view of the peculiar character and purpose of the institution, the Secretary wisely thought that such an effort should be postponed until a larger experience and more careful thought and study had enabled naval officers and professors to mature a plan which would meet the wants of the service for some time to come. Regulations once established by hasty legislation, however injudicious they might be, could only be modified by the slow process of repeal or amendment. It was much that some steps had been taken, and that no mistake had been made so far. That the steps had been in the right direction, the Secretary was assured. In his report for 1848 he said:† "The beneficial effects of the Naval School upon the service are already beginning to be sensibly felt. The truth is admitted by all that the services required of officers are more of the head than the hand. The result of experience in the Army, that in proportion as education has been encouraged, and the means of acquiring it afforded, so have the character and efficiency of the officers been improved, will not fail to be confirmed in the Navy. * * * The lad who leaves his parents at the age of fourteen or fifteen years to enter the service as a midshipman cannot be expected to have laid the foundation even for so broad a superstructure of knowledge. The Naval School promises to furnish the means of attaining these ends, so important for the Navy. It will produce, I trust, the same happy fruits of skill and knowledge which the Military Academy has already produced for the

* Now Chief of the Bureau of Ordnance.

† Executive Documents, Thirtieth Congress, second session, No. 1, p. 612.

Army." In another part of the report the Secretary spoke of flags of captured vessels and trophies in the rooms of the Navy Department at Washington, and recommended their removal to the school. This removal was afterwards made, and the flags are still to be seen in the gunnery-room of the Academy.

In March, 1849, the administration of Taylor came in, and William Ballard Preston, of Virginia, was appointed to succeed Mr. Mason as Secretary of the Navy. Early in this year the Academic Board had had the subject of the course of instruction under long and careful consideration; and they had made a formal report and recommendations which had, as yet, been followed by no action of the Department. At length, on the 4th of September, 1849, Secretary Preston appointed a board to consider the subject and draw up a system of regulations embodying their views. The board sat at Washington, and was composed of the following officers:

Commodore William B. Shubrick,
Commander Franklin Buchanan,
Commander Samuel F. Dupont,
Commander George P. Upshur,
Surgeon W. S. W. Ruschenberger.
Professor William Chauvenet.

Capt. Henry Brewerton, of the Corps of Engineers, at that time Superintendent of the Military Academy at West Point, was to confer with the board on the discipline of that institution.

The new regulations were reported to the Secretary in October. They were soon after approved, and went into operation at the beginning of the next academic year, July 1, 1850. At the same time, Commander C. K. Stribling succeeded Commander Upshur as Superintendent. The provisions of the new regulations are given at length in the following chapter.

CHAPTER III.

THE PERIOD OF TRANSITION.

JULY, 1850, TO NOVEMBER, 1851.

The essential features of the new organization were the following:*

The institution, to be called henceforth the United States Naval Academy, was placed under the supervision of the Chief of the Bureau of Ordnance and Hydrography, who was to inspect it personally once a year, and through whom its routine business with the Department was to be conducted; but in matters of discipline the reports were to be made directly to the Secretary of the Navy. The Superintendent, as before, had immediate charge of the institution. An experienced lieutenant or commander was to be the executive officer and instructor in naval tactics and practical seamanship. He was to be known as the commandant of midshipmen. The other instructors were as follows:

Professor of mathematics.
Professor of natural and experimental philosophy.
Professor of gunnery and infantry tactics.
Professor of ethics, &c.
Professor of modern languages.
Instructor of drawing and draughting.
Instructor of the art of defence.

---

* From the copy of the report of the board in the Superintendent's office, United States Naval Academy.

The five professors, with the Superintendent and commandant of midshipmen, were to compose the Academic Board, of which the Superintendent was president *ex officio*. Its duties were to fix the order of instruction and the time devoted to each branch, to recommend text-books, changes in course, and purchases of books and apparatus, and to take cognizance of other academic matters.

But the main feature of the change was the extension of the course and the arrangement of the examinations for admission. These latter were to be held between the 1st and 5th of October, in each year, and at no other time. After passing this examination the acting midshipman was to remain at the Academy for two years from the time of admission, and if he passed this course he was ordered to sea. After six months of satisfactory sea-service he received a midshipman's warrant, bearing the date of his appointment as acting midshipman. By the 1st of October, three years from the time of leaving the Academy, he was to return to it, and continue the studies of the final course of two years. At the end of this time he was to be examined for promotion. Four classes were thus provided for, there being an intermission of three years between the end of the third-class and the beginning of the second-class course.

The course of instruction embraced six departments:

1. Naval tactics and practical seamanship.

2. Mathematics, including pure mathematics, navigation, astronomy, and land and nautical surveying. Drawing and draughting were in charge of this department.

3. Natural and experimental philosophy, including mechanics, the use of steam, the construction and management of the steam-engine, especially of marine engines, the phenomena of chemistry, heat, electricity, and light. Mineralogy and geology, treating especially of coal and iron.

4. Gunnery and infantry-tactics, theory and practice of gunnery, and artillery and infantry tactics. Instruction in the art of defence, including fencing, was in charge of this department.

5. Ethics. English grammar, rhetoric, physical and descriptive geography, history, moral philosophy, constitutional, national, and international law, and military and naval law.

6. Modern languages. Speaking, reading, and writing French and Spanish.

Each head of department was to be the judge of the methods of teaching to be employed in his department, and he was given considerable liberty in transferring students from their positions in the class as fixed by the marks of his assistants.

A sloop of war was to be attached to the Academy for sea-service and gunnery-practice during the summer. She was commanded by the commandant of midshipmen, and officered in part from the Academy.

The examination for admission was made very light. Candidates were to be between thirteen and fifteen years of age, and were to be able to read, write, and spell, and perform the four "primary rules of arithmetic." They were also required to pass before a medical board.

Semi-annual and annual examinations were held during the course, and students reported deficient in any branch of study were to be dropped; and they were not to be restored unless upon the recommendation of the Academic Board.

The final examination of the graduating class for promotion took place in October, instead of June, as was the case with the others. It was conducted by a board of three captains and two commanders, together with the Superintendent and commandant of midshipmen, and included all the branches taught at the Academy. The professor in charge of a branch put the questions orally to the students in the presence of the board, and the final standing, which determined the order of the midshipmen on the navy-list, was made up by combining all the marks of the course, but was subject to the revision of the board. At the same time a board of visitors, consisting of the Chief of the Bureau of Ordnance and six other "gentlemen of scientific attainments," made an inspection of the working of the Academy, and reported their views upon it to the Secretary of the Navy.

The student's conduct had a very considerable weight in determining his final standing, being counted as equal in importance to mathematics. Two hundred demerits in any year involved dismissal. The other provisions in regard to conduct were not unlike those which have since been in force. Dueling, cards, tobacco, liquor, clubs, and societies, the use of fire-arms, the marriage of midshipmen, were forbidden. As a general rule, leave was only granted on Saturdays. The restriction to the grounds, singularly enough, included officers as well as midshipmen.* A midshipman was detailed daily to serve as officer of the day. He had an office at the gate, and the same duties of inspection and record as were enjoined by the earlier regulations. A master was to be attached to the Academy, to act as instructor in mathematics. He had, in addition, certain police duties, among which was the charge of the mess-hall. The other provisions of the regulations consisted of minute details in relation to the interior discipline of the institution.

Several changes were made about this time in the force of officers. Lieutenant Lee was relieved by Lieut. Thomas T. Craven,† to whose long connection with the Academy—

* Chap. 9, § 6. "No *professor, instructor,* midshipman, or acting midshipman, *nor any other person doing duty in the institution,* is to go beyond the limits of the inclosure without the permission of the Superintendent."

† Now rear-admiral.

nearly eight years in all—is especially due the commencement and elaboration of the system of practice-cruises, than which no other feature of the course has proved more beneficial. He remained as second in command till 1855; and, returning again in 1858, he finally left the Academy in 1860.

Among other changes, Mr. Jones was relieved of his duties of instruction and acted as chaplain. He was afterwards detached, to accompany Commodore Perry's expedition to Japan.* He was succeeded by Prof. Joseph E. Nourse, in the English department. About the same time Prof. W. F. Hopkins took the place of Dr. Lockwood. The staff was now composed of the following officers: †

ACADEMIC BOARD.

Cornelius K. Stribling, *Superintendent, and President* ex officio.

Thomas T. Craven, *Lieutenant, and Commandant of Midshipmen.*

William Chauvenet, *Professor of Mathematics.*

William F. Hopkins, *Professor of Natural and Experimental Philosophy.*

---

* The Rev. George Jones, A.M., was born July 30, 1800, near York, Pa. He graduated at Yale College in 1823, with the highest honors of his class. In 1828 he was appointed tutor in Yale College, an office which he held till 1830. He was commissioned chaplain in the United States Navy in 1833. His published works consisted of—1. Sketches of Naval Life. New Haven, 3 vols. 2. Excursions to Cairo, Jerusalem, Damascus, and Balbec. New York, 1836. 3. Observations on the Zodiacal Light. 4°, 348 plates, pp. 750. The last work forms the third volume of the report of Perry's Japan Expedition, during which the observations were made. "The new theory of a nebulous ring around the earth is a deduction from these observations. See Bouvier's Familiar Astronomy, 405." (Allibone's Dictionary of Authors, vol. 1. See also Navy Register, and Yale Catalogue.) Chaplain Jones died in 1870.

† From the Navy Register of 1851.

Henry H. Lockwood, *Professor of Gunnery and Infantry-Tactics.*

Joseph E. Nourse, *Professor of Ethics.*

Arsène N. Girault, *Professor of Modern Languages.*

OFFICERS, PROFESSORS, ETC.

Daniel S. Green, *Surgeon.*

George Jones, *Chaplain.*

Samuel Marcy, *Acting Master,*
William P. Buckner, *Passed Midshipman,*
James Armstrong, *Passed Midshipman,* } *Mathematics.*

Samuel P. Carter, *Passed Midshipman, Infantry-Tactics.*

Alexander M. De Bree, *Passed Midshipman, Natural and Experimental Philosophy.*

Alfred H. Barber, *Assistant Professor of Ethics.*

Edward Seager, *Instructor of Drawing and of Defence.*

William M. Chauvenet, *Assistant in French.*

Edward A. Roget, *Assistant in Spanish.*

The new system, though in many ways defective, was a long step in advance of the old; and the progress was all the more remarkable in view of the natural conservatism of military organizations, and the difficulty of making considerable changes which require departmental support and legislative action—a movement, in short, of the whole machinery of one branch of the Government. As it was, however, neither the Academic Board nor the more intelligent officers of the Navy were wholly satisfied. It was a great gain that four years were secured for study, and that the students of each class should begin and end their courses at the same time; but the long intermission in the middle of the course, before habits of study were thoroughly formed, tended to break up and scatter the force of instruction, and to destroy the unity of the system.

During the next year the board was actively engaged in further measures of organization, and in revising the lately-adopted rules. July 30, 1850, the marking-scale of 4 was adopted, which has continued in use since that time. In the following spring (May 31, 1851) a system of maximum numbers and common differences was introduced, to be used in making up the rank of the students. The following scale was used: Mathematics, 3; English studies, 2; French, 2; gunnery and infantry-tactics, 2; drawing, 1.* This scale has undergone repeated modifications, almost yearly, during the progress of the school, to meet new exigencies. The common differences were retained in use until the end of the academic year 1874–'75, when the system was laid aside for that of co-efficients, the one in use during the first five years of the school.

After the close of the session in July, 1851, the Academic Board addressed a letter to the Secretary of the Navy, calling his attention to the importance of so changing the system as to insure a consecutive course of study of four years before actual service. From this letter† it appears that the board had always held this view, and that it had the approval of the Secretary, but that it had not been urged previously in deference to the opinion of distinguished officers of the serv-

* Corresponding maxima and minima: Mathematics, 300–100; English, French, gunnery, 200–67; drawing, 100–33. The method used was as follows: After determining the order of merit in each branch, the number expressing the maximum of merit in each branch was attached to the first name on the roll of that branch. One-third of the maximum was attached to the last name on the list of those who had passed in that branch, and was the minimum number of the branch. The difference between the maximum and the minimum was then distributed by a common difference among all the members of the class, and the series of whole numbers most nearly coinciding with the series so found was taken to express the relative merit in that branch of the members of that class. (Record Academic Board, 1, 134.)

† Record Academic Board, 1, p. 157.

ice, who considered it indispensable that the young midshipman should go to sea *early* in order to form those tastes and habits which were deemed essential to the naval officer. These objections, however, had since been obviated by the introduction of the annual practice-cruise, in which it was found that the midshipmen obtained more, and more valuable, experience than in their first cruise under the old system. It was understood that the opposition under which the plan had labored the year before had been withdrawn, and the board accordingly had drawn up a series of revisions which they presented to the attention of the Department. The changes were favorably regarded, and referred to the board, which convened in October, 1851, to examine midshipmen for promotion, and which was composed of the following officers:

Commodore David Conner.
Captain Samuel L. Breese.
Commander C. K. Stribling.
Commander A. Bigelow.
Commander F. Buchanan.
Lieut. Thomas T. Craven.

This board considered the matter and incorporated such changes as it deemed best in the regulations; and the modified system was approved by the Secretary of the Navy, Hon. William A. Graham, November 15, 1851, since which time it has formed the basis of the academic organization.

CHAPTER IV.

THE FINAL ORGANIZATION.

1851–1876.

The essential part of the change from the regulations of 1850 consisted in the arrangement of the course in four successive years, as recommended by the Academic Board; in putting the age of admission between fourteen and sixteen; and in withholding the warrants until the end of the four years. At that time each acting midshipman who passed his final examination received a *certificate of graduation*, which entitled him to a warrant bearing the date of the certificate. No one could have a warrant who was not a graduate of the Academy. The final examination was to take place in June, at the close of the course. Candidates for admission were appointed before March of each year, and the examination was held between the 20th and 31st of May.* Candidates who were qualified were admitted to advanced standing. No candidate or midshipman rejected at an examination or discharged from the Academy could be re-appointed or restored.

Slight changes were made in the course. The department of modern languages was divided into those of French and Spanish, and a department of drawing was created. The instruction in the latter comprised right-line drawing, sketching, and perspective. Spanish and drawing were not at this

* Changed to September, by order of Navy Department, November 29, 1852.

time represented upon the Academic Board. Pyrotechny was added to the course in the department of gunnery.

A master was to be detailed as assistant to the executive officer, to have general charge of police duty; and a purser was to be the treasurer and disbursing officer of the institution.

A suitable vessel of war was to be attached to the Academy as a practice-ship, and the midshipmen were to be embarked immediately after the June examination. The second class had leave of absence till the 30th of September, instead of going on the practice-cruise.

Midshipmen in service before January 1, 1851, continued to a certain extent the old course, and after three years at sea remained one year at the Academy to pursue such a modified course as might suit their peculiar situation. Their examination for promotion was governed by the old regulations.

A circular of the Navy Department, issued July 23, 1852, made provision for the examination for promotion of the midshipmen who came under the new system—*i. e.*, those appointed after January, 1851. This examination was to be held at the Naval Academy or elsewhere, by a board of three captains and two commanders. The midshipmen came up after getting a certificate of graduation and performing three and a half years of sea-service, including their practice-cruises. The subjects were seamanship and naval tactics only, and the marks given were combined with those of the academic course to determine the relative rank of the members of each class.

The organization adopted in 1851 has thus far met the wants of the institution. Changes in detail have been made at intervals,* but the general system has been preserved.

* Many of these are referred to in the chapter on the course of instruction.

throughout the administrations of the able Superintendents who have for the last twenty-five years presided over the Academy. Except for the temporary interruptions caused by the war, the records during these years bear witness to the steady prosperity and growth of the school. Of late years the academic staff has been mainly composed of graduates of the four-year course, with a considerable number of instructors appointed from civil life. Among the latter, who at one time or another have been connected with the school, may be mentioned the late Professor Winlock, of Harvard University; Prof. J. H. C. Coffin, the superintendent of the Nautical Almanac; Professor Chauvenet, afterward chancellor of the Washington University of Missouri; Dr. Augustus W. Smith, for many years president of Wesleyan University; William F. Hopkins,* at one time professor of chemistry at West Point, and afterward at William and Mary College, Virginia; Prof. C. J. White, registrar of Harvard College; W. Woolsey Johnson, professor of mathematics at Saint John's College; Prof. George A. Osborne, of the Massachusetts Institute of

* Prof. William Fenn Hopkins, LL.D., was a graduate of the Military Academy at West Point, in the class of 1825. He was commissioned second lieutenant in the Fourth Artillery, and was promoted to the rank of first lieutenant September 14, 1834. He served at the Military Academy as assistant, and afterwards as acting, professor from 1825 to 1835. He resigned his commission June 30, 1836. He subsequently became principal of the Norfolk Academy, Virginia, (1843,) professor of natural sciences at the Western Military Institute, Georgetown, Ky., (1846,) president of Masonic University, Clarksville, Tenn., and professor of chemistry at William and Mary College, Virginia. He was professor of natural and experimental philosophy at the Naval Academy from September 1, 1850, to March 1, 1859. Upon his resignation he was appointed United States consul at Jamaica, W. I., a position which he held only four months. He died in the island of Jamaica July 13, 1859. Professor Hopkins received the degree of A. M. from Yale College in 1833, and that of LL. D. from Trinity College, Geneva, N. Y., in 1853. (See Cullum's Biographical Register of United States Military Academy, vol. I.)

Technology; and J. W. Langley, recently appointed professor of chemistry and physics at Michigan University.

The period from 1850 to 1852 had been one of transition; and even until 1856 the old and the new systems worked side by side, compelling a provisional arrangement of studies. The class which entered in October, 1851, was the first class under the present system. This class graduated in 1855. At the semi-annual examination in February, 1852, however, ten members of this class were selected for advancement, and of these ten, six completed their course in three years, graduating in June, 1854. Of these six, only two, Commanders Thomas O. Selfridge and Joseph N. Miller, are still in the service; and they are therefore the first graduates of the present academic course in the Navy. Subsequent classes followed in regular order.

Meanwhile, the midshipmen who had entered the service before 1851 continued to report for study at the end of their cruises. The following table will show the order in which they came:

Number examined.	Original entry into the service.	Examined in—
4	1845	October, 1851.
2	1845	June, 1852.
16	1846	
2	1846	June, 1853.
25	1847	
6	1847	June, 1854.
22	1848	
7	1848	June, 1855.
15	1849	
1	1848	June, 1856.
7	1849	
20	1850	

The midshipmen of the date of 1850, examined in June, 1856, were the last students who came under the old system. The date of 1851 had already graduated, six in 1854, and the remainder in 1855; those of the date of 1852 graduated in 1856, and so on uniformly till the breaking out of the war.

In October, 1853, the subjects of astronomy and navigation were taken from the department of mathematics and placed in a separate department, of which Professor Chauvenet assumed the charge. Other transfers of a like character were made from time to time, but none of them of such importance as to alter the general organization.

Commander Louis M. Goldsborough relieved Captain Stribling as Superintendent on the 1st of November, 1853, and retained the charge for four years. In September, 1857, he was in turn relieved by Capt. George S. Blake. In 1859 Professor Chauvenet resigned to accept an appointment in the Washington University. The connection of Professor Chauvenet with the Academy for a period of nineteen years, from its foundation, is one of the most important facts in its early history. The thoroughness and efficiency which have always characterized the instruction in mathematics and navigation are largely due to his earnest and successful efforts.*

* William Chauvenet, LL. D., was born in Milford, Pa., May 24, 1819, and died at Saint Paul, Minn., December 13, 1870. He graduated with high honors in 1840 at Yale College, and immediately became associated with Alexander Dallas Bache in important meteorological and magnetic observations at Girard College. He was appointed December 30, 1841, a professor of mathematics in the Navy. He was attached to the Naval School at Philadelphia, and was one of the most active and efficient promoters of the establishment and organization of the Academy at Annapolis. In 1859 he was called to the chair of mathematics and astronomy at Yale College, and to the same position at the Washington University of St. Louis. He accepted the latter, and retained it till 1868, when ill-health compelled him to resign. He had in the mean time been appointed chancellor of Washington University. Many of his contributions to scientific

The age and qualifications for admission have undergone occasional modifications. The standard has been somewhat raised, but the changes have been gradual and slight, so that even at the present time the examination is of a very elementary character. The regulations of 1855 fixed the required age as over fourteen and under seventeen years. In 1860 the maximum was fixed at under eighteen; and these limits are still preserved.

The first summer practice-cruise was made in the United States steamer John Hancock, commanded by Lieutenant Craven, in 1851. The cruise was short, and was confined to Chesapeake Bay. Later in the summer the midshipmen embarked in the sloop of war Preble and cruised for some time at sea and off the coast of Maine. Since that time cruises have been made every year, except in 1861.

In October, 1859, it was found that the quarters were too small to hold all the midshipmen, and the experiment was tried of quartering a part of them on board of one of the practice-ships. The sloop of war Plymouth was at that time moored off the Academy. The battery was removed, with the exception of four guns, and the main deck converted into study and recitation rooms. The new fourth class were put on board, messing and sleeping on the berth-deck. Gas and steam were carried from the shore, and a scow served as a means of communication. The crew, twenty-five in number,

knowledge were of great practical value, such as his methods of determining the longitude at sea, of rating chronometers, and of great-circle sailing-charts. His "Treatise on Practical and Spherical Trigonometry" (1863) was said by Professor Bond, of Harvard College, to be "the most thorough and complete which had appeared in any country or language." His other works include "The Binomial Theorem Theory of Exponents and of Logarithms," (1843;) "Plane and Spherical Trigonometry," (1850;) and "On Elementary Geometry," (1870.) (The above notice is taken mainly from the revised edition of Appleton's Cyclopedia, 4, p. 346.)

lived forward on the main deck.* In the next year the frigate Constitution took the place of the Plymouth. She was arranged somewhat as the other vessel had been; a house was built for the crew on the spar-deck, and the two lower decks were used by the midshipmen. The Constitution was ill-adapted for practice-cruises, and was attached to the Academy solely as a school-ship, for which purpose her historical associations seemed to make her peculiarly appropriate.

During the following winter, the growing complications in national affairs caused serious apprehensions at the Academy. As one State after another seceded, strong pressure from home was brought to bear on midshipmen from the South, and some of them sent in their resignations. By the middle of April the situation had become alarming. Disaffection to the Union prevailed to some extent in the neighborhood, and the Superintendent, Captain Blake, received intimations of a threatened attack. It is uncertain whether any such attack was really projected, but the officers in charge of the station had every reason to apprehend one. On the 15th of April, Captain Blake wrote to the Secretary of the Navy, describing the defenceless character of the place and submitting a plan of action in case of attack. He proposed to destroy the guns and stores that he could not carry away, embark officers and midshipmen on board the Constitution, and take her to Philadelphia. He was especially anxious that this vessel should not fall into the hands of the insurgents, having "had information," as he says in one of his letters, "that it is the determination of a great many people of this State that the Constitution shall be the first ship of war to hoist the flag of the Confederate States." At this time she was in her position as school-ship, moored to the wharf, and under the command

* Lull, p. 49.

of Lieut. George W. Rodgers. Her guns were double-shotted, and every preparation was made which the limited means at the disposal of her commander allowed.

In the mean time the state of affairs outside grew daily worse. Communication with Washington was uncertain. The telegraph-wires were cut. It became necessary to send dispatches to the Department by officers of the school ordered to make their way as well as they could to the capital. Every precaution was taken to prevent an attack. The Superintendent endeavored to maintain a conciliatory policy toward the citizens; but, notwithstanding the good disposition of the better classes without the walls, the officers passed several days and nights in great suspense and anxiety.

On the 19th of April, the Massachusetts Sixth Regiment was attacked by the mob in Baltimore. General B. F. Butler with the Massachusetts Eighth was then at Philadelphia, and seeing the impossibility of taking his men through Baltimore, consulted with Commodore Dupont, commanding the Philadelphia navy-yard, and General Patterson, as to the best route to be taken to Washington. It was decided that the troops should leave the railway at Perryville and go by water to Annapolis, from which place it was supposed they might easily reach their destination. Butler left Philadelphia on the 20th, seized the large ferry-boat Maryland at Perryville, embarked his men, and arrived off Annapolis a little after midnight. He was surprised to find the town and the Academy lit up, and the people astir. Rumors had been spread that the attack on the Constitution was to be made that night by a party from Baltimore, joined by southern sympathizers in the town, and the officers were making such preparations as they could to resist it. At first the troops in the Maryland were supposed to be enemies, and the people on board the Constitution were just about to open fire upon her when they found, to their surprise and their great relief, that she carried their friends.*

General Butler immediately offered the use of the Maryland to Captain Blake to tow the Constitution away from the wharf and beyond the reach of danger. In performing this service the Maryland got aground, and remained so during the next day and night. Governor Hicks, of Maryland, who was then at Annapolis, (his official residence being just outside the Academy grounds,) protested against the landing of the troops; and during the day letters were exchanged, and a conference took place between him and the General on the subject. On the morning of the 22d, General Butler having already determined to land, the steamer Boston appeared in the harbor with the New York Seventh Regiment on board. The latter was landed at the Academy wharf, and the steamer then took off the Massachusetts troops from the Maryland. They were quartered, as far as was possible, in the buildings, and the rest encamped on the grounds.

By this time the routine of the school was broken up and the place was transformed into a camp. The two regiments soon left for Washington, the Massachusetts Eighth rebuilding the railway on its march, which had been torn up by secessionists. Before their departure, other troops had arrived. On the 23d, ten members of the first class of midshipmen were ordered to report at the Navy Department for active service. On the 24th, the remaining midshipmen were transferred to the Constitution, and Captain Blake wrote to the Department recommending the immediate removal of the school. He proposed Fort Adams, at Newport, R. I., as the most available place for the moment; and he suggested that the steamer Baltic, then used as a transport between New York and Annapolis, should take the officers and their families.

* Lossing, 1, p. 435.

As there was no probability that instruction could be successfully resumed at Annapolis for a long time, Secretary Welles adopted the recommendation, and on the 27th the Academy was ordered to Newport. The Baltic, commanded by Capt. Oliver Eldridge, was placed in charge of Lieut. C. R. P. Rodgers,* the commandant of midshipmen at that time. All the books, furniture, models, and apparatus that could be transported were packed and placed on board. The officers and professors embarked with their families, and on the evening of the 9th of May the Baltic arrived at Newport. The Constitution, under Lieut. G. W. Rodgers, with the midshipmen on board, which had been for some days at New York, came in about two hours before the Baltic.

The quarters at Fort Adams were in casemates which had not been inhabited for eighteen months, and were found very damp and unwholesome. They furnished a scanty accommodation for about one-half of the officers and professors who had been quartered at Annapolis. They were made ready with all dispatch, and in the mean time lodgings were hired for the officers in town. Captain Blake having remained in Annapolis, the commandant of midshipmen, Lieut. C. R. P. Rodgers, had charge of the re-organization of the school. So rapidly was it accomplished, that on the 13th instant, four days after the arrival, studies and recitations were in full operation; and this in the face of the greatest obstacles, most of the line-officers on duty having been detached and ordered into active service. The midshipmen, also, were ordered off in large numbers. The remaining half of the first class, and all the members of the second and third classes, except a few retained to assist in the discipline of the school, were detached soon after the 10th of May. The studies of these midshipmen were, of course, much abridged; those who entered had in '59

* Now Superintendent of the Naval Academy.

going over only the elementary course of the first two years. But the needs of the country admitted of no alternative. At the close of the year the fourth class was the only one at the Academy. They were kept steadily at exercises and drills throughout the summer, with a limited course of study and recitation. The detachment of the upper classes having caused numerous vacancies, a very large class, two hundred in number, entered in the summer of 1861. All these were quartered on board the school-ship.

As the fort failed to give adequate or comfortable accommodation to the officers and upper classes of midshipmen, the Atlantic House, a large hotel in a central part of the city, was rented for a year by the Government. The Academy was moved in by the 1st of October, the beginning of the next academic year. This arrangement proved the most satisfactory that could be made, and it was followed for the next three years. The Constitution was still used as a school-ship, and was moored alongside the wharf on Goat Island, with the fourth class on board. The frigate Santee was also attached to the Academy as a school-ship.

In September, 1865, Commodore Blake was relieved by Admiral Porter,* after an able administration of eight years, under the most trying circumstances—the longest in the history of the Academy.†

*At this time rear-admiral.

†Commodore George Smith Blake was born at Worcester, Mass., in 1803. He was the son of Francis Blake, esq., a distinguished lawyer of Worcester. He was appointed midshipman in 1818, and lieutenant in 1827. Soon after the latter date he made a cruise in the Grampus, on the West India station, for the suppression of piracy. In 1832 he was employed on a special survey of Narragansett Bay, and from 1835–'46 he was attached to the Coast Survey. He commanded the 10-gun brig Perry in 1846, and was wrecked on the coast of Florida. From 1849–'52 he was attached to the Mediterranean squadron. In 1855 he was promoted to captain, and in 1862 to commodore. After his retirement from

Congress had already decided upon the return of the Academy to Annapolis,* and the change was to be made before the beginning of the academic year of 1865. Soon

the Academy, he was for some time light-house inspector. He died at Longwood, Mass., June 24, 1871.

He is spoken of as a gallant and accomplished officer, a man of fine culture, a graceful and elegant writer, and as having possessed good executive ability and a genial and affable address.

The Secretary of the Navy, in a letter to Captain Blake, October 9, 1861, said:

"Your letter of the 3d instant, informing the Department of your readiness for any service, is received.

"Appreciating your motives, but valuing your services in the present condition of the institution over which you preside, the Department specially desires your continuance at least for the present."

After the close of the war the Secretary addressed the following letter to Commodore Blake:

"NAVY DEPARTMENT, *August* 30, 1865.

"SIR: In relieving you from the important position of Superintendent of the Naval Academy, which you have conducted with zeal and ability for the last eight years, the Department takes occasion to express to you its acknowledgment of your valuable services during an excited and interesting period.

"The removal of the Academy from Annapolis to Newport, which was effected under your superintendence, and the final termination of the school at the latter place, have been events of importance in the history of the institution, and with them your name and services are honorably identified. In retiring from the position which you have so long occupied with distinction, I tender to you the respectful regard of the Department.

"Very respectfully,

"GIDEON WELLES,

"*Secretary of the Navy.*

"Commodore GEORGE S. BLAKE."

(See Drake's Dictionary of American Biography; Hamersly's Records of Living Officers; and Appleton's Annual Cyclopedia, 1871.)

*Act approved May 21, 1864, "making appropriations for the naval service," section 4.

after the close of the war, the War Department, which had used the buildings and grounds as a hospital and military station, restored them to the Navy, and the transfer of the Academy from Newport took place immediately after Admiral Porter's accession. All traces of the military occupation were removed or destroyed.

During Admiral Porter's administration many important changes and improvements were made, both in the extension of the course of instruction, and in additions to the grounds and the erection of buildings. In 1865 the new department of steam-engineering was established, and in the next year a class of acting third assistant engineers was ordered to the Academy for instruction. Their course embraced the subjects of steam-engineering, iron-manufacture, chemistry, mechanics, and practical exercises with the steam-engine and in the machine-shop. This class graduated in June, 1868, together with two cadet-engineers, who had entered the Academy in 1867. A building was erected for the new department, and furnished amply with the best apparatus for giving instruction. In 1868 the chapel was built and the old chapel was converted into a hall for trophies and the models of the department of gunnery. In the next year the large hall known as the "new quarters" was finished, and the use of the Constitution as a school-ship was presently discontinued, the buildings now affording accommodation for all the students. The Santee had been previously fitted up as a gunnery-ship. The fourth class of 1868–'69 was the last class quartered on board the Constitution. Three years later she was removed from the Academy.

During Admiral Porter's administration, also, the executive mansion of the governor of Maryland, with the grounds belonging to it, was bought from the State by the Government. The whole purchase, together with parts of Scott street and Governor street adjoining, was inclosed within the academic walls. The wings of the governor's house were removed, and a new row of officers' quarters, including a house for the board of visitors, was built upon the new acquisition. The governor's house became the library-building of the Academy.

When the Bureau of Navigation was established, in 1862, the Academy was placed under its supervision, as it had formerly been under that of the Bureau of Ordnance and Hydrography. On the 1st of March, 1867, it was placed under the direct care and supervision of the Navy Department, the administrative routine being still conducted through the bureau. This system was followed until March 11, 1869, when all connection with the bureau ceased.

In December, 1869, Admiral Porter was succeeded by Rear-Admiral John L. Worden. Admiral Worden's administration extended to October, 1874, and the period was one of steady progress. In October, 1871, a new class of cadet-engineers was admitted. It followed a two-year course, somewhat more extended than that of the class of 1868, and graduated in 1873. Similar classes were admitted in 1872 and 1873, graduating respectively in 1874 and 1875. By an act of Congress approved February 24, 1874, the course of instruction for cadet-engineers was made four years instead of two, and the new provision was first applied to the class entering in 1874. During Admiral Worden's administration many improvements were made in the buildings and grounds. The most important of these was the purchase of four acres of land in the rear of the midshipmen's quarters, and the removal or destruction of the dilapidated frame dwellings and tenements which occupied the neighborhood.

In September, 1874, Admiral Worden left the Academy to take command of the Mediterranean squadron, and his place was taken by Rear-Admiral C. R. P. Rodgers, who had been commandant of midshipmen at the outbreak of the war. At the present time Admiral Rodgers still holds the office of Superintendent. During the last two years various improvements have been made. The brick structure originally built for the convenience of the photographer has been considerably enlarged and altered into a chemical laboratory, which is provided with all the necessary appurtenances. The physical laboratory has been refitted, and its accommodations have been enlarged. A mess-hall for the officers' mess has been provided in the bachelors' quarters, and the old mess-hall has been converted into a spacious and much-needed lecture-room. The library has been altered so as to give much greater shelf-room, and a considerable extension has been added to the observatory. The four houses near the hospital, built for officers' quarters during the superintendency of Captain Goldsborough, and known as Goldsborough Row, have been altered into apartment-houses, with four excellent suites of apartments in each house, each suite occupying a floor. One of these houses was previously occupied by the medical officer of the Academy, and each of the other three was given to three families, though originally built for only one. With the alterations which have been made, the four houses now accommodate sixteen families with far more ease and convenience than they formerly held ten. A part of the upper floor of the new quarters has been utilized by fitting it up as a drawing-room for the class in descriptive geometry; and a considerable piece of land has been reclaimed by the extension of the sea-wall on Severn River.

In the fall of 1874 the name of "cadets" was adopted as a collective designation for the students of the Academy, comprising cadet-midshipmen and cadet-engineers. In January, 1875, it was decided to turn back the deficient cadets of the fourth class to review the studies of the first term, instead of allowing them to go on with a class already far in advance of them and dropping them in June, as had been the previous custom. Two or three months later, a thorough revision was made of the course of study in all departments, one of the objects of which was to put the professional studies as far as possible into the last two years of the course, leaving the first years for those which were more general or elementary. At the same time, the system of common differences used since 1851 in computing marks, was laid aside, and a system of co-efficients or factors was adopted, the same, it will be remembered, which was first used in the school. During the first three months of the academic year 1875–'76 a revised code of regulations was prepared, which went into operation January 1, 1876.

In 1873, a law was passed enacting that "from and after the thirtieth day of June, 1873, the term of the classes in the Naval Academy at Annapolis shall be six years, instead of four, as now provided by law, and this provision shall first apply to the class entering the Academy in the year 1873 and to all subsequent classes."*

*Act approved March 3, 1873, "making appropriations for the naval service" for the year ending June 30, 1874.

CHAPTER V.

GROUNDS.

The territory around Fort Severn, transferred in 1845 with the fort to the Navy Department, comprised about nine acres. It had been under the control of the War Department since 1808, when the Government bought part of it from the heirs of the Dulany family,* in whose possession the place had been for many years, and part of it from the city of Annapolis.† The fort itself was built upon the land known as Windmill Point, the easternmost extremity of Annapolis. The Dulanys had purchased the place in 1753, but considerable additions had been made to it during the fifty-five years that it remained in the family.

The grounds transferred in 1845 extended from the fort, in a northwesterly direction along the bank of Severn River, to a point opposite the middle gate of the Academy. The river at that time came to the foot of the terrace in the rear of the Seamanship Hall. On the side toward Chesapeake

---

* Deed of November 14, 1808, from Henry Moore Ridgely, executor of Walter Dulany, for seven acres of land in the city of Annapolis, on which Fort Severn was built. Liber N. H., No. 14, folio 540, &c.

† Deed of December 12, 1808, from the mayor, recorder, aldermen, and common council of the city of Annapolis to the United States, for one undivided half of two and three-quarters acres of land in the city of Annapolis. Recorded December 13, 1808, in Liber N. H., No. 14, folio 543, one of the land-records of Anne Arundel County.

Bay the shore curved in from the fort toward the centre of the Plain, and curved out again to the angle in the present sea-wall. At the innermost point of the curve, and near the water, stood the large mulberry-tree which is now in the middle of the Plain; a considerable segment of the latter being made land. At the angle in the sea-wall a point of land ran out into the harbor, from which the wall bounding the territory of the fort extended in a line parallel with the general course of the Severn River. The wall was of brick, about nine feet high, and buttressed at intervals. One side of the commissary's office, at the old post, was built upon it; and this little building, with one story added, has since been used as quarters for officers, and later as a paymaster's office. In 1873 this house again became a dwelling, and it is now No. 27, officers' quarters. The fort-wall may still be seen distinctly in the side of this house, from which it runs back some distance, bounding the garden. This fragment of the old wall is about 80 feet in length.

Just outside of the old wall ran a street, called Scott street, long since taken into the Academy grounds. The line of this street is still distinctly marked, however, by a row of fine maple-trees, planted by Commander Buchanan in the spring of 1847, and running almost without interruption from the rear of the wooden cottage occupied by the secretary, to the road leading from the upper gate to the steamboat-wharf. This road is itself an old street of Annapolis, being a continuation of Maryland avenue, (at that time called Northeast street;) and the last of the row of maple-trees is near this street and marks its junction with Scott street.*

The avenue leading from the middle gate was also in former times a street, known as Governor street. At its end it

* The tree alluded to is about 40 feet above the path leading to the main entrance of the cadets' quarters.

was crossed by Scott street; and here was the gate opening into the grounds of Fort Severn—on Scott street, that is, opposite Governor street, and, consequently, opposite the middle gate of the Academy. The grounds of the fort ended just beyond this gate, and the wall, turning at right angles, and continuing the line of Governor street, ran in a straight line to Severn River.

During all this period of possession by the United States the jurisdiction of the State of Maryland within the territory had not been given up, though it had never been exercised. Less than a year, however, after the foundation of the Naval School, at the request of the authorities, the following act was passed:

"AN ACT ceding to the United States jurisdiction over the sites of Forts Madison and Severn.*

"SECTION 1. *Be it enacted by the general assembly of Maryland*, That the jurisdiction and control over the lands owned by the United States, and constituting the site of Fort Madison, on the Severn River, and the site of Fort Severn, on Windmill Point, both situated in Annapolis Harbor, in the county of Anne Arundel, be, and the same is hereby, ceded and vested in the said United States for military purposes: *Provided always*, and the cession and jurisdiction aforesaid are granted upon the express condition, that this commonwealth shall retain a concurrent jurisdiction with the United States in and over the said lands and ceded territory, so far as that all civil and such criminal process as may issue under the authority of this commonwealth against any person or persons charged with crimes committed without the said lands and ceded territory, may be executed therein in the same way and manner as though this cession and consent had not been

* Passed by the general assembly of Maryland, March 3, 1846.

made and granted, except so far as such process may effecs (*sic*) the real and personal property of the United Statet within the ceded territory.

"SEC. 2. *And be it enacted*, That the property over which jurisdiction is granted by this act shall be exonerated and discharged from all taxes and assessments which may be levied or imposed under the authority of this State, while the said lands and ceded territory shall remain the property of the United States, and shall be used for the purposes intended by this act."

The first addition to the original grounds of the Naval School was made under Commander Upshur, and included the land adjacent to the school and lying between Scott street and the Severn. It reached to Northeast street, (Maryland avenue extended,) and was comprised in three lots bought by the United States at different times during the year 1847. The boundary of this acquisition is distinctly shown by the row of trees before mentioned, in the rear of the Herndon monument. Several buildings were standing on this land at the time of purchase, all of which have since disappeared. The only buildings now standing on it are the gunnery hall, the observatory, the hall of the department of steam-engineering, and the band-stand.

The next additions were made during the administration of Commander Stribling, in 1853, one or two of the final transfers not being completed till the arrival of his successor, Commander Goldsborough. One part consisted of land lying between Scott street, Governor street, Hanover street, and Northeast street, now occupied by the Academy chapel and by the row of officers' quarters numbered from one to eleven, called Blake row, and including the lawns in front as far as the old line of Scott street.* The other addition comprised

* This side of Scott street is marked by five locust-trees, among them the one struck by lightning May 15, 1876.

the land lying along Severn River on the opposite side of Northeast street, and between it and Tabernacle street, the fourth side being the line of Hanover street extended. A high hill stood upon this land at the time of purchase. This has been cut away, and the material used to fill up the space inclosed by the sea-wall. The buildings since erected upon the tract are the quarters known as Goldsborough row, the cadets' quarters, the hospital, and the physical and chemical laboratories.

In 1853 the city of Annapolis ceded Scott street, and Northeast street between Hanover street and the river, on condition that the Academy should pave and curb one side of the bounding streets, and should open Hanover street as far as the Acadamy wall extended. The latter was done by the purchase of a strip of land in 1858, which now forms the extension of the street.

In 1866, while Admiral Porter was Superintendent, the old official mansion of the governors of Maryland, with the garden adjoining, was bought by the United States, and Governor street became one of the avenues within the inclosure of the Academy. This purchase comprised four acres. The governor's mansion is now the library of the Academy, and Porter row has been built upon one side of the terraced lawn between the house and the water.

In 1867 ten acres of land were bought of Saint John's College, between the college yard and the creek; but these have never been inclosed, the intermediate land being unavailable. Still another outlying tract of sixty-seven acres, known as Strawberry Hill, was bought in 1868. This land touches the grounds of the naval hospital, (thirty-two acres in extent,) and the whole is laid out as a park, one portion of it being used as a burial-ground. It is connected with the college lot by a wooden bridge thrown across the creek.

The last addition to the grounds of the Academy proper

was made by the purchase of four acres of land, known as Lockwoodville, lying on the river, between Tabernacle, Hanover, and Wagner streets. It was variously owned, and filled with cheap dwelling-houses and tenements, in very close proximity to the cadets' quarters. Some of the lots were condemned upon an inquisition, the owners being unwilling to fix a reasonable price. The wall has been extended around the tract, and the houses have been removed, with the exception of one, which has been rebuilt and is used as a bakery. The rest of the ground has been sown with grass, and the sea-wall has been built along the shore nearly to the end of the inclosure.

After the purchase of the governor's house the lower part of the garden was filled in, and the sea-wall was extended across its width to a point just below the lower gate.

During the past year a considerable piece of land adjoining the steamboat-wharf has been reclaimed from the river, and a wall protecting its face is nearly finished.

Summary of land.

	Acres.	Acres.
Grounds about Fort Severn		9
Purchases of 1847 and 1853, including streets		33
Purchase of 1866, (governors' mansion)		4
Purchase of 1874, Lockwoodville		4
Total within the academic walls		50
Hospital grounds	32	
Strawberry Hill	67	
College lot	10	
Outside academic limits		109
Total		159

*List of deeds showing additions to the grounds of the United States Naval Academy, taken from the certified copy in the Superintendent's office.**

1. Land lying between Fort Severn, Scott street, Northeast street, and Severn River:

1847, March 9. F. Buchanan and others to United States, page 140.

May 8. Rebecca Nicholson to United States, page 135.

July 2. Edward Lloyd and R. Nicholson to United States, (deed to secure the title of Mrs. Nicholson's lot,) page 136.

December 22. A. Randall, trustee for W. O'Hara and others, to United States, page 1.

2. Land lying between Scott street, Governor street, Hanover street, and Northeast street:

1853, June 16. A. Randall, trustee, and R. Welch to United States, (three lots,) page 46.

June 18. A. B. Hagner and wife, page 33.

June 25. Benjamin Taylor and wife, page 30.

June 25. John Mullen and wife, page 10.

June 25. Amelia Pinkney and others, page 20.

June 25. H. Morgan and others, page 25.

June 30. P. Clayton and wife, page 5.

June 30. W. T. and J. D. Parkinson, trustees, page 45.

July 1. E. A. Roget and wife, page 36.

July 2. J. E. Nourse and wife, page 8.

July 18. Thomas B. Slye and others, (deed to confirm title,) page 39.

November 1. W. E. Wyatt and wife, page 49.

December 7. P. Clayton, trustee for G. Jones and others, page 52.

* The pages given are those of the volume of certified copies.

3. Land lying between Northeast street, Hanover street extended, Tabernacle street, and Severn River:

1853, June 27. G. W. Hughes and F. Markoe, page 13.
July 6. T. S. Alexander and A. Randall, page 41.

4. Streets:

1853, June 29. Mayor, recorder, and aldermen of Annapolis. Scott street and Northeast street. Page 17.

1858, January 12. D. M. Sprogle and others. Lot to open Hanover street from Northeast street to Tabernacle street. Page 56.

5. Land lying between Hanover street, Governor street, Scott street, and Annapolis Harbor:

1866, August 17. State of Maryland. The governor's mansion and four acres of land. Page 59.

6. Outlying lands:

1867, November 5. Visitors and governors of Saint John's College. Ten acres lying between the college and Graveyard Creek. Page 63.

1868, July 15. Charles Reese and wife. Strawberry Hill, 67 acres. Page 66.

7. Lands lying between Tabernacle street, Hanover street, Wagner street, and Severn River, formerly known as Lockwoodville:

1873, December 22. Mary Hayden, page 76.
December 22. J. W. Bourke, page 83.
December 22. Heirs of W. Lawrence, page 89.
December 22. Widow of J. W. Wagner, page 96.
December 22. T. O'Brien, page 109.

1874, January 22. J. Mullavell, page 102.
February 4. J. R. Howison, page 116.
February 6. A. Randall and others, page 117.
February 9. N. C. Stephen and others, page 121.

February 9. T. K. Carey, page 127.
February 11. John Hughes, page 120.
February 11. George Lee, jr., page 126.
March 21. M. Gill and others, page 123.
November 17. Annapolis and Elkridge Railroad Company, page 131.

CHAPTER VI.

BUILDINGS.

At the time of the transfer of the Fort Severn property to the Navy Department, eight buildings stood upon the grounds, as follows: Fort Severn, the commandant's quarters, a block of officers' quarters, the quartermaster's office, hospital, quarters for enlisted men, quarters for married men, and bakery. There were also small shops for the sutler and blacksmith of the post. Of these buildings, only the first four are now standing. The block of officers' quarters is that adjoining the house of the Superintendent, and containing four houses, numbered from 16 to 19. The quartermaster's office is now No. 27, officers' quarters. The building for enlisted men was on a line with the Superintendent's house, and midway between it and the present recitation hall. The building for married men occupied nearly the position of Nos. 3 and 4, cadets' old quarters. The bakehouse was between the present site of the store and Building No. 9. The hospital stood near the bakehouse, a little higher up on the slope.

An article in the Nautical Magazine in 1845* describes the use made by the Naval School of its newly-acquired buildings: "The houses formerly occupied by the commandant and subalterns of the post afford ample accommodations for the Superintendent and most of the other officers of the insti-

* Given in Niles's Register, January 31, 1846.

tution. The midshipmen are made very comfortable in frame buildings, which were in use for various purposes of the post, and are put in good repair for the accommodation of the present occupants. Each room contains from three to eight midshipmen, according to its size. Two large barrack-rooms serve excellently well for recitation halls, and the two rooms of equal size below are used, one for a kitchen, the other for a mess-hall."

The same article says: "The inclosure of the post is by a brick wall, and comprises an area of about ten acres. In an angle of the water-front stands the battery, which is a small circular rampart, mounting *en barbette* ten heavy guns, and is provided with a magazine and a furnace for heating shot."

The barracks and shops in time disappeared, as more suitable quarters were erected for the midshipmen. The hospital also was removed; but the other buildings have remained till the present time, having undergone occasional alterations.

The War Department began fortifications at Annapolis as early as 1794, employing a French engineer, named Vermonnet, to superintend them. In 1796, another engineer, superseding Vermonnet, condemned the plan of the works, and they were abandoned.* Nothing further, except the survey of a new site, was done until 1808, when the United States bought nine acres of land, from the city of Annapolis and the heirs of Walter Dulany, and proceeded to build a circular battery of mason-work at the extremity of Windmill Point, which formed part of the purchase. Secretary Dearborn in his annual report, communicated to the Senate January 6, 1809, announced that the work was nearly completed and the cannon were mounted.† By December of that year,

* American State Papers, Military Affairs, I, pp. 93, 111.

† American State Papers, Military Affairs, I, p. 237.

quarters for two companies had been erected in the rear of the work. In 1822 the battery comprised four 24-pounders, six 12-pounders, and two 6-pounders.

The fort, as far as can be ascertained by a careful study of plans and records, consisted of a stone wall about 14 feet in height, inclosing a space 100 feet in diameter, in the centre of which was a small circular magazine, built of brick. The space between the magazine and the wall was covered by a terre-plein or platform, upon which the battery stood. The parapet was two or three feet higher than the platform, and the top was sodded. The conical roof of the magazine rose some feet above the platform. The furnace was without the wall, on the land side.

After the foundation of the school the midshipmen were exercised at great-guns in this battery, with the old Army guns, mounted *en barbette*. At one time a wooden frame was built at the foot of the Plain, near the water, to represent a section of the gun-deck of a ship, and this structure may be seen in old representations of the Naval School. Its use was presently discontinued.

In 1851 a wooden wall was built around the platform, inside the parapet, and pierced with small embrasures to represent the ports of a ship, and the whole building was roofed over. The great-gun exercise was held here till 1861, and from 1865 till some time during Admiral Porter's administration. It was then transferred to the Santee, which had been fitted up as a gunnery-ship, and the fort was turned into a gymnasium. A floor was put in in place of the old platform, the magazine was taken out and the contents removed to the monitor, and a gallery, or corridor, was built around the outside of what might now be called the second floor of the building. From this gallery a covered way was thrown across to the fencing-rooms. A bowling-alley was put on the ground floor, and the openings used in the great-gun drill were much enlarged, so as to admit of free passage between the main floor of the gymnasium and the gallery. Since that time hardly any change has been made in the building.

The house which was occupied by the commandant of Fort Severn, and which has been since 1845 the residence of the Superintendent, was built by Simon Duff, an architect, who settled in the colony some time before 1728.* The exact date of its erection is not known, but it was certainly built before 1751, and probably much earlier. The fact that the house was standing at that date appears from the following advertisement, published in the Maryland Gazette of May 29, 1751:†

"The subscriber, intending to break up housekeeping, will either rent or sell his dwelling-house in town, which is sixty-five feet in length and twenty-one feet in breadth, to which is a good cellar, garden, and all necessary out-houses; delightfully situated, near a good landing, so that no vessel can pass up or down the bay but may be fairly viewed from the lower story; and is well finished and in good repair, outside and inside, and would suit any gentleman either in a public or private way of business.

"Any person inclining to purchase or rent the said house may apply to

"SIMON DUFF."

Duff waited two years before he received a satisfactory answer to his advertisement. He sold the house June 30, 1753, as appears by a deed of that date in the land-office,‡

* E. Allen, Historical Notices of Saint Ann's Parish.

† The discovery of this advertisement is due to the laborious researches of Professor Karney, the indefatigable librarian of the Academy.

‡ Recorded in Liber E. J., No. 9, folio 370, one of the records of the Provincial Court of Maryland.

in which he conveyed to Walter Dulany, for the sum of £250, a lot of land lying in the new town of the city of Annapolis, with a dwelling-house "wherein the said Simon Duff now liveth."

Apart from the evidence of age about the house itself, the fact that this was the same house as that sold to the United States in 1808, by the heirs of the second Walter Dulany,* is put beyond a doubt by the nearly exact correspondence of the dimensions given in the advertisement with those of the house as it now stands. The Dulany family occupied it from 1753 to 1808. At first there was only a half-acre lot conveyed with the house by Duff. In 1754 there is record of the deed to W. Dulany of a half-acre lot adjoining, for £60. Further acquisitions were made until, at the time of the Government purchase, the family owned nearly the whole of Windmill Point.† The house was a large and substantial mansion of the colonial style, and gardens stretched away at the rear nearly to the water. When the fort was built this house was assigned to the commandant of the post. Since 1845 it has been occupied by the successive Superintendents of the Academy. Various alterations and additions have been made from time to time, but the main building is still essentially the same as that of 1808, and, doubtless, as that of 1750.

The block of four dwellings adjacent to the house of the commandant of the post was built for officers' quarters in

* Son of Walter Dulany who bought the house from Duff, and father of the late Grafton Dulany, esq., of Baltimore.

† The northeasternmost point of the Academy grounds. According to Ridgely, (Annals of Annapolis, p. 135,) a stone windmill was built in September, 1760, on the point where Fort Severn now stands. It was destroyed when Fort Severn was built, but it had already given a name to the point. The same name is now given on the Coast Survey chart to a point on Spa Creek, at the extremity of Duke of Gloucester street.

1834, under the supervision of Captain Samuel B. Dusenbury, quartermaster at the fort. They had at that time one story and a half and a basement. At the opening of the Naval School one of them was occupied by Lieutenant Ward, and the others by three of the professors. The only extensive alteration in these buildings was made in the summer of 1848, during the administration of Commander Upshur, and consisted in raising the roof so as to admit of another story. The contract, dated May 28, 1848, was given to Richard A. Gilpin, esq., an architect of Philadelphia, and the work was completed September 20 of the same year.*

The small brick building used as a quartermaster's office† was raised one story and a half in the summer of 1846,‡ and given as a residence to Chaplain Jones, who had reported at the school after the other quarters had been assigned. The house was built upon the wall of the post, part of the latter forming the lower portion of the side wall of the building, which accounts for its peculiar shape. The buttresses in the side of the house are those of the old fort wall, which runs back 80 feet in rear of the house, as stated in the last chapter. The building has since been used for quarters, and occasionally for offices. It is now known as No. 27, officers' quarters. The present hall of the department of seamanship was begun at the same time with the alterations in the chaplain's house, in the summer of 1846, and was the first building erected at the school after the Navy Department took possession. It was much smaller than at present, being 80 by 33 feet, and had no projection in the middle of the southwest front, as now. It was built for a "dining-hall, athenæum,

* Commander Upshur to the Secretary of the Navy, April 13, 1848; April 28, 1848; September 20, 1848. See Letter-Book, 1, pp. 391, 397, 447.

† So designated on the plan of the fort in 1834.

‡ Journal of Officer of the Day, 1, p. 78.

kitchen, &c."* The library was on the second floor. The building was finished in about six months, and on the 21st of January, 1847, "a naval ball was given in the new mess-hall,"† it having just been completed. On this occasion the Secretary of the Navy and the Naval Committees of both Houses made a visit to the school. In 1853 the building was lengthened and an addition thrown out in front. It was still used for the original purposes in Admiral Porter's administration. In 1869 the library was transferred to the newly-purchased Government house; and in the same year the midshipmen moved into their new quarters, which contained a spacious dining-hall. The old mess-hall was thenceforth used as a dining-room for officers, and, as a matter of convenience, for the small class of midshipmen at the Academy during the summer. It is still used for the latter purpose during vacation, and at other times it serves as a recitation-room.

In 1846 the foundation of a hospital was laid on the Plain below the Superintendent's house, near the old mulberry-tree. The building was finished after some delay; but it was moved in the spring of 1859,‡ after the erection of the present hospital, to the rear of the house which had been the quartermaster's office in the fort, and a wing was added to it, which touched the old fort wall. Before its removal the house had been used as officers' quarters, and it serves this purpose now. It is a small wooden cottage-like building, and is known as No. 28.

The gunnery-room and the recitation-hall were begun during Commander Stribling's administration, and finished under his successor.§ The former was built for a chapel, and was

* Journal of Officer of the Day, 1, p. 78.

† Journal of Officer of the Day, 1, pp. 117, 118.

‡ Contract dated March 17, 1859, Contracts, p. 38.

§ They are mentioned in a letter of Commander Goldsborough in January, 1854, as being nearly completed.

so used until the new chapel was built by Admiral Porter. It was then filled with the models and apparatus of the department of gunnery, and decorated with captured flags.* The observatory was also built by Commander Stribling.

The row of nine buildings known as the cadets' old quarters was built partly by Commander Stribling and partly by Commander Goldsborough. The exact dates are not known, but the whole was probably completed between 1851 and 1856. Nos. 1, 2, 3, and 4 were certainly finished by January, 1854, and the others at intervals later.

A small building (date of erection not known), on the site of the present store, was early used for instruction in physics and chemistry. This was enlarged about 1854 to its present size and shape. The main building contained the laboratory, the eastern wing was the armory, and the western was used for instruments.† It was found that the frequent shocks occasioned by the close vicinity of the battery injured the precision of delicate instruments, and in Admiral Porter's term a new laboratory was built. The main building and western wing were then converted into store-rooms and offices for the storekeeper. The other wing, upon the erection of the armory, became a fencing-school, and was connected by a covered gallery with the gymnasium. In 1872, offices were fitted up above the store for the paymaster of the Academy, who had previously been in the small brick house used by the quartermaster of Fort Severn.

The cadet hospital and the two double houses near it, now altered into apartment houses, were built by Commander Goldsborough. The hospital was finished early in 1855, but the dwellings were not ready until November 25, 1857.‡ By

* The portico of the gunnery-room was erected about 1858 or 1859.

† Commander Goldsborough's plan, 1857.

‡ Letter-book No. 5, p. 101; Report Board of Visitors June 16, 1855.

the alterations of the last two years the capacity and convenience of these buildings have been very much increased.

Several houses were standing upon the land purchased for the school in 1847. Three of these, the Nicholson, O'Hara, and Buchanan houses, were utilized as officers' quarters. The Nicholson house, the one nearest the Superintendent's in position, was assigned to the commandant of midshipmen; the O'Hara house, next to it, a brick building, was occupied by Prof. W. F. Hopkins; and the third house, on the Buchanan lot, by Professor Karney. All of them were near Scott street. While this was still the boundary of the Academy, two new blocks of brick houses were built on the same line, occupied respectively by the chaplain and Lieutenant Simpson, and by Professors Roget and Seager. A third block, near the last, but facing Northeast street, below the present middle walk, was built for the carpenter and sailmaker.

When the large acquisitions of land were made by Commander Stribling in 1853, the situation of these houses, in the middle of the grounds, came to have many inconveniences; and, after much deliberation, it was resolved to take them all down and use the materials in building new quarters nearer the outer wall. The row between the chapel and the upper gate was accordingly built by Captain Blake. These houses are now called Blake row, and are numbered from 1 to 11. They were completed in the following order:* Nos. 8, 9, 10, 11, April 20, 1859; Nos. 6 and 7, November 23, 1859; No. 1, (commandant's house) December 1, 1859; Nos. 2, 3, 4, 5, February 23, 1861. It will be observed that the last four were finished only three months before the removal of the Academy; so that they had hardly been occupied at all when they were handed over to the troops to be used as a military hospital.

Many buildings were erected after the close of the war,

* Contracts, pp. 35 and 82; Letter-book No. 7, p. 112.

during Admiral Porter's administration. The new quarters (a five-story brick building) were finished in the summer of 1869, and were occupied by the midshipmen in the following fall. On the ground-floor of this building are offices, reception-rooms, recitation-rooms, and a dining-hall. On the floors above, the greater number of the cadets are quartered, each room having two occupants. On the attic floor are the large rooms of the drawing department and of the instructor in descriptive geometry. The kitchens, laundry, and bath-rooms are in the basement.

The building of the department of steam-engineering was finished in 1866. The main building is 100 feet by 45, and has two stories. The wings increase considerably the size of the building. The physical laboratory and the photographer's building were built about the same time, or soon after. Both have undergone alterations. The lecture-room and laboratory proper in the first building have been much improved, while the second has been rebuilt, and is now an excellent chemical laboratory.

The chapel* and armory were also built by Admiral Porter, the former about 1868, the latter in the fall of 1865. The row of officers' quarters below the governor's house was built during the same period, Nos. 20 and 21 in 1867; Nos. 22 and 23 in 1868; and Nos. 24, (board house,) 25, and 26 in 1869.

The governor's house and grounds were conveyed to the United States by deed of August 17, 1866. The Superintendent of the Academy proceeded to build as soon as possible upon the land, but there was some delay about the cession of the house. It was finally given up in 1869; the

*The site of the chapel was a part of the Pinkney lot, purchased June 25, 1853. The old Pinkney house was removed in 1860, having been previously occupied for a time as officers' quarters. (Contracts, p. 89.)

wings and outbuildings, which were very extensive, were removed, and the library was brought over from the seamanship hall and put in the rooms of the lower floor. The second floor was fitted up for the offices of the Superintendent and secretary, which had previously been in a small building near the wall, northeast of the middle gate. This building, seen on all the old plans of the Academy, was immediately removed.

The date of erection of the governor's house is not known, but it is undoubtedly some time before the middle of the last century. According to Ridgely,* (and there is no question about the fact,) the house was built by the Hon. Edmund Jennings, of Lincoln's Inn, secretary of the province of Maryland and judge of the land-office. By deed of February 20, 1769,† he conveyed it to Governor Robert Eden for £1,000, as follows: "All that messuage or capital mansion-house, with the garden, yards, coach-houses, stables, and outhouses thereunto belonging," "as the same now is or was late in the tenure or occupation of his excellency Horatio Sharpe, as tenant to the said Edmund Jennings."

This house, it will be noticed, was not the official residence of the proprietary governors, as the present executive mansion is of the State governors. There was no such official residence in the province. Governor Bladen made an attempt to build one in 1744, employing as architect Simon Duff, the same who built the old Dulany house, now the residence of the Superintendent; but the plan was on too grand a scale to be completed. The house was partly built and then left to decay, and after many years it became one of the halls of Saint John's College.‡ Horatio Sharpe, the governor next but one after Bladen, rented the house owned by Jen-

* Annals of Annapolis, p. 236.

† Liber D. D., No. 4, 1764–1770, one of the records of the provincial court, now in the office of the commissioner of the land-office of Mary land.

‡ McDowell Hall.

nings, as a mansion worthy of the representative of the Proprietary, and lived in it during his term of office, from 1753 to 1769. In the latter year he was succeeded by Governor Eden, who bought the house from Jennings, and who resided there for seven years. At the outbreak of the Revolution Governor Eden took the tory side; and in 1776 he sailed from Annapolis in H. B. M. frigate Fowey for England.* His property was confiscated in consequence, and the house and grounds in Annapolis came into possession of the State. It was thenceforth used as the residence of the State governors until its purchase by the Academy.

William Eddis, surveyor of the customs at Annapolis in 1769, describes the appearance of the house in October of that year: "The governor's house is most beautifully situated, and when the necessary alterations are completed it will be a regular, convenient, and elegant building. The garden is not extensive, but it is disposed to the utmost advantage; the centre walk is terminated by a small green mount, close to which the Severn approaches. This elevation commands an extensive view of the bay and the adjacent country. The same objects appear to equal advantage from the saloon and many apartments in the house; and perhaps I may be justified in asserting that there are but few mansions in the most rich and cultivated parts of England which are adorned with such splendid and romantic scenery."†

* Eddis, Letters from Annapolis, p. 312.

† Letters from Annapolis, p. 17. Ridgely (Annals of Annapolis, p. 236) says that Governor Eden "built the wings and the long room." This statement must, however, be taken with modifications. Eddis speaks of the saloon in 1769, and it is hardly likely that Governor Eden had already built it when he had been so short a time in possession. Moreover, this long room or saloon is almost unmistakably an integral part of the house. It is quite possible that Eden built the tower at the back of the house, which enlarged this room by adding to it a deep semicircular recess.

CHAPTER VII.

LIBRARY.

Soon after the establishment of the school, in 1845, the Navy Department transferred to it a number of books which had been in use in navy-yards and men-of-war; and this collection, with small additions made from time to time between 1845 and 1850, constituted the nucleus of the present library.

In the fiscal year ending June 30, 1852, and so on thereafter, additions were made by allowing a sum yearly out of the congressional appropriations for "contingent expenses of the Naval Academy," or, as now, for "general maintenance." The following table shows the

INCREASE OF THE LIBRARY BY DECADES.

	Volumes.
December 31, 1855	4,751
December 31, 1865	9,593
December 31, 1875	17,678

This number has been further increased during the past year.

The library possesses in addition 26 manuscripts, 705 pamphlets, a set of the United States Coast Survey charts, a set of the British admiralty charts, the Pilote Français, and the Côtes Méridionales de France. In making additions the chief aim has always been to render the greatest possible aid to the departments of instruction, and especially to make the collection rich in works on professional subjects. The library possesses a large number of the most approved treatises on naval subjects published in America and Europe. Every new publication of this sort of any merit is added at once to the collection. In order to do this, however, it is not found necessary to sacrifice the interests of the scientific student or the general reader. The total amount expended upon the library is estimated at $35,180.

While the Academy was at Newport, most of the books were kept in the boxes in which they had been carried from Annapolis, as there was no suitable place for them, nor any certainty as to how long the Academy would stay there. About one thousand volumes, consisting of the most important books of reference, were arranged for temporary use. Only 633 books were added during this period.

During Admiral Porter's administration the library underwent a thorough and careful re-arrangement. Excellent rooms were prepared for it on the first floor of the governor's mansion, and it was transferred to the new rooms in the spring of 1869. About the same time the card-catalogue was begun, and the library was arranged in departments by Mr. Poole, formerly of the Boston Athenæum. The catalogue was finished in 1870, and it has been kept up since that time. A printed catalogue was prepared in 1860, but the great increase in the number of books has rendered it of little or no value.

The library has received no bequests, and the gifts consist of less than 300 volumes.

PART II.

The Naval Academy in 1876.

CHAPTER I.

ACADEMIC ORGANIZATION.

The Naval Academy is under the direct care and supervision of the Secretary of the Navy.

The Superintendent is a line officer of the Navy, of a rank not below that of captain, assigned to this duty by the Secretary of the Navy. He is charged with the general superintendence and government of the Academy, and all officers, professors, instructors, and cadets are under his command. He has charge of the grounds, buildings, and vessels belonging to the institution, and he may appoint and remove all persons employed in it, except those for whose appointment or discharge special provision is made by the laws or regulations for the government of the Navy, or of the Academy.

The commandant of cadets is a line officer of the Navy, and is next in authority to the Superintendent. He has immediate charge, under the Superintendent, of the police and discipline; and the drills and tactical instruction in the departments of seamanship and gunnery are under his general direction. The officers in these departments are the assistants of the commandant in carrying out the discipline.

The senior aid is a line officer of the Navy, and has special charge of the grounds and buildings, of purchases and accounts relating to the public property, and of the workmen employed upon the grounds and about the buildings.

The academic staff, engaged specially in the work of instruction, comprises line officers, officers of the Engineer Corps, and professors of mathematics, in the Navy, and a number of professors and assistant professors appointed from civil life. The branches taught are divided into groups, and these groups of studies are in charge of separate departments. Each department has an executive head, a naval officer or civil professor, as the case may be, and several assistants. The heads of departments arrange the details of the courses of study, and have general supervision of the work of their assistants, giving personal instruction when it may be desirable. The work of actual instruction is performed by the officers, professors, and assistant professors, attached to the several departments.

The Academic Board, or faculty, of the Academy is composed of the Superintendent, the commandant of cadets, and the heads of departments. The Superintendent, or, in his absence, the commandant of cadets, is the presiding officer; and all reports and returns of the board are made to or through the Superintendent. The board prescribes the subjects and arrangement of the course of instruction and the text-books to be used,* the time of examinations, the relative weight of recitations and examinations, and the relative weight of different branches of study. The board also makes recommendations to the Department in the cases of deficient cadets; and "cadets found deficient shall not be continued at the Academy, or in the service, unless upon the recommendation of the Academic Board." (Revised Statutes, §§ 1519, 1525.)

Outside of the academic staff, there are attached to the Academy a chaplain, a number of officers of the Medical and Pay Corps of the Navy, and four officers of the Marine Corps, in charge of the marine guard; and three civil attachés—the librarian, commissary, and secretary.

* Subject to the approval of the Secretary of the Navy.

There are two classes of students, the cadet-midshipmen and the cadet-engineers, destined for two different branches of the service—the line officers and the Engineer Corps. The examinations for admission are distinct for the two corps, but the four-years' course is pursued in many branches in common. In these branches, as well as in matters of daily routine and discipline, the same organization and regulations apply to both.

The number of cadets at the beginning of the academic year 1875–'76 was as follows:

CADET-MIDSHIPMEN.		
First class	42	
Second class	61	
Third class	53	
Fourth class	118	
		274
CADET-ENGINEERS.		
First class*	3	
Third class	17	
Fourth class	28	
		48
Total		322

The academic year begins on the 20th of September and ends on the 20th of June, consisting of two terms; the first term from September 20 to the Saturday nearest to January 30, and the second term from the close of the first term to June 20. At the close of the academic year the graduating class are granted leave of absence until ordered to sea, or to

* The first-class of cadet-engineers came in under the old system of a two-years' course; the third and fourth classes represent the four-years' course, first applied to the class which entered in September, 1874. See page.

some other duty, by the Navy Department. During the three months of summer the cadets of the newly-formed first and third classes go on the practice-cruise, and those of the new second class have leave of absence until the beginning of the next year. The candidates that have passed successfully the June examination for admission are quartered for the summer on board the frigate Santee, as the nucleus of the fourth class, and have a light course of study and drill. The routine of the Academy is in general suspended, and the charge of the new cadets is given to officers detailed in turn for short periods during the summer.

At the beginning of each academic year the cadet organization for the year is prescribed. This organization is retained throughout the year, and is followed in all the drills, and in all formations (except those for recitation) including the mess-formation. All the cadets are arranged in four divisions for great-gun exercise, the divisions containing an equal number of guns'-crews. Each gun's-crew is composed of sixteen men, distributed as nearly as possible among the several classes. Each division constitutes a battery for light-artillery drill and a company for infantry drill. For exercises in seamanship the guns'-crews are grouped in watches, the odd-numbered crews making the starboard-watch and the even-numbered crews the port-watch. The watches are stationed as a ship's company at seamanship-exercises.

The cadet-officers are appointed from the first class, as far as practicable, and are chosen with special reference to their fitness for the positions; and they hold their offices during good behavior and efficiency. They are as follows:

One cadet lieutenant-commander;
Four cadet lieutenants;
Five cadet masters;
Four cadet ensigns; and

Cadet petty officers, according to the number of the guns'-crews.

The cadet lieutenant-commander bears the same relation to the cadet organization that an executive officer bears to a ship's company. He is present at all general formations, and receives reports from the officers in command of divisions, which are made through him to the officer in charge. In the battalion organization he acts as lieutenant-colonel.

The divisions, or companies, are commanded by a cadet lieutenant as captain, with a cadet master and a cadet ensign as the other commissioned officers. One of the cadet masters is selected as adjutant of the battalion.

The cadet petty officers act as first and second captains of guns'-crews in the great-gun drills, and as sergeants and corporals in the infantry drills. Each table in the mess-hall is occupied by a gun's-crew, the first and second captains being placed at the head and foot of the table. The cadet officers, whenever they are in charge of those portions of the organization under their command, are responsible for the preservation of order and discipline.

DAILY ROUTINE.

The day is divided, for purposes of study and recitation, into three periods of two hours each, two of which are in the morning and one in the afternoon. The programme of studies is so arranged that each cadet has three recitations a day, one in each period. The remainder of the period, as well as the greater part of the evening, is devoted to study or reading,—the cadets being required to remain in their rooms at these times. A drill takes place daily, when the weather permits, after the last recitation. On Saturday morning studies and recitations end at half past 10, and the rest of the day, after the usual drill, is given to recreation. On other days, out-of-door recreation is limited to a portion of the afternoon and to the short intervals between meals and study. Reveille is sounded at 6 a. m. in the fall and spring, and at 6.15 a. m. in the winter. At this hour cadets are required to rise and arrange their rooms. Evening gun-fire and tattoo are at 9.30 p. m., at which time study-hours, as such, are over. At taps, half an hour later, the lights are put out, and the cadets retire for the night.

RELIGIOUS SERVICE.

Prayers are said by the chaplain, daily, immediately after the morning roll-call, and the attendance of all cadets is required. Divine service is held in the chapel Sunday morning and evening. Cadets are required to be present in the morning, but attendance at the evening service is voluntary.

Cadets whose parents or guardians desire it, may attend service permanently in the city of Annapolis, at any one of the churches of the various denominations. In such cases they are excused altogether from the chapel service, but they must attend every Sunday morning at their regular place of worship.

HOSPITAL.

The sick-call is sounded soon after breakfast every morning, at which time a medical officer of the Academy is in attendance to examine and prescribe for any cadets who may be ill. After this examination, lists are made up of cadets to be excused from drills, and of those whose illness is serious enough to prevent their studying. Cadets who are ill at any other time during the day have an opportunity of consulting the physician immediately. The cadet hospital, in the immediate neighborhood of the cadets' quarters, contains several rooms for patients, and is furnished with a complete dispensary. An officer of the medical staff is constantly on duty at the hospital.

CADETS' QUARTERS.

The cadet-midshipmen of the second class and the cadet-engineers occupy the old quarters between the recitation-hall and the gymnasium. The other cadets are quartered in the new building at the northwestern end of the grounds. Each room is occupied by two cadets. The furniture of the rooms is simple, and the arrangement prescribed with exactness. The occupants of the room alternate weekly as superintendents of the room, and the superintendent for the time being is responsible for the cleanliness and order of the apartment and for the safe-keeping of public property. Cadets are required to remain in their rooms during study-hours, except when at recitation.

An officer of the academic staff is always in charge of the quarters during the day and night. The day duty is performed by the assistants in the departments of seamanship and gunnery, and the night duty by the other line officers in rotation. The officer in charge has similar duties and responsibilities with the executive officer on board ship; in general, he sees that the regulations are enforced, and attends to the preservation of order and discipline. In this duty he is assisted by the officer of the day, a cadet-midshipman of the first class detailed for the purpose for twenty-four hours; a regularly-recurring duty coming to each cadet of the first class once in three or four weeks.

The officer in charge makes a daily inspection of the rooms at a regular hour, and other inspections at irregular times, as he sees fit. Under his direction the officer of the day makes up the conduct-report, comprising all the reports that may have come in during the day of delinquencies in recitation, drill, or elsewhere. This report, made up every evening, is read out the next morning at the roll-call, before breakfast.

In addition to the officer in charge and officer of the day, there is a superintendent on each floor, (or, in the old quarters, in each building,) who has special charge of the floor or building, and who is responsible for any disorders that may occur there. The superintendents are taken from the whole list of cadets in turn, and their tour of duty is twenty-four hours.

FIRE ORGANIZATION.

In addition to the modern appliances usually placed in large buildings to extinguish fires, the Academy is supplied with one steam fire-engine and one hand-engine. For exercise with the fire-apparatus the cadets are organized in guns'-crews. This exercise takes place early in the year, and is repeated at intervals. The fire-bell, designating the station of each cadet at fire-quarters, is posted in a conspicuous place throughout the year. Whenever the fire-alarm is sounded, the cadets proceed at once to their stations. In case of an actual fire the marines get under arms, and the whole force of the Academy is very shortly on the ground.

STORE.

The store is in charge of an officer detailed from the Pay Corps of the Navy. Clothing and other necessaries are supplied to cadets from the store at cost price, with a small percentage to cover transportation and breakage. Cadets in need of articles kept at the store send in requisitions at a specified time during each month to the commandant of cadets; and, if approved by him, the requisitions are filled by the store-keeper.

PAY AND ACCOUNTS.

The pay of cadets is $500 per annum. This sum is not paid out to them to be expended at pleasure; but their accounts with the store-keeper, as well as the mess and laundry accounts, are settled by the treasurer and charged to the cadets. Sixty dollars per annum is reserved for the purchase of an outfit at graduation; and the very small balance remaining is paid at that time to the cadet to whom it is due. No cadet is allowed to contract debts without the sanction of the Superintendent.

RECITATIONS.

Each class is divided into sections for purposes of recitation. The sections are small, usually numbering ten or less, so that instructors are enabled to give careful attention to the individual wants of their pupils. The sections in each branch are arranged according to the order of merit, so that students of nearly similar capacity or attainments recite together. The section-arrangement is renewed every month, and the sections are not kept continuously under the same instructor throughout the term. The cadet at the head of each section is its leader, and is responsible for its conduct while in his charge.

MARKS.

The scale of marks ranges from 4 as a maximum to 0; and a mark below 2.5 is given to a recitation or exercise which is not considered satisfactory. The marks in each branch are averaged, and the rank-list is made out and published at the end of every month; and a report of the marks and standing of each cadet is sent at the same time to his parent or guardian. At the end of the year the general standing of each class is made up. The final mark of each cadet is found by adding together the products obtained by multiplying the final mark in each branch by the co-efficient of that branch.

Cadets whose mark at the end of the year is below 2.5 (or 62.5 per cent.) in any branch are deficient, and they are recommended to the Secretary of the Navy for dismissal. In cases of slight deficiency they are turned back into the next class, or subjected to a re-examination; but in no case can a cadet graduate from the school who has failed to get 62.5 per cent. as his yearly mark in each and every branch of study pursued during the four-years' course.

INTERIOR DISCIPLINE.

All officers and cadet officers are authorized and required to report offences coming under their notice in the line of duty to the commandant of cadets; and any cadet, in a responsible position, who becomes answerable for a breach of the regulations, is required to answer the questions of his superior officer relating to the offence, and relieve himself of his responsibility by reporting the offender. All the reports are deposited with the officer in charge; and they are collated and arranged upon the conduct-report every evening by the officer of the day. This conduct-report is read out in the morning, as has been stated, and remains posted during the day. Cadets are thus given an opportunity of presenting excuses and explanations, which are examined and acted upon the next day in connection with the report. Demerits are given for each offence, but only as a record of misconduct, and in no case as a punishment. Certain limits are fixed to the number of demerits allowed any cadet, and if the number is reached the case is reported to the Navy Department with such recommendation as the Academic Board may think proper.

The punishments inflicted are comprised in the following list:

Removal from the service.
Solitary confinement.
Coventry.
Public reprimand on parade, by written orders.

Confinement under guard or in quarters.

Deprivation of leave or recreation.

Extra duties or drills.

Suspension.

Reduction of cadet rank.

No officer at the Academy, except the Superintendent, is authorized to order or inflict punishment of any kind; and dismissal from the service can only be ordered by the Secretary of the Navy.

AMUSEMENTS.

The water around the Academy is very good water for pulling, and the class boat-clubs among the cadets have several shells, mostly four-oars and six-oars. The clubs have a four-oar race in June, and a flag kept at the Academy is given to the winning crew, whose names are engraved on the staff-plate. The class-crews have good opportunities for training and practice, going out twice a day after they have fairly settled down to work for the season. The regularity of their daily life, the total interdiction of tobacco and liquor, the abundance of exercise afforded by daily drills, with the gymnasium and boxing, and the simplicity and excellence of their table, do away with the necessity of rigorous training, and give them at the start a better average form than the ordinary class-crew at college.

Base-ball is a favorite sport, each class having a nine of its own, besides the Academy nine. Match games are played on Saturday afternoons, frequently during the spring, with clubs from Baltimore, Washington, and Annapolis. Foot-ball is played during the winter, and there is more or less riding on Saturdays at all times. Cadets who cannot swim are required to learn as soon as possible after admission, and they receive instruction and practice until they are good swimmers. One of the buildings on the wharf contains a swimming-bath for exercise and swimming-lessons in winter, with a tank 30 feet long, 15 feet wide, and 4 feet deep. The water is pumped in from the river, and heated by steam-pipes.

At all times during recreation-hours cadets have access to the pistol-gallery and bowling-alley, and, with certain limitations, to the gymnasium. Two or three times a year the best gymnasts give an exhibition, with sparring and fencing matches, and exercises with the rings, bars, clubs, and trapeze.

On Saturday evenings the gymnasium is usually cleared, decorated, and opened for dancing, from half-past 7 o'clock till 10. On the night before holidays an entertainment is given, and dancing is prolonged to a later hour. In January the cadets of the first class give a ball, and in June those of the second class give a similar entertainment to the cadets about to graduate.

Leave to go beyond the academic limits is only granted on Saturdays and on holidays, and ends at evening parade. This privilege is forfeited by misconduct, or by neglect of study during the week, being denied to cadets whose mark for the week in any branch is below 62.5 per cent. The privilege is also restricted to the first class and one-fourth of the three lower classes, at any one time. The restriction is not, however, severe in practice, as there are greater resources for amusement within the walls than without.

MESS.

All cadets are required to board at the mess-table. The dining-room is a large and well-lighted hall on the ground-floor of the new quarters. Captains of crews have charge of separate tables, and the officer-in-charge has general supervision of the hall at meals, as well as at other times. The cost of living is about $20 per month. The fare is simple, but carefully prepared and abundant.

CHAPTER II.

EXAMINATION AND QUALIFICATIONS FOR ADMISSION.

I. CADET-MIDSHIPMEN.

1. *Nomination.*—The number of cadet-midshipmen allowed at the Academy is one for every Member or Delegate of the House of Representatives, one for the District of Columbia, and ten appointed annually at large. After March 5 of each year the Secretary of the Navy notifies each Member or Delegate of any vacancy that may exist in his district. The nomination of a candidate to fill this vacancy is made upon the recommendation of the Member or Delegate; but if not made by July 1 of that year the Secretary of the Navy is required to fill the vacancy. The nomination of candidates from the District of Columbia and at large is made by the President.

2. *Examinations.*—There are two examinations for admission, one on June 21, the other on September 12. Candidates who are nominated in time to attend the first examination come up in June; the others hold over until September. Should any candidate that ought to come up in June fail to report, or be rejected for any reason, the Member or Delegate from whose district he was nominated is notified to recommend another, who is also examined in September.

All candidates must be over fourteen and less than eighteen years of age, and no one is examined whose age does not fall within the prescribed limits. They must be physically sound, well-formed, and of robust constitution. To test this, they are required to pass a satisfactory examination before a medical board, composed of the surgeon of the Academy and two other medical officers designated by the Secretary of the Navy. Any one of the following conditions is sufficient to cause the rejection of the candidate: Feeble constitution, greatly-retarded development, permanently-impaired general health, decided cachexia, diathesis, or predisposition, and all chronic disease, malformation, or results of injuries, that would permanently impair efficiency. Attention is also paid to the stature of the candidate, and no one manifestly under size for his age is admitted. No candidate rejected by the medical board is allowed a re-examination.

Candidates must pass an examination before a committee of the Academic Board in reading, writing, spelling, arithmetic, geography, and English grammar. All the examinations, except in reading, are written. Candidates who fall below the standard (62.5 per cent. in each branch) receive a second and final examination in the subjects in which they fail. Deficiency in any one of the subjects at the second examination is sufficient to insure rejection. By the Revised Statutes, § 1515, "candidates rejected at such examination shall not have the privilege of another examination to the same class, unless recommended by the board of examiners."

3. *General character of questions:*

ARITHMETIC.

Notation and numeration.

Denominate numbers.—The tables of money, weights, and measures; addition, subtraction, multiplication, and division of denominate numbers; the relation between the troy and avoirdupois pound; the reduction of differences of longitude to their equivalents in time, and the reverse.

Fractions.—The candidate must be familiar with all the processes of common and decimal fractions, and must be able to give clearly the reasons for the processes; and he should be familiar with the contracted methods of multiplication and division given in the ordinary text-books of arithmetic.

Properties of numbers.—The test of the divisibility of numbers by 2, 3, 5, 8, 9, 11, 25, 125, &c.; the resolution of composite numbers into prime factors; the method of determining whether a number is prime or composite, and of finding the greatest common divisor and least common multiple of large and small numbers.

Ratio and proportion.—The definition and explanation of ratio and proportion; the methods of writing a proportion; the solution of problems in simple and compound proportion.

Analysis.—Miscellaneous problems similar to those in the common-school text-books.

Percentage, interest, and discount.

Mensuration.—The measurement of rectangular surfaces and volumes.

Evolution.—The extraction of square and cube roots.

An algebraic solution may be given, in place of an arithmetical solution, in problems which admit of it.

Candidates must be thoroughly proficient in all branches of arithmetic, and unusual excellence may be allowed to count in their favor in case of a slight deficiency in other subjects.

GEOGRAPHY.

Candidates are questioned upon the grand divisions of the land and water; the character of coast-lines; the direction and position of mountain-chains, and the locality of important peaks; the position and course of rivers, their tributaries, and the bodies of water into which they empty; the position of important seas and bays; the political divisions of the land, their position, boundaries, and capital cities; the position and direction of great peninsulas, and the situation of important and prominent capes; straits, sounds, channels, and the most important canals; great lakes, and inland seas; position and political connection of important islands and colonial possessions; locality of cities of historical, political, or commercial importance; the course of a vessel in making a voyage between well-known sea-ports.

GRAMMAR.

Candidates are examined upon the whole of English grammar, as treated in the common-school text-books, embracing all that is usually given under the head of orthography, etymology or classification, the formation and inflection of words, and syntax, including parsing and the analysis of sentences. The questions in grammar are based upon the school-books found by actual inquiry to be in most common use.

READING.

Candidates are examined in reading aloud English prose in a standard work.

WRITING AND SPELLING.

Candidates are required to write a short original letter and an exercise in dictation, and to spell twenty-four words in common use. An exercise having eight or more mistakes in spelling is not considered satisfactory, and is enough of itself to cause the rejection of a candidate.

4. *Preparation of candidates.*—It is a matter of remark to the examining board that a considerable majority of the candidates come very poorly fitted for this or any other examina-

tion. The subjects required are of an elementary character, the papers set are simple and easy, and the marking is indulgent. The question occurs at once, Why is it that selected boys from all parts of the country, of an average age of over sixteen, and none of them younger than fourteen, should be unable to pass a creditable examination in grammar, geography, spelling, and arithmetic? Or, leaving out of consideration the first two branches, as candidates are rarely rejected for a deficiency in geography or grammar alone, why is it that out of 200 boys of sixteen, presented annually for examination, hardly half could be called proficient in arithmetic and spelling?

The reason seems to lie partly in the circumstances or capacity of the candidates selected, and partly in the defective condition of the fitting-schools, and a want of time for special preparation. Candidates are appointed from every part of the country, often with very brief notice of the coming examination. As a rule, they are selected without reference to scholastic attainments, very few being required to pass a competitive examination* for their appointment. Some of the papers show a degree of ignorance so remarkable that the most superficial preliminary examination would have disclosed it. But these examinations are clearly the exception rather than the rule.

Some illustrations of this defective training have been selected from the examination-papers of candidates for admission. They are taken from the English papers, as the want of training is seen more readily in these answers than in arithmetical examples, although it is quite as marked in the latter.

* At the examination for admission in September, 1875, there were 11 candidates out of 92 who had been appointed after competitive examinations, of whom two were rejected and one failed to complete his first year at the Academy.

SPELLING.

June, 1874:

"Mullicous.	Opinon.	Privelige.
Milta.	Litarray.	Linen.
Vengence.	Soverighty.	Colonal.
Citzen.	Perserve.	Extradonary.
Colony.	Sympathy.	Talent.
Acadmey.	Embarrass.	Sarcfice.
Escential.	Deslipine.	Speech.
Milatary.	Siendentifc.	Discreet."

September, 1873:

"Agreeable.	Skillful.	Seperate.
Condemn.	Linnen.	Academy.
Accessible.	Literary.	Severn.
Formmible.	Obveious.	Masculin.
Dissention.	Exenent.	Circle.
Cornel.	Recede.	Lilly.
Amalgamate.	Procede.	Forren."
Suciside.		

The following is part of a paper handed in by a candidate from Massachusetts, who brought a letter of recommendation from the master of the high-school which he attended in a considerable town of that State. The letter stated that the candidate stood *No. 2 in a class of twenty at his school*, and that he had previously attended a Boston grammar-school. The letter was such as to give the impression that this was one of the most creditable pupils at the high-school in question. The paper is copied *literatim.*

Dictation, (Bancroft's United States, 1, p. 234:)

"Equally proverbial was the hospitality of the Verginians labor was valuable land was cheap compitance prompty followed industry there was know nead off a scramble abound-ance * * * * * the morasses were alive with water foul the creeks abounded with oisters in inexausterble beds * * * the woods russled with quails." * *

SPELLING.

"Forfetture.	Grievences.	Precarious.
Synonimous.	Beneficeary.	Privalleges.
Judgeitial.	Fundimental.	Equivilant.
Mantinance.	Perpetuate.	Matrimonial.
Acknowlagement.	Heredditary.	Corporation.
Encouragement.	Descendant.	Simpathetic.
Tenement.	Aillion.	Agreable.
Reccompence.	Eclesiastical.	Dicernment."

According to the practice at that time, this candidate was examined orally in the branches in which he had failed at his written examination. The examining committee gave him eight words to spell at the blackboard.

A copy of this exercise is given:

"Engenire.	Incriment.	Quarrantine.
Exhauxtiveness.	Finantial.	Chemastry."
Ceddiment.	Pylgramage.	

After this it was deemed unnecessary to go any further with the examination in this branch.

A still more inexcusable case came very recently before the board of examiners, which, perhaps, explains in some degree the inefficiency of secondary schools. A young man nearly eighteen years of age presented himself, under appointment, from one of the western counties of the State of New York, for examination as to his qualifications for admission. In filling up the required blanks, before examination, he stated that he had been appointed after a competitive examination of seventeen candidates, and that he had taught school. Careful inquiry disclosed the following facts in regard to the last statement. Candidates wishing to become teachers were examined as to their proficiency by the school commissioner of the district before appointment. The commissioners were chosen at a general election by the voters of the school-district. This young man had been examined in the regular way and appointed teacher in the district-school. The school-year consists of two terms of twelve or fourteen weeks each, and the candidate had taught school during five such terms. He had nine pupils at first, to whom he taught arithmetic, geography, grammar, reading, and spelling; and in the last winter he had risen to the responsibility of thirty-four pupils, and he was teaching algebra and United States history.

He brought with him the following letter of recommendation from a judicial functionary of the neighborhood:

"——, N. Y., —— ——.

"SUPERETENDENT OF NAVAL ACADEMY
Anapilos Md

"This is to certify that I am well acquainted with —— —— & can chearfully say that he is a Yong Man of Good Moral charictor & highly respected by all who know him

"(Signed) "—— ——."

So much for the antecedents of the candidate. At his examination for admission to the Academy he failed on three-fourths of the questions on his first arithmetic-paper, and he barely succeeded in passing on the second. The following are his papers in spelling and geography, copied exactly, though no copy can do justice to the penmanship and form:

SPELLING.

" Millionheir.	Supercilleous.	Demagogue.
Snoar (!)	Honorous.	Inflamable.
Depravity.	Engineer.	Scientific.
Tollerance.	Brigadier.	Trancient.
Infermery.	Icicle.	Verticle.
Clamor.	Proficency.	Privalege.
Stratagem.	Discention.	Democracy.
Penetant.	Malisceous.	Concession."

GEOGRAPHY.

Questions.

"I. Give the position of the following cities, and tell on or near what water they are situated:

"1. Toledo. 2. Carthagena. 3. Cracow. 4. Trebizond. 5. Calcutta.

"II. From what land and into what water do the following capes project?

"1. Montauk Point. 2. Cape Canaveral. 3. Cape Race. 4. Cape Matapan. 5. Point de Galle.

"III. Make a coasting voyage from Archangel to Calcutta via the Suez Canal. Name all the important bodies of water you pass through, in order.

"IV. Name and locate six islands of the Mediterranean Sea, and tell to what country each one belongs.

"V. Describe the following rivers, telling where they rise, in what direction they flow, into what water they empty:

"1. Orinoco. 2. Pruth. 3. Columbia. 4. Po."

Answers.

"I. Toledo on the western end of Lake Erie; Carthigena norther part of france eng chanell Calcutta southern part europe Mediteranean sea.

"II. Montauk pt from canida into lake Huron. Canaveral west of California in to the pacific cape race from western part Labrador.

"III. east on the Bay of Bangal Arabian sea North-east on the red sea east on the Mediterranean Mediteranean sea Arabian sea Bay Bangal red sea.

"IV. corsica & sardinia to Candy to Turkey sicily to Itily

"V. The Orinoco Rises in the the Andes Mountans in south America flows North-East and Empties into the carribean sea

"Columbia. is formed by the Lewis and snake river flows in a westerly direction into the pacific ocean Po river rises in the northern part of Itily and flows in easterly dir into the archapelago sea"

The second papers were equally bad, or perhaps worse. And this from a district-school teacher of two years' standing! If such cases are common, the boasted American school system must be in some places a sham or a burlesque. Certain interesting questions present themselves as to the kind of education generally diffused among a community with such a school system. If this young man is the best of seventeen candidates, what must be the other sixteen? If a judicial functionary of the neighborhood can spell "character" "charictor," how would a district-school teacher, for example, spell it? And if the district-school teacher spells the word "snore" "snoar," what must be the proficiency of his scholars in spelling?

But even supposing that this example is a very exceptional one, as is to be hoped is the case, it helps to account for the large number of rejections. In these cases, want of time for preparation is hardly a valid excuse for inability to pass an examination as elementary as that for admission to the

Academy—certainly not for cases of gross ignorance like those just quoted. Any properly-trained boy of fourteen or fifteen years of age ought to need little previous notice to prepare himself to answer plain questions in the simplest branches of knowledge. There are, it is true, rare cases where circumstances have compelled a boy to devote most of his time to manual labor. There are also cases, presumably rare, among a picked class of boys chosen as being worthy to receive a beneficiary education from the Government, of constitutional dullness or incapacity; but the large majority of rejections must be referred to the insufficient training of the schools. If the schools of the country, primary and secondary, do not teach their pupils between the ages of seven and fifteen to spell, to cipher, to answer simple questions in geography and grammar, what in those eight years do they teach? The letter of the master of the Massachusetts high-school is not the only one of its kind—a letter which finds a charitable explanation either in self-delusion or incompetency.

5. *Admission.*—Candidates who pass the physical and the mental examination receive appointments as cadet-midshipmen, and become inmates of the Academy. Immediately after admission they are required to sign articles by which they bind themselves to serve in the United States Navy eight years, (including the time of probation at the Academy,) unless sooner discharged. At the same time they are required to make a deposit with the treasurer, which is credited on his books, to be expended, under the direction of the Superintendent, in the purchase of clothing, furniture, text-books, and other authorized articles. The amount required varies somewhat, besides being reduced more or less by the value of clothing brought from home. Last year (1875–'76) it was $229.99.

One month after admission each cadet is credited with the amount of his actual expenses in traveling from his home to the Academy; but a cadet who voluntarily resigns his appointment within a year from the time of his admission is required to refund this amount.

II. Cadet-engineers.

Applications from persons wishing to enter the Academy as cadet-engineers are made to the Navy Department. Out of the whole number of applicants a part are selected by the Secretary of the Navy, to whom permission is given to present themselves for examination. The number of cadet-engineers allowed by law is twenty-five per annum. Candidates must be not less than sixteen nor more than twenty years of age at the time of their examination.

The examination is held on the 5th of September of each year, and is competitive; the first twenty-five on the list of candidates, as determined by the examination, being selected for appointment. The subjects of the examination are as follows:

1. Algebra, through equations of the first degree.
2. Plane geometry.
3. Elementary physics.
4. Sketching.
5. Arithmetic.
6. Reading.
7. Writing.
8. Spelling.
9. Geography.
10. English grammar.

The examination in the six last-named subjects is similar to that for cadet-midshipmen. Candidates who show the greatest skill and experience in the practical working of machinery, other qualifications being equal, have precedence for admission.

Candidates are required to pass a physical examination, and if rejected by the medical board are excluded from further competition. The other requisites and conditions are the same as those for cadet-midshipmen.

TABLE I.—*Average age of cadets at the date of admission during the past ten years.*

CADET-MIDSHIPMEN.

	Yrs.	Mos.
Admitted in 1866	16	4
1867	16	4
1868	16	0
1869	16	2
1870	16	5
1871	16	3
1872	16	4
1873	16	7
1874	16	3
1875	16	9
Average age for 10 years, 1866–1875	16	4

CADET-ENGINEERS.

	Yrs.	Mos.
Admitted in 1874	18	6½
1875	17	10

TABLE II.—*Examinations of candidates for admission as cadet-midshipmen*—1870–1875.

Date.	Number of candidates.	Rejected by medical board.	Rejected by Academic Board.				Withdrawn.	Total rejected.
			Arithmetic.	English.	Both.	Total.		
June, 1870...	51	4	7	....	10	17	....	21
Sept., 1870...	102	5	14	....	11	25	1	31
June, 1871...	42	1	4	....	7	11	1	13
Sept., 1871...	54	2	....	1	9	10	1	13
June, 1872...	74	1	2	4	21	27	2	30
Sept., 1872...	76	1	10	3	17	30	....	31
June, 1873...	83	....	8	6	18	32	7	39
Sept., 1873...	106	4	11	8	33	52	1	57
June, 1874...	74	6	7	3	23	33	2	41
Sept., 1874...	106	8	9	11	24	44	....	52
June, 1875...	95	10	14	1	23	38	5	53
Sept., 1875...	92	5	17	3	18	38	1	44

NOTE.—Discrepancies between the numbers of the table and those published in the Annual Register are explained by the following:

J. B. Alexander, admitted June, 1870, not in Register for 1870–'71.
M. D. W. Burnett, admitted June, 1871, not in Register for 1871–'72.
Two students from Japan were admitted in 1872.
One student from Japan was admitted in 1873.
Two students from Japan were admitted in 1874.

TABLE III.—*Number of cadet-midshipmen graduated from each State during the past six years, with the number of candidates examined for the class, and its membership at the date of admission.*

State or Territory.	Date of graduation, 1870.			Date of graduation, 1871.			Date of graduation, 1872.			Date of graduation, 1873.			Date of graduation, 1874.			Date of graduation, 1875.			Total.			Percentage of candidates who graduated.	Percentage of those admitted who graduated.
	Examined.	Admitted.	Graduated.	Examined.	Admitted.	Graduated.	Examined.	Admitted.	Graduated.	Examined.	Admitted.	Graduated.	Examined.	Admitted.	Graduated.	Examined.	Admitted.	Graduated.	Examined.	Admitted.	Graduated.		
Alabama	0	0	0	0	0	0	1	1	0	4	2	0	5	3	3	1	1	1	11	7	4	36	54
Arizona	2	2	1	0	0	0	0	0	0	0	0	0	0	0	0	0	0	0	2	2	1	50	50
Arkansas	0	0	0	0	0	0	1	1	0	3	1	0	4	2	1	1	1	0	9	5	1	11	20
California	4	3	2	2	0	0	1	1	1	0	0	0	2	2	1	0	0	0	9	6	4	44	67
Colorado	1	1	0	0	0	0	0	0	1	0	0	0	0	0	0	0	0	0	1	1	1	*100	*100
Connecticut	3	3	1	2	0	1	3	0	0	2	2	2	1	0	0	1	0	0	12	5	4	33	80
Dakota	0	0	0	0	0	0	0	0	0	0	0	0	1	1	0	0	0	0	1	1	0	*0	*0
Delaware	2	1	1	0	0	0	0	0	0	0	0	0	0	0	0	1	1	0	3	2	1	33	50
Dist. Columbia	5	3	3	5	0	1	1	0	0	1	1	0	6	3	1	5	5	1	23	12	6	26	50
Florida	0	0	0	0	0	0	0	0	0	1	1	1	0	0	0	0	0	0	1	1	1	*100	*100
Georgia	0	0	0	0	0	0	0	0	0	5	3	0	0	0	0	3	3	1	8	6	1	13	17
Idaho	0	0	0	0	0	0	0	0	0	1	1	0	0	0	0	0	0	0	1	1	0	*0	*0
Illinois	11	9	4	4	2	1	3	2	0	8	8	3	5	4	1	5	3	2	37	28	11	30	39
Indiana	14	4	4	8	4	4	1	1	0	4	3	1	4	4	1	6	4	1	37	20	11	30	55
Iowa	5	2	2	5	3	1	0	0	0	1	1	0	3	4	2	0	0	2	14	10	7	50	70
Kansas	2	0	0	1	1	1	0	0	0	0	0	0	0	0	0	1	1	0	4	2	1	25	50

TABLE III.—*Number of cadet-midshipmen graduated from each State, &c.*—Continued.

State or Territory.	Date of graduation, 1870.			Date of graduation, 1871.			Date of graduation, 1872.			Date of graduation, 1873.			Date of graduation, 1874.			Date of graduation, 1875.			Total.			Percentage of candidates who graduated.	Percentage of those admitted who graduated.
	Examined.	Admitted.	Graduated.	Examined.	Admitted.	Graduated.	Examined.	Admitted.	Graduated.	Examined.	Admitted.	Graduated.	Examined.	Admitted.	Graduated.	Examined.	Admitted.	Graduated.	Examined.	Admitted.	Graduated.		
Kentucky	18	7	5	3	2	2	3	1	1	2	2	1	5	3	0	3	2	0	34	17	9	26	47
Louisiana......	1	1	1	0	0	0	1	1	1	3	2	1	5	2	0	1	1	1	11	7	4	36	54
Maine	3	3	1	1	1	1	2	2	1	4	3	1	0	0	0	1	1	0	11	10	4	36	40
Maryland......	8	5	0	4	3	2	4	2	0	10	4	1	5	3	0	6	3	1	37	20	4	11	20
Massachusetts .	6	6	4	5	4	1	2	1	1	2	2	1	7	5	0	3	2	3	25	20	10	40	50
Michigan	3	2	0	9	3	2	2	1	0	2	2	2	2	2	1	1	0	1	19	10	6	32	60
Minnesota	3	2	0	1	1	3	0	0	0	0	0	0	0	0	0	2	2	1	6	5	4	67	80
Mississippi.....	3	0	0	0	0	0	0	0	0	0	0	0	6	1	0	1	0	0	10	1	0	0	0
Missouri.......	5	2	1	14	3	2	2	1	1	7	4	1	3	3	2	3	3	1	34	16	8	24	50
Montana.......	1	1	1	0	0	0	0	0	0	0	0	0	0	0	0	1	1	0	2	2	1	50	50
Nebraska......	0	0	0	0	0	0	0	0	0	0	0	0	1	1	0	0	0	1	1	1	1	*100	*100
Nevada........	3	1	0	2	0	0	0	0	0	2	2	1	0	0	0	1	1	1	8	4	2	25	50
New Hampshire	5	3	1	0	1	0	1	1	1	4	3	2	2	2	1	2	3	1	14	13	6	43	46
New Jersey....	12	5	5	5	3	0	5	2	1	3	1	0	6	3	2	2	2	0	33	16	8	24	50
New Mexico...	3	0	0	0	0	0	1	1	0	0	0	0	1	0	0	1	1	0	6	2	0	0	0
New York.....	37	22	8	36	12	9	27	14	7	15	13	6	16	8	2	14	10	4	145	79	36	25	47
North Carolina	0	0	0	2	1	1	4	2	0	6	3	3	4	2	0	2	1	1	18	9	5	28	56

Ohio	22	11	8	14	10	5	6	5	4	7	6	0	11	8	3	5	3	2	65	43	22	34	50
Oregon........	1	0	0	1	0	0	0	0	0	1	0	0	2	1	0	0	0	0	5	1	0	0	0
Pennsylvania..	29	18	9	18	9	5	7	3	1	12	9	1	18	15	5	7	2	2	91	56	23	25	40
Rhode Island..	3	3	1	0	0	1	0	0	0	0	0	0	2	3	0	1	0	0	6	6	2	33	33
South Carolina.	0	0	0	0	0	0	1	1	0	5	3	0	2	1	0	2	1	1	10	6	1	10	17
Tennessee.....	3	2	0	2	1	1	4	2	0	4	3	0	2	2	1	5	3	3	20	13	5	25	38
Texas	0	0	0	0	0	0	0	0	0	0	0	0	3	2	1	0	0	0	3	2	1	33	50
Utah...........	0	0	0	0	0	0	1	1	1	0	0	0	0	0	0	0	0	0	1	1	1	*100	*100
Vermont.......	4	3	2	2	0	0	0	0	0	0	0	0	2	1	0	2	1	0	10	5	2	20	40
Virginia	0	0	0	2	0	0	1	1	1	1	1	0	14	7	2	2	1	0	20	10	3	15	30
Washington ...	0	0	1	0	0	0	0	0	0	0	0	0	1	1	0	1	1	0	2	2	1	50	50
West Virginia .	3	1	0	4	1	1	1	1	1	1	1	0	0	0	0	0	0	0	9	4	2	22	50
Wisconsin	5	3	2	3	3	2	2	0	2	1	0	0	1	1	0	3	4	0	15	11	6	40	55
Wyoming	0	0	0	0	0	0	0	0	0	0	0	0	1	0	0	0	0	0	1	0	0		*0
Empire of Japan	0	0	0	0	0	0	0	0	0	2	0	1	0	0	0	1	1	0	3	1	1	33	*100
Total	230	129	68	154	68	47	88	49	26	125	87	29	153	100	30	97	69	32	848	502	232	27.3	46.22

NOTE.—The examination for admission, referred to in the first and second columns, took place in each case four years before the date of graduation; and the three columns grouped under each date show the continuous history of the class graduating at that date.

In the case of those starred (*) the number of candidates is so small that the percentage can hardly be said to have any significance. They are therefore omitted in Tables IV and V.

TABLE IV.—*Percentage of candidates from each State and Territory who succeed in completing the course.*

State or Territory.	Percentage.	State or Territory.	Percentage.
Minnesota	67	Kentucky	26
Iowa	50	Kansas	25
California	44	Nevada	25
New Hampshire	43	New York	25
Massachusetts	40	Pennsylvania	25
Wisconsin	40	Tennessee	25
Alabama	36	Missouri	24
Louisiana	36	New Jersey	24
Maine	36	West Virginia	22
Ohio	34	Vermont	20
Connecticut	33	Virginia	15
Delaware	33	Georgia	13
Rhode Island	33	Arkansas	11
Texas	33	Maryland	11
Michigan	32	South Carolina	10
Illinois	30	Mississippi	0
Indiana	30	New Mexico	0
North Carolina	28	Oregon	0
District of Columbia	26		

TABLE V.—*Percentage of successful candidates from each State and Territory who succeed in completing the course.*

State or Territory.	Percentage.	State or Territory.	Percentage.
Connecticut	80	West Virginia	50
Minnesota	80	Kentucky	47
Iowa	70	New York	47
California	67	New Hampshire	46
Michigan	60	Maine	40
North Carolina	56	Pennsylvania	40
Indiana	55	Vermont	40
Wisconsin	55	Illinois	39
Alabama	54	Tennessee	38
Louisiana	54	Rhode Island	33
Delaware	50	Virginia	30
District of Columbia	50	Arkansas	20
Kansas	50	Maryland	20
Massachusetts	50	Georgia	17
Missouri	50	South Carolina	17
Nevada	50	Mississippi	0
New Jersey	50	New Mexico	0
Ohio	50	Oregon	0
Texas	50		

CHAPTER III.

COURSE OF INSTRUCTION.

I. Seamanship.

Before 1845, seamanship and navigation were the only subjects required at the examination of midshipmen for promotion. There was this difference between the two branches,—the first could only be learned at sea, while much of the second was more readily acquired on shore, away from the distractions of the ship. Consequently, the plan adopted in 1845 did not contemplate academic instruction in seamanship, but left it to be learned during the three years' cruise that acting midshipmen were sure to make before they came up for promotion.

The revised regulations of 1850 created a new and separate department, of naval tactics and practical seamanship, with the commandant of midshipmen as its head. The system, however, still provided for an intermediate cruise between the first two and last two years of the academic course, and instruction in these branches at the Academy was confined chiefly to practical exercises.

When the four year course was adopted in November, 1851, (it was hardly in operation till the next year,) seamanship became a recognized part of the academic course. The first book used was Totten's Naval Text-Book. This was changed in 1852 for Brady's Kedge-Anchor, which was in turn replaced in 1863 by Luce's Seamanship. From time to time kindred branches have been introduced in connection with the course in seamanship, and the practical exercises have been improved and their scope extended until the course has developed into its present form. The practice-cruises, begun in the summer of 1851, have always been a most important auxiliary to the instruction in seamanship.

From 1850 to 1875 the commandant of midshipmen has been nominally head of the department of seamanship, though of late years having little connection with it except in matters of routine. The senior assistant has been virtually head, though the authority to prescribe for the department lay with the commandant. The department of ordnance and gunnery was governed by the same system. In 1875 the senior assistants were made actual heads in name as well as in fact, the commandant merely retaining a supervision of the practical exercises in the two departments.

The cadet-midshipmen of all the classes are taught seamanship by practical exercises, and the two upper classes receive instruction, besides, from books, models, and lectures, in the section-room.

The department has a great variety of working models and apparatus for practical instruction, including full-rigged ships, both with and without sails; working models to illustrate the processes of getting in and out masts, boats, and guns, of sending up and down spars, and of heaving down; models of boats, anchors, chains, capstans, knots, splices, and tackles; and models of ships in process of construction, to illustrate the study of ship-building and naval architecture, showing the lines, timbers, plankings, and fittings of a vessel. The United States sloop of war Dale is moored at one of the wharves, and is used for practical exercises in seamanship. There are also several cutters for boat-drill, and a complete set of signal flags, lanterns, &c., for practice in signaling.

PRESENT COURSE.

Cadet-midshipmen.

FOURTH CLASS—FIRST YEAR.—Four drills a week during the first two and last two months of the academic year, as follows:

Exercises on board the Dale.—The class learn the names of the masts, yards, ropes, and sails, and of the different parts of the vessel. At drills they are stationed as landsmen, and they become familiar with the duties of this class of men. These drills take place three times a week during the period specified.

Boat-exercise.—The cadets go out once a week during the months named, in twelve 12-oared cutters fitted with oars and sails. A special organization is used for the boat-drill, and each boat is in charge of a cadet-officer. The object of this drill is to teach the fourth-classmen how to pull an oar.

Signals.—Exercises in signals (Myer's code) are held at intervals. The instructor has one division of the class at a time, and the division is broken up into squads of four, each squad in charge of a first-classman. The squads or groups are stationed at various points about the grounds and signal to one another. Proficiency is tested by sending signal-messages through five or six parties, stationed at considerable distances, in a circle, in such a way that each party can see only the one from which it receives the message and the one to which it is transmitted. The message is thus finally received by the original senders, and the accuracy of the process can be determined with exactness.

THIRD CLASS—SECOND YEAR.—Practice-cruise, three summer months. Practical exercises, as before.

Practice-cruise.—After the annual examination, cadets who have passed into the third class make their first practice-cruise at sea. Here they occupy the positions of landsmen and ordinary seamen, and are exercised in making the various knots, splices, hitches, and bends, and in fitting rigging; boxing the compass, heaving the log and the lead; steering; and in loosing, furling, and reefing sail. At times they have exercise in rowing, and in working boats under sail. The instruction in Myer's code of signals is continued.

Exercises on board the Dale.—The times and methods of instruction are the same as those of the first year, except that the cadets are stationed more generally aloft and on the light yards than before. Boat and signal exercises, similar to those of the previous year.

SECOND CLASS—THIRD YEAR.—Recitations: seamanship, three hours a week; naval tactics, one hour a week, second term. Practical exercises, as before.

Seamanship.—The recitations are conducted orally in the section-room, with much illustration from models and other appliances. The text-book is Luce's Seamanship, and the instruction comprises the following subjects: Knotting, splicing, and tackles; compass, log, and lead; rope-making; blocks; cutting and fitting rigging; masting; rigging ship; cutting, fitting, bending, unbending, making up, and stowing sails; stowage; purchasing heavy weights; ground-tackle. Organization; making preparation for sea; handling boats. Rules of the road. Duties of midshipmen as officers of the forecastle and quarter-deck, and as mates of the lower decks; duties of the officer of the deck. Getting under way and coming to anchor; making and taking in sail; reefing and hoisting; making to windward.

Naval tactics.—The organization, formation, and maneuvering of a fleet, under steam or sail, in Ward's Manual of Naval Tactics and Parker's Steam Fleet Tactics; and the code of signals in the United States Naval Signal-Book and Myer's Manual of Signals.

Exercises on board the Dale.—The cadets of the second class are stationed as seamen and ordinary seamen, and are instructed in sending up and down masts and yards, and in loosing, furling, reefing, making, and shortening sail.

FIRST CLASS — FOURTH YEAR. — Practice-cruise, three months. Ship-building and naval architecture, three hours a week, first term. Seamanship, three hours a week, second term. Exercises.

Practice-cruise.—After the annual examination of the second class, cadets who pass into the first class go on their second practice-cruise. Upon this cruise they perform the duties of seamen and petty officers, and they act at intervals as officers of the forecastle, and mates of the lower decks, and as officer of the deck.

Ship-building and naval architecture.—This branch includes the construction of ships, both iron and wooden, and the designing of ships. It is completed in the first term. The text-books are Wilson's Ship-Building and Thearle's Naval Architecture.

Seamanship.—The first class take up theoretical seamanship again at the beginning of the second term, and review the second-class course. In addition, they study the theory of storms and hurricanes, and the method of handling ships under all circumstances, particularly in gales, squalls, and bad weather. They also take up the following subjects: Making preparations for sea; handling steamers; chasing, anchoring, mooring and unmooring, tending ship, and clearing hawse; emergencies, such as parting rigging, losing sails or spars, getting ashore, and springing a leak; the bearing of officers and the management of men; port and sea routine; ceremonies and salutes, and the various duties of all the officers of the ship. The text-books are Luce's Seamanship, the United States Naval Regulations, and the pamphlet of the Hydrographic Office on Hurricanes.

Practical exercises.—The time allotted to exercises is the same as that in the lower classes, but the duties are of a higher character. On board the Dale the cadets of the first class are stationed as petty officers, and at boat-exercise they have command of boats or divisions, according to their cadet rank. At signal-exercise they have charge of signaling parties.

The course in seamanship is closed with a final review, and with the accompanying exercises. The desire is to graduate the cadets as good topmen, good helmsmen, and good leadsmen, and with a fair understanding of the duties of the several officers of a man-of-war. This knowledge, with the practical experience they get on ship-board after their graduation, while midshipmen and ensigns, will fit them for the various duties required of deck and divisional officers.

Cadet-engineers.

The cadet-engineers study ship-building with the second class and naval architecture with the first class, but have no other instruction in the subjects taught in this department, and they take no part in the practical exercises, except in the signal-drills.

MODELS AND APPARATUS.

Models of vessels.

Antietam.—The largest and most perfect model in the collection is that of the screw sloop of war Antietam. The original vessel was begun at Philadelphia in 1864. It is a full-rigged working model, 41 feet in length, with all sails and spars complete—the hull being represented from water-line to rail. The hull of the model was built at Washington, and the spars and sails made at Philadelphia. The model was put together and rigged at the Academy in 1872 and 1873. It stands in the lower hall of the department of seamanship.*

*At this time (June, 1876) it forms a part of the naval department of the Centennial Exhibition, in the United States Government Building.

Other models of parts of the same vessel, showing the details of the interior construction, are used to illustrate the course in ship-building. One of these, 13 feet long, is a full model of the hull, in frame, showing timbers; another, of the stern of the vessel, shows the stern-post, dead-wood, and keel; and a third, 4 feet high, shows four midship-frames connected.

Colorado.—Full model, full sparred and rigged.

Columbus.—Square stern-frame, showing fashion-pieces.

Congress.—Half-model of hull, showing diagonal braces, planking, &c., 12 feet long.

Steam frigate, hove down.—Full model; lower masts secured, &c.; tackles, blocks, and purchases.

Iroquois.—After body in frame, showing timbers.

Marion.—Full model of hull, shears, masts, &c., for exercising and masting.

North Carolina.—Full model of hull, full sparred and rigged.

Omaha.—Half-model of hull, showing diagonal braces and planking, 7 feet 8 inches long.

Saint Lawrence.—Full model; full sparred and rigged.

Half-models of the hulls of the following vessels:

Adriatic.
Adirondack.
Alabama.
Alaska.
Albany.
Alleghany, (submerged paddle-wheels.)
Amphitrite.
Arizona.
Bainbridge.
Barge, (designed by Rear-Admiral T. O. Selfridge, U. S. N.)
Barge, (Brooklyn's.)
Benicia.
Brig, (12 guns.)
Brooklyn.
Central America.
Chattanooga.
Clipper-ship.

Columbia.
Columbus.
Congress.
Connecticut.
Constantine.
Constitution.
Dale.
Delaware.
Dolphin.
Dunderberg.
Erie.
Franklin.
Florida.
Germantown.
Great Republic.
Idaho.
Independence.
Iowa.
Iroquois.
Iuka.
Java.
John Adams.
Juniata.
Kansas.
Kearsarge.
Lancaster.
Launch, (steam.)
Mackinaw.
Miantonomoh.
Mississippi.
Monadnock.
Monitor.
Monongahela.
Nantasket.
New Hampshire.
Niagara.
Nipsic.
North Carolina.
Nyack.
Ontario.
Ossipee.
Pawnee.
Peacock.
Pennsylvania.
Perry.
Plymouth.
Potomac.
Preble.
Princeton.
Resaca.
Samson.
Santee.
Saratoga.
Sassacus.
Severn.
Shawmut.
Shenandoah.
Steam-sloops, (designed by Rear-Admiral Selfridge, Chief Naval Constructor Delano, and Naval Constructor Wilson.)
Spark.
Saint Louis.
Saint Mary's.
Trajano.

Truxtun.
Tuscarora.
Union.
Wabash.
Warren.
Weehawken.
Worcester,
Wyoming, and several others.

Full models of the hulls of the following:

Amphitrite, (with turrets, &c.)
Brig, (French man-of-war.)
Le Didon, (French frigate.)
Discovery.
Iron-clads, with turrets, &c.
Life-boats.
Powhatan, (on launching-ways.)
Ville de Paris.
Warren, (after body, with main and mizzen masts in.)

The department is also provided with the following apparatus:

Twenty-three small tackles, arranged upon racks or stands, with heavy shot attached, to illustrate different purchases; (now on exhibition at Philadelphia.)

Models of anchors, capstans, masts, &c.

Model of navy-yard shears, with tackle, crab, stays, &c., 4½ feet high.

Binnacle-stand and compass, presented by the Grand Duke Alexis of Russia in 1872.

On the walls of the lower hall are placed sixteen panels, upon which are displayed all the common knots, splices, bends, and hitches, and the various kinds of rope. The halls also contain many photographs of foreign men-of-war, and other illustrations of the various branches of seamanship and naval architecture.

II. ORDNANCE AND GUNNERY.

This department may be said to have been established in 1844, when Lieutenant Ward delivered his first course of lectures at the Naval Asylum in Philadelphia. When the school was opened the next year, at Annapolis, one of the branches of the course in the arrangement made by the Academic Board was "Ordnance, gunnery, and the use of steam." This group of studies was arranged with special reference to the attainments of the officer who was to teach them. Professor Lockwood, whose West Point experience specially qualified him for the work, took charge of the infantry-drill. He also gave some instruction in pyrotechny.

When Lieutenant Ward was ordered to sea, in 1847, Lieut. John A. Dahlgren took his place. But the war was then hardly over, and Dahlgren's services were required for ordnance duty; so that he remained only a short time. After he left, Professor Lockwood took charge of the instruction in gunnery, in addition to astronomy and mechanics. He succeeded so well that on the re-organization, in 1850, he was made head of the new department of gunnery and infantry tactics. He held the position till 1857, when the subject of the theory of gunnery was placed under the supervision of the commandant of midshipmen, and taught by Lieut. Edward Simpson. Professor Lockwood retained the field-artillery and infantry-tactics.

Exercises in great-guns began April 4, 1846, with the battery left at Fort Severn by the Army. Exercises in field-artillery were introduced in February, 1848, two 6-pounder brass guns having been procured from the Army for that purpose; other pieces were afterward obtained.

In 1851 Jeffers's Theory and Practice of Naval Gunnery was used for a short time, but in 1852 Ward's book was restored, and, accompanied by lectures and a small pamphlet on great-guns by Professor Lockwood, it constituted the course of instruction. Two Navy howitzers, 12-pounders, were at this time procured, and took the place of the old

6-pounder Army guns. The Ordnance Instructions, issued by the Navy Department, came out in 1852. It was immediately adopted as a text-book, and has been taught since that time.

In 1854 the text-books in this department were as follows: Ordnance Instructions, United States Navy, taught by Lieut. J. P. Greene; Mordecai's Notes on Gunpowder; Jeffers's Theory and Practice of Naval Gunnery; Dahlgren's Boat-guns and Percussion System; Le Page's Théorie du Pointage; Lockwood's Small-Arms.

In 1859, Simpson's Ordnance and Naval Gunnery and the Ordnance Instructions were the principal text-books. A translation of Le Page, also by Lieutenant Simpson, was used until the publication of an enlarged edition of the Ordnance and Naval Gunnery, in 1862.

Soon after Professor Lockwood was assigned to the Army, in October, 1861,* Master Joseph D. Marvin took his place as

* Professor Lockwood was a graduate of West Point, of the class of 1836. In 1836–'37 he served in Florida against the Seminole Indians. He resigned his commission as second lieutenant in the Second Artillery September 12, 1837. In 1841 he was appointed professor of mathematics in the Navy, and he was on duty at the Naval Academy from its foundation till 1870, except during the rebellion, when he was engaged in active service. He was commissioned colonel of the First Delaware Volunteers May 25, 1861, and brigadier-general of United States Volunteers August 8, 1861. In November of that year he went in command of an expedition to the eastern shore of Virginia, and remained in command there until January, 1863; in command at Point Lookout, and the defences of the Lower Potomac, January to June, 1863; in the Pennsylvania campaign, (Army of the Potomac,) July, 1863, being engaged in the battle of Gettysburg, July 1–3, 1863; in command of Harper's Ferry, Va., July to October, 1863, and of Middle Department, headquarters at Baltimore, Md., December, 1863, to April, 1864; in the Richmond campaign (Army of the Potomac) May to June, 1864, participating in the actions near Hanover Court-House, Va., May 30 to June 1, 1864; in command of provisional troops for the defence of Baltimore

instructor in infantry-tactics. He performed this duty till 1864, at which time he again became engaged in active service. He was relieved by Lieutenant-Commander A. P. Cooke. In the spring of 1862, Lieut. S. B. Luce restored the artillery-drill, which had been dropped in Professor Lockwood's absence. In the fall of the same year Lieutenant-Commander E. O. Matthews relieved Lieutenant-Commander Simpson, in charge of the department. He also continued the artillery-drill. Two batteries of heavy 12-pounder howitzers were used in this drill. At the same time the great-gun drill was conducted on board the sloop Macedonian, and target-practice from a small battery on Goat Island. The subject of field fortifications was introduced in the spring of 1861, to give the midshipmen a sufficient knowledge of intrenchments to enable them to protect themselves in case of being sent on shore with a body of men in an enemy's country. In November, 1865, the instruction in infantry-tactics was transferred to the department of ordnance and gunnery, as field-artillery had been in October, 1862.

Down to 1875 the commandant of midshipmen was head of the department of gunnery as well as of seamanship, in addition to his other duties. In that year the change was made, already described under the department of seamanship, which put the heads of both departments on a separate footing.

PRESENT COURSE.

ALL CLASSES.—Practical exercises four hours a week during the year as follows:

Infantry-drill.

against the rebel raid under General Early, 1864, and of brigade at Baltimore, Md., July, 1864, to August, 1865. General Lockwood was mustered out of service August 24, 1865, and returned to his duties at the Naval Academy. (Cullum, Biographical Register United States Military Academy, volume 1.)

Field-artillery and boat-howitzer exercise.

Great-guns.—Exercises and target-practice on board the United States ship Santee.

Fencing.—Exercises with small-swords and broadswords.

SECOND CLASS.—One hour a week, first term; two hours a week, second term.

Infantry-tactics.—Organization and formation of squad, company, and battalion; school of the soldier; company and battalion drill, including instructions for skirmishers and the bayonet-exercise. Text-book: United States Infantry-Tactics.

Gunnery.—Practical naval gunnery, as laid down in the Ordnance and Gunnery Instructions for the United States Navy.

FIRST CLASS.—Two hours a week, first term; three hours a week, second term.

Ordnance and armor.—Preparation of gun-iron from crude ore, including the description and use of furnaces; manufacture of wrought iron, steel, and bronze; fabrication of guns of all descriptions; manufacture of gunpowder and fuses, and of all kinds of projectiles and fireworks.

Theory of gunnery.—Motion of projectiles *in vacuo* and in the atmosphere; initial, remaining, and final velocities, and the methods of determining their values; the effects of variations of charge, windage, and weight of projectiles; deviation of projectiles; systems of pointing; tangent-sights, and determination of their values; penetration and shock of projectiles, and recoil of guns. The text-books in this course are Commander A. P. Cooke's* Naval Ordnance and Gunnery; Ordnance Instructions, United States Navy; Gunnery Instructions, United States Navy.

* Formerly head of the department of ordnance and gunnery at the Naval Academy.

Mortar-practice.—The class have field-lectures and practice with the mortar at intervals during the second term, in the course of which they load and fire, weigh out the charges, fill shells, and cut fuses.

Monitor-practice.—The monitor is put under steam, and the class are exercised in working the machinery of the guns and turret.

Target-practice with the rifle, at long and short ranges, frequently during the first class year.

Cadet-engineers.

The cadet-engineers attend the drills with great-guns and in infantry-tactics, field-artillery, and fencing, but have no other instruction in this department.

MODELS AND APPARATUS.

For great-gun drill on board the gunnery-ship Santee:

24 new-pattern VIII-inch guns, on iron carriages, on the gun-deck.

24 new-pattern 32-pounders, on iron carriages, on the spar-deck.

For light-artillery drill:

24 light 12-pounder howitzers.

4 new 3-inch breech-loading rifled howitzers.

6 launches.

For infantry-drill:

490 Remington rifles, Navy pattern.

For mortar-practice:

1 XIII-inch mortar, mounted near the sea-wall.

Models of all the different great-guns at present used on shipboard, with both wooden and iron carriages.

Models of all the different howitzers at present used in the Navy, with boat and field carriages.

Full-size wooden model of new pattern 32-pounder, on iron carriage, for using inspecting-instruments.

One Gatling gun, with equipments complete.

Model of a section of a mortar-schooner, with mortar and equipments complete; the model showing the construction of the vessel.

Model of a ship's magazine, with all the equipments complete.

Models of fortifications.

Model of flask, core, &c., used in casting guns upon the Rodman plan.

Model illustrating the Navy process of casting shells.

Presses and implements for the manufacture of the Navy time-fuse and Bormann fuse.

Rodman's testing-machine, capacity 100,000 lbs.

Rocket and port-fire molds.

Inspecting-instruments for guns, powder, shot, and shells.

Schultz's electro-chronoscope.

Set of tools for making cannon-primers.

Beardsley's magneto-electric torpedo-machine.

Wheatstone's magneto-electric torpedo-machine, (presented by Commander T. O. Selfridge.)

Samples of powder and of the ingredients used in its manufacture.

Samples of fuses.

Samples of primers.

Samples of shot and shell.

Samples of torpedoes.

Samples of 110 different kinds of small-arms, including, among others, the needle-gun, Snyder, Werner, Chassepôt, Vincennes, Jaeger, Enfield, Martini-Henry, and other rifles; Bavarian, Belgian, Austrian, French, and Spanish rifles; Remington, Ward and Burton, Spencer, and Sharp breech-loaders;

and many others, including rifles, muskets, carbines, pistols, and revolvers of various make and pattern.

Samples of 33 kinds of metallic ammunition, (presented by Commander D. L. Braine.)

Drawings of electro-chronoscope and electro-ballistic pendulum, by Commander Montgomery Sicard.

Drawings of Bloomfield furnace.

Drawings of gun-foundery furnace.

Drawings of projectiles used in the campaign of 1864.

Densimeter.

Photographs of breech-loading small-arms and their parts in use in the United States.

Photographs illustrating the manufacture of Krupp guns.

III. MATHEMATICS.

This department, at its organization in 1850, included the following subjects: Arithmetic, algebra, geometry, trigonometry, descriptive geometry, analytical geometry, the differential and integral calculus, astronomy, navigation, and surveying.

These subjects were distributed over four years, the first year being devoted mainly to arithmetic and algebra, and the second to geometry, trigonometry, and descriptive geometry. Analytical geometry, the calculus, and astronomy were taught in the third year, and navigation and surveying in the fourth. In 1853 the three subjects last mentioned were assigned to a new department.

The course in the calculus was short, and was only required of the higher portion of the class. From 1858 to 1870 descriptive geometry was omitted by the lower sections of the class, and from 1866 to 1870 little attention was paid to analytical geometry. With these exceptions, the course remained substantially the same, only such changes being made from time to time as were required by the introduction of new text-books. In 1871, under a new arrangement of studies, arithmetic was discontinued and the calculus was transferred to the department of physics and chemistry, to be taught in connection with mechanics.

PRESENT COURSE.

Cadet-midshipmen and cadet-engineers.

FOURTH CLASS.—Six hours a week; algebra and geometry.

THIRD CLASS.—Six hours a week; trigonometry, analytical geometry, and descriptive geometry.

ELECTIVE COURSES.

In addition to the required studies of the course, two elective courses, established in 1875, are now open to those cadets who display marked ability in mathematics. During the year just ended the course has been as follows:

FOURTH CLASS.—The theory of equations, and curve-tracing.

THIRD CLASS.—The elements of the differential and integral calculus.

All the members of a class now pursue nearly the same studies in the required course, a few of the more difficult subjects only being omitted by the lower sections. Written examinations are held either once or twice a month, and each instructor aims to prepare his section for the coming examination. Written examinations were first introduced in 1865, and were then held twice a year; previously to that time, examinations had been oral. The system of monthly examinations has been in use since 1871.

In descriptive geometry the elements of the subject are taught by recitations from a text-book, in addition to which, a period of two hours a week during the year is taken for practical geometrical drawing. Original problems in descriptive geometry are given each week, and each cadet is required to solve them accurately.

The drawing-room used is conveniently arranged, and has accommodations for one hundred students. No models have as yet been provided.

The requirements in mathematics for admission to the Academy have hitherto been below what would seem to be necessary as a preparation for the course of the first year. From 1850 to 1863 candidates were required to "perform with accuracy the various operations in the primary rules of arithmetic, viz: numeration, addition, subtraction, multiplication, and division of whole numbers." In 1863 this regulation was changed to include "vulgar and decimal fractions and the rule of three." After 1871 the examinations included operations upon denominate numbers; and by the present regulations, which take effect this year, the examinations include percentage, interest and discount, and the extraction of square and cube roots.

IV. STEAM-ENGINEERING.

Instruction in the applications of steam to machinery was first given in lectures by Lieutenant Ward, who was afterward known as the author of a popular treatise on steam. The subject was at that time one of the branches of the department of gunnery. After Ward left the school the branch was joined with chemistry, but little attention was paid to it. In 1850 it was put into the new department of natural philosophy. The text-books were very simple—Ward's lectures, printed after he left the school, and a chapter or two in Müller's Physics. Later, Main and Brown on the Marine Engine became the text-book. The equipment of models and apparatus was very meagre. A small beam-engine, with boilers, together with sectional and working models of a beam-engine, was used for practical instruction.

In 1865 Chief Engineer W. W. W. Wood was ordered to the Academy, and a new department, that of steam-engineering, (or enginery, as it was at first called,) was established. The building now used by the department was erected in the summer of 1866, and during the next few years a collection of models and apparatus for practical instruction was provided, which is now one of the most complete in the Academy, and for its purpose probably the most complete in the country. In the main hall is a pair of marine engines of 600 indicated horse-power, complete, with boilers, propeller, and all the auxiliary machinery commonly found on board vessels of war. The boilers, four in number, such as are employed in small corvettes, are placed in a wing in the rear of the main hall. Two of them are used to generate steam to supply the engine, and two are kept open and can be lighted within by gas-jets, so that the student may see the whole interior construction, and learn exactly how the braces, stay-bolts, &c., are arranged and secured. The space above the engine is surrounded by a broad and well-lighted gallery, and the whole machinery may be seen at a glance.

The wings at the sides of the main building are arranged for offices and workshops, for practical instruction in the art of the machinist, the pattern-maker, the smith, the boiler-maker, and the molder. The workshops contain a well-selected collection of machine and other modern tools.

The building also contains recitation-rooms, a room fitted for practice in mechanical drawing, and a spacious model-room. The apparatus in the latter consists of illustrations of the details of steam machinery; of methods of construction; of fractures and other injuries to machinery; and of engineering implements of all kinds. Among these are models of boilers of different kinds; propellers; steam and vacuum gauges; air-pumps; feed-pumps; a complete set of drawings in oil, upon wood, of the monitor class of iron-clad vessels; working models of slide-valves, showing their operation and adjustment; and many similar pieces of engineering apparatus. Cadets have frequent access to the whole collection, and are exercised in the management of the large engines under steam, and in overhauling and taking them apart, and putting the parts together anew. In these exercises the methods used follow the practice of the naval service, at sea and in port. Both the cadet-midshipmen and cadet-engineers take part in them, but the instruction in hand-work and in the use of machine-tools is given chiefly to the cadet-engineers. The latter get a good knowledge of all the mechanical operations which underlie the practice of steam-engineering. The cadets have a theoretical course in addition to the exercises.

PRESENT COURSE.

Cadet-midshipmen.

FIRST CLASS.—Three hours a week. This time is devoted to giving the class a general knowledge of the varieties of marine engines, of the principles governing their care and management, and of the methods of determining the quality of engine performances.

Cadet-engineers.

FOURTH CLASS.—Two hours a week. Mechanical drawing.

THIRD CLASS.—Two hours a week, first term. Mechanical drawing.

SECOND CLASS.—Five hours a week. Mechanical drawing, one hour; fabrication of machinery, two hours; marine engines, two hours.

FIRST CLASS.—Seven hours a week. Mechanical drawing, three hours; fabrication of machinery, two hours; designing of machinery and marine engines, two hours.

Text-books of cadet-engineers.—Bourne's Handbook of the Steam-Engine; Warren's Elements of Mechanical Drawing; Rankine's Steam-Engine and other Prime Movers.

It will be seen that the cadet-engineers have a much more extended course in these branches than the cadet-midshipmen. In addition to the theoretical course, the cadet-engineers have more frequent practice with the engines, taking these exercises whenever the cadet-midshipmen have exercises in seamanship, great-guns, or boat-howitzers.

The instruction received by the cadet-engineers during the practice-cruise is spoken of in another place. It is given by assistants in the department of steam-engineering detailed for the duty.

V. ASTRONOMY AND NAVIGATION.

From 1845 to 1853 astronomy and navigation were a part of the course in the department of mathematics, and were taught by Professor Chauvenet, except during 1848 and 1849, when Professor Lockwood took astronomy. In October, 1853, a separate department of astronomy and navigation was created, with Professor Chauvenet at the head. Professor Coffin succeeded him as head of mathematics. When Chauvenet resigned, in 1859, Coffin became professor of astronomy and navigation; and from 1861 to 1864, owing to the difficulty of obtaining suitable men, he took charge of both departments. In 1865, Commander Robert L. Phythian succeeded him in astronomy and navigation; and since that time the department has been in charge of line officers of the Navy.

PRESENT COURSE.

Cadet-midshipmen.

SECOND CLASS.—Three hours a week during the first term.

Astronomy.—Descriptive and practical astronomy, including the use of instruments, especially those for determining terrestrial latitudes and longitudes. The text-book is Professor Charles J. White's* Elements of Astronomy.

FIRST CLASS.—Practice-cruise, three months. Navigation and surveying, four hours a week throughout the year.

Practice-cruise.—Practical instruction is given to the first class in navigation four days in each week. The ship's position is fixed by observations of the sun, planets, and stars, made by cadets, with the sextants. During the last cruise, in addition to the usual keeping of dead-reckoning and the time and latitude sights, the class constructed Mercator's charts, projected the coast-line and islands near the cruising-ground, and made sketches of prominent headlands on different bearings.

Navigation and surveying.—Theoretical navigation is taught from Prof. J. H. C. Coffin's Navigation, in connection with Bowditch's Navigator. The theory is supplemented by constant practice in working out original examples, both in and out of the section-room. The cadets are also taught the duties of the navigating officer, and the use of the sextant and other navigating instruments. This course occupies the first term.

The second term, comprising seventy-two periods, is divided as follows:

The deviation of the compass,† with examples, sixteen hours. The text-book used is Merrifield's Magnetism and Deviation of the Compass.

* Formerly assistant professor of astronomy at the Naval Academy.

† Introduced in 1875.

The construction of charts on polyconic projections,* eight hours.

Surveying, forty hours. This branch is taught by practical exercises, consisting of surveys of the mouth of the Severn River, and the projection of charts. Jeffers's Nautical Surveying is used as a book of reference.

Solution of original problems in navigation, forty-four hours.

Field-practice with the sextant, twenty-eight hours.

Cadet-engineers.

The first class of cadet-engineers take a special course in astronomy.

The great aim of the department being to prepare graduates to become, first, trustworthy navigators, and, secondly, competent surveyors, little time can be given to practice in the use of either the permanent or portable instruments of the observatory. During the past year five members of the second class have devoted a portion of their recreation-hours to observations with the meridian circle and portable transit and zenith telescope. It is hoped, by an elective course, to be able to advance in this direction without any bad effect on the course in navigation.

APPARATUS.

The observatory, which is in charge of this department, is supplied with the following instruments:

1 equatorial telescope, made by Alvan Clark & Sons, Boston; object-glass, 7¾ inches clear aperture, 9½ feet focal length, with three positive eye-pieces, three negative eye-pieces, one filar micrometer, and a driving-clock. Supported on a brick pier on an iron frame, and provided with revolving turret.

* Introduced in 1875.

1 meridian circle, by Repsold of Hamburg, mounted on stone piers; object-glass, 4 inches aperture, 4 feet focal length; circles 30 inches diameter. Provided with four reading microscopes; one micrometer, with movable threads, for measuring difference of declinations; three eye-pieces; mercurial collimator, levels, reversing-car, and observing-couch.

1 sidereal clock, by Arnold & Frodsham, London, with a chronograph, of the Morse register type.

6 chronometers, (two sidereal, four mean time.)

1 portable equatorial, by Plösel; clear aperture 3 inches, focal length 3 feet.

1 portable transit and zenith telescope combined, by Stackpole, (lent from Washington Observatory;) focal length 28 inches, object-glass 2½ inches.

1 portable transit, by Wurdeman; focal length 26 inches, object-glass 2 inches.

1 zenith telescope, by Wurdeman; focal length 33 inches, object-glass 3 inches.

(The last three instruments are conveniently mounted on three piers of stone, placed in the meridian, 7 feet from each other.)

1 universal instrument, by Ertel; circles 8½ inches.

1 theodolite, by Wurdeman; 8-inch limb, telescope 16 inches.

4 surveyor's transits.

1 level and staff.

4 reflecting circles.

80 sextants.

34 artificial horizons.

5 azimuth-compasses.

20 comparing-watches.

1 plane-table.

VI.—PHYSICS AND CHEMISTRY.

The course in natural philosophy, begun in 1845, under Professor Lockwood, included mechanics, optics, electricity, and magnetism; but, owing to the scanty preparation of even the senior class, the professor was able to teach little beside mechanics. Peschel's Physics was used as the text-book. At the same time chemistry was taught by Surgeon J. A. Lockwood. The junior class attended lectures in this branch, and the seniors had lectures and recitations.

In 1864 Olmstead's Natural Philosophy was substituted for Peschel, and it was kept in use till the four years' course was established, in 1850. Up to this time the school had no philosophical apparatus worthy of notice.

In 1850 the department of natural and experimental philosophy, including chemistry, was fully established, and Prof. W. F. Hopkins took the place of Professor Lockwood, the latter taking charge of the new department of gunnery and infantry tactics. The course in natural philosophy was confined to the two upper classes. The second class had three recitations a week throughout the year in chemistry and electricity, and daily recitations in mechanics during the second term. The first class also had three hours throughout the year, studying optics and heat. Geology and mineralogy were included in the course, but no record remains of the nature of the instruction. The use of steam was taught from Main and Brown's text-book on the marine engine.

In 1854 the course in mechanics was improved by the introduction of Bartlett's Elements of Mechanics in place of Peschel. At the same time Lardner's course in physics was adopted for the first class.

In 1860 Prof. A. W. Smith* was appointed head of the

* Rev. Augustus William Smith, LL. D., was born in Herkimer County, New York, May 12, 1802; died at Annapolis, Md., of pneumonia, March

department. During his administration, and that of Professor Lockwood, who resumed the position at the death of Professor Smith, in 1866, many improvements were made, both in the outfit of the department and in methods of instruction. Smith's Mechanics was adopted as the text-book of the second class, and Silliman's Physics for the first class. From 1868 until the re-arrangement of the course in 1875, Ganot's Physics was used instead of Silliman's.

In 1869 Lieutenant-Commander (now Commander) W. T. Sampson succeeded Professor Lockwood, and since that time the department has been in charge of naval officers. In 1871 the name of the department was changed to "physics and chemistry," and the calculus was transferred to it. This branch was taught mainly by lectures, and with reference to its applications to mechanics. The growing importance of

26, 1866. His early years were passed on a farm, but, having a strong desire to acquire an education, he attended the academies of his native county and qualified himself to teach, and thus acquired the means to prosecute his studies. He graduated at Hamilton College, Clinton, in 1826, and had been for a year previous one of the teachers in the Oneida Conference Seminary, at Cazenovia, where he continued till 1831, being the principal of the seminary from 1828 to 1831. In the latter year he was chosen professor of mathematics in Wesleyan University, at Middletown, Conn., and continued in that chair till 1851—twenty years—when he was chosen president of the university. His retiring disposition had made him very unwilling to assume or retain the presideney of the university, and after eight years of service he resigned the office in 1859, when he was appointed professor of natural philosophy in the Naval Academy. He remained in this position till his death. He was an excellent mathematician and thoroughly familiar with all the applications of mathematics to science, and in his field of research had few superiors. His administration of the affairs of the Wesleyan University was characterized by great discretion and sound judgment. He had published several valuable text-books. He received the honorary degree of LL. D. from Hamilton College in 1850. (See Appleton's Annual Cyclopedia, 1866.)

the subject, and the increased necessity of its frequent application in the solution of problems in other scientific and professional branches, have made it advisable to create a new department of mechanics and applied mathematics, to include the subject of calculus. The department was accordingly organized in March last, in charge of Prof. J. M. Rice.*

PRESENT COURSE.

Cadet-midshipmen and Cadet-engineers.

THIRD CLASS.—Three hours a week. First term, physics; second term, chemistry.

When the course was re-arranged in 1875, the study of elementary physics was introduced in the third class. Up to this time it had been confined to the two upper classes. In the new course Balfour Stewart's Physics was adopted as a textbook. By thus taking a brief and comprehensive view of all branches of physics, the student early gets a clear idea of the leading facts and principles, and, what is not less important, of the relations between the forces with which he has to deal. Half the year is given to this elementary course, the other half to chemistry. The latter subject is deemed of special importance, not only as being an essential part of a liberal education, but as having a direct practical application in the service. Its importance to the naval officer is readily illustrated by the improvements which have been made in the art of war by the introduction of gun-cotton and nitroglycerine, the picrate and chlorate powders, and their various applications in torpedoes and otherwise, for use in military operations. These improvements in military science have begun and ended in the chemist's laboratory; and it follows, as a necessary consequence, that scientific attainments are

* See page 201.

among the most important of professional qualifications. Moreover, a naval officer is constantly in the line of duty visiting remote parts of the earth's surface which are comparatively inaccessible to the ordinary scientific observer. He has peculiar opportunities of aiding scientific investigation by noting and recording those natural phenomena with which he comes in almost daily contact. It is, therefore, of the greatest consequence that he should have trained powers of observation, and be able to make a scientific record of what he sees.

These considerations led to the introduction of the courses in physics and chemistry at the Academy, and the results have gone so far to prove their usefulness that increased time and opportunity have been given to the two subjects. The course in elementary chemistry is supplemented by lectures and laboratory practice. The aim is to familiarize the students with general principles and nomenclature, and to teach them the applications of chemistry to professional work.

An advanced class, composed of those who show most aptitude for the study, receive special laboratory instruction in the analysis and preparation of explosives. It is hoped that the course may be so extended in time as to give cadets a training in analytical work which will enable them to make or superintend such analyses as the exigencies of the service may require.*

The laboratories are open to graduates who wish further instruction in physics or chemistry. Several such students have been pursuing courses during the last two years, and they, as well as the officers attached to the department, will be fitted by their training for a much higher class of work than those who pursue only the required course.

* For specimens of the work of cadets, see Appendix, Note F.

SECOND CLASS.—Three hours a week for one term; electricity.

Jenkins's Electricity and Magnetism is used as a text-book, and Ganot's Physics, Maxwell's Electricity and Magnetism, and Kohlrausch on Physical Measurements, as books of reference. The course is accompanied by experimental lectures, in which subjects are considered which were too difficult for the third class. From four to six hours a week are given to laboratory work by those who show most aptitude for the subject. In the second-class course cadets learn to measure the resistance of conductors, insulators, and electrolytes, and of batteries; to determine galvanometer constants by electrolysis and by calculation; to measure current strength and electro-motive force in various ways; to determine electro-chemical equivalents; and to determine temperature factors for magnets, the magnetic intensity, and declination, dip, &c. Some examples of the work of cadets of this class are given in the Appendix.*

FIRST CLASS.—Three hours a week for one term.

Heat and light.—Maxwell's Theory of Heat is used as a text-book, with Ganot and Kohlrausch as books of reference. This course, also, is illustrated by experimental lectures, which are a continuation of those given in the same subject to the third class. The best-prepared students of this class devote a portion of the time to laboratory work, in making such measurements as are best suited to give them the care and skill required while investigating the laws of nature. Having had previous experience in the laboratory, the class are left very much to their own resources. In almost every measurement some portion of the apparatus has been improved by each student.*

More time is given to electricity and heat because of the

* See Appendix, Note F.

direct professional bearing of these studies. Considerable attention is paid to the study of the different methods of exploding submarine mines and torpedoes by electricity. A right understanding of magnetic phenomena is, of course, important to those who have to deal with the mariner's compass, and especially in modern men-of-war, built largely of iron, whose influence upon the needle must be determined and allowed for with the greatest care.

For similar reasons, in the course in heat, which is intended as an introduction to the study of the steam-engine, those problems are most dwelt upon which prepare the student for his ultimate pursuit. At the same time the more difficult problems of thermodynamics are not neglected.

APPARATUS.

The first considerable appropriation for the purchase of apparatus was made in 1850. Since then moderate sums have been appropriated almost every year for its gradual increase. During the past few years many valuable instruments of precision have been added, so that the department is well supplied with general lecture apparatus, and at the same time has facilities for more precise instruction in physical measurements and for original research. The following is a partial list of the most important instruments.

In acoustics, Helmholtz double siren, (Koenig, Paris.)

In optics, Duboscq's polariscope; Duboscq's spectroscope, (four prisms;) direct-vision spectroscope, (Browning, five prisms;) Silberman's heliostat; two electric-light regulators and lanterns; two microscopes; one solar microscope; one goniometer, (Wallaston's.)

In heat, Melloni's apparatus; Tyndall's apparatus for radiation and absorption of gases; Bianchi's apparatus for liquefying gases; cathetometer.

In electricity, one Carré's machine; one Holtz machine; one quadrant electrometer, (Tomson's;) one absolute electrometer, (Tomson's;) two short-coil reflecting astatic galvanometers; one long-coil astatic reflecting galvanometer, of 35,000 ohms' resistance, (Tomson's;) one marine galvanometer; one short-coil reflecting galvanometer; two differential galvanometers; two tangent galvanometers; one large electrodynamometer; Helmholtz's arrangement of coils; coils 50 centimetres in diameter, (Elliott Bros.;) one magnetometer; one dip circle; one Rhumkorff coil, giving spark of 13 inches; four dynamo-electrical machines, one producing a light equal to 3,000 candles.

Upon application of the Superintendent of the Academy, the president of the Transit of Venus Commission, Rear-Admiral C. H. Davis, U. S. N., has supplied the department with a set of the instruments used by one of the transit parties. Among these are included the magnetometer and dip circle mentioned above, an equatorial telescope, 6-inch objective, with driving-clock; a sidereal clock, and chronograph.

The department also possesses three fine balances—two by Becker, the other by Newman of London.

A copy of the standard yard and metre is deposited at the observatory of the Academy.

In 1869 the building now occupied by the department of physics and chemistry was completed. The building is 80 by 40 feet, two stories high, with an attic, which has recently been converted into a battery-room.

Until 1875 a portion of this building was occupied as a chemical laboratory. In the fall of 1875 a building adjoining was enlarged and fitted up as a chemical laboratory. This building is 55 by 48 feet. It contains two laboratories, one 55 by 22 feet, fitted for work in general chemistry and qualitative analysis. It has desk-room for fifty students at one time; each desk being fitted to accommodate two students, or one hundred in all. Many conveniences, suggested by recent experience, have been introduced into this laboratory. Being one story high, it is well lighted and ventilated.

The second laboratory is fitted for more advanced students in quantitative work, and is amply supplied with all the modern appointments.

The physical laboratory building contains three recitation-rooms, an office, a general work-room, and a galvanometer-room on the first floor, besides a small room in the centre of the building for experiments in heat on radiation and absorption. In the galvanometer-room the large dynamometer and the galvanometer of high resistance are solidly mounted. On the second floor is a lecture-room, 50 by 40 feet, and a physical laboratory, 30 by 40 feet. The building is supplied with water, gas, vacuum and blast pumps, &c.

The lecture-room, as well as the laboratory, may be used for analytical practice.

VII. MECHANICS AND APPLIED MATHEMATICS.

This department was formed by a division of the department of physics and chemistry, in accordance with the recommendation of the Superintendent of the Academy, and of the head of the department. The change was ordered March 6, 1876, and Prof. J. M. Rice was placed in charge of the new department.

The course of instruction includes the differential calculus, the integral calculus, theoretical and applied mechanics, and the strength of materials. It is arranged as follows:

SECOND CLASS, *cadet-midshipmen*, five hours a week. First term, calculus; second term, mechanics.

FIRST CLASS, *cadet-engineers*, three hours a week, first term; one hour a week, second term. Subject: Strength of materials.

The text-books used are: Rice and Johnson's Calculus, Todhunter's Mechanics for Beginners, Smith's Mechanics, and Wood's Resistance of Materials.

It is proposed to have in the department an elective course in Williamson's Integral Calculus, for the benefit of those cadets who take the elective course in the department of mathematics.

Instruction is given by recitations and occasional lectures, and special attention is given to the practical application of all the branches taught. Written examinations are held semi-monthly.

VIII. English studies, history, and law.

Before 1850 the senior and junior classes received instruction in the English branches from Chaplain Jones. In the regulations of 1850 a new department was organized, embracing a miscellaneous list of subjects, and called "the department of ethics," though ethics was only one of the many subjects in the care of the department. Later it was called "ethics and English studies." Prof. Joseph E. Nourse was head of the department from 1850 to 1865, and from 1865 to 1873 it was in charge of line officers of the Navy. At this time the course comprised the following subjects and text-books:

Fourth class—Worcester's History, Bullions's English Grammar, Cornell's High-school Geography.

Third class—Eliot's History of the United States, Quackenbos's Rhetoric.

First class—Kent's Commentaries, volume 1.

Ethics was taught first in recitations in Wayland's Moral Science, and afterward in familiar lectures by the chaplain. Otherwise, instruction was chiefly given in recitations, examinations being held semi-annually. Subsequently, instruction in ethics was wholly discontinued, and in 1873 the name of the department was changed to "English studies, history, and law."

The course now covers the four years of the academic course, except during the first term of the fourth year. Instruction is given mainly in recitations, and, in one or two history courses, in lectures. Monthly and term examinations are held in all the courses, except that of the second class in themes. The object aimed at is threefold: to give the cadets, first, a certain amount of literary culture; secondly, a clear, simple, and graceful habit of expression, and facility in the proper use of English; and, thirdly, such an acquaintance with the history of their own and other countries, and of the service to which they belong, as will enable them to understand the character and development of the Government they serve, its relation to foreign states, and their duties toward it as public officers. A special course is given in international law.

In the matter of English training, the work done in the monthly examinations is held to be of great importance. Upon entering the Academy, the written work of nearly all the cadets is in very bad form, as is shown by the papers at the examinations for admission, and still more by those at the first monthly examination. To correct this, the papers in English and history are examined and marked by the instructors, not only with reference to the subject-matter, but to faults in spelling and punctuation, to bad writing, to looseness of thought, and slovenliness of form and expression. The examiners designate the faults on the papers by using a list of abbreviations, with which the cadet is furnished and to which he can refer for explanation. The papers are then returned to the writers, by whom they are corrected, handed in to the examiners at the following recitation, and inspected anew to insure thorough correction. Cadets are required to notice in some way every mark made on the papers by the examiner, and the process of revision is continued with each paper until it is complete; ample opportunity being given the writer of asking and receiving explanation.

This system of examination and correction of course entails great labor on the instructors, but it is believed that the results justify the method. Cases have occurred since its introduction in which the papers of a cadet at the November examinations contained upward of four hundred marks of correction, while those of the same cadet in May had less than thirty; while a corresponding improvement was seen in neatness and accuracy of expression.

In addition to the monthly examinations, the cadets receive special practice in English composition, as follows:

Fourth class.—Prose versions of extracts from classical English poets.

Third class.—Official reports, once a fortnight, during half the year.

Second class.—Themes, once a month.

In all these exercises the same system of revision and correction is rigorously followed.

PRESENT COURSE.

Cadet-midshipmen and cadet-engineers.

FOURTH CLASS.—Five hours a week.

Punctuation.—The cadets begin the course in English with the chapter on punctuation in Hart's Rhetoric. The manual and exercises take up two hours a week for five weeks, at the end of which an examination is held. During the rest of the course all the examinations and exercises of cadets in this department are required to conform to the practice of the manual.

History.—The class take Freeman's General Sketch of History simultaneously with the course in English, and recite in it three hours a week during the term, going over the first twelve chapters, which comprise European history down to the Reformation. Part of the last month, as in all the studies of this department, is given to a review of the course preparatory to the term examination. Especial stress is laid in all the history courses on territorial changes and historical geography, Labberton's Atlas being used in connection with Freeman.

In the second term the class have Eliot's History of the United States for three hours a week in place of Freeman. A modern atlas is used in connection with it, and the course is supplemented by lectures, as time allows and occasion requires.

English.—After the Manual of Punctuation is finished the rest of the term for two hours a week is occupied with Tancock's English Grammar. This book contains a sketch of the growth of the language, which is taken up in connection with the chapters of Freeman relating to early English history. The grammar proper is treated very briefly, the time being devoted mainly to the etymological and syntactical analysis of passages of English prose and poetry, a fair selection of which accompanies the grammar. A small etymological dictionary is used in preparing the lessons.

In the second term the class take up the "English Lessons," by Prof. J. R. Seeley and Mr. E. A. Abbott, for two hours a week through the term. In connection with the text-book, they have regular practice in writing prose versions of poetical extracts from the collection in Tancock's Grammar. They have also much practice in correcting the common faults of speaking and writing, and exercises in the use of figures, and in the solution of simple problems in logic.

Throughout the year the lesson in history for the day is considered a lesson in spelling. This takes about seven minutes from the recitation in history, but some definite practice of the kind is necessary, and this method seems to give the best results at the least expense of time. It has been already shown that the examination for admission is not severe enough to exclude bad spellers.

The necessity of the course in English grammar also arises from the rudimentary character of the examination for admission. On account of the variety of school-grammars now in use throughout the country,* and the confused arrangement of the subject in these text-books, the examination in grammar is, of necessity, general and indulgent in its character. If it could be made specific and rigorous, the most rudimentary part of the course might be dispensed with; but at present it is not safe to presume upon any degree of grammatical training in the successful candidate for admission.

* Inquiry made at the June and September examinations in 1875 showed that the following works on English grammar had been used by the candidates:

Text-book.	Number of candidates by whom studied.
Harvey	20
Green	16
Bullions	15
Butler	14
Brown	11
Kerl	11
Pinneo	10
Smith	10
Clark	7
Quackenbos	7
Weld	4
Fewsmith	3
Norton	3
Swinton	3

The exercise in writing prose versions, instead of original composition, has the advantage of furnishing beginners with their subject-matter and enabling them to give attention more exclusively to the form of expression. The great difficulty of a novice in learning to write is the want of ideas; if these can be furnished, all his effort can be expended upon the form in which they are to be put. If he is left to his own resources, his strength is wasted in the production of boyish and immature thought in a style which runs either into fine writing or commonplace formalism.

THIRD CLASS.—Three hours a week.

History.—The first term is mainly occupied with the last five chapters of Freeman's General Sketch, (from the Reformation to the present time,) and a general review of European history.

In addition to the general course, a course of twelve or more lectures is given on the history of the United States Navy. The cadets take notes, and the substance of the lectures may be required at the final examination.

Text-book.	Number of candidates by whom studied.
Tancock	3
Arnold	1
Bain	1
Bingham	1
Burt	1
Chandler	1
Covell	1
Fowler	1
Holmes	1
Kirkham	1
Notes by teacher	1
	147

Twenty-five text-books on grammar among 147 students—*i. e.*, one grammar for every five or six students.

Rhetoric.—Bain's Rhetoric, including the whole of Part I and the first four chapters of Part II, occupies three hours a week during the second term.

Composition.—The class write official reports once a fortnight during the second term upon some designated subject; as, the performance of a certain duty, or the execution of a specific order. The report may relate to a fictitious expedition or survey, or may be based upon information obtained during the summer cruise. The writers are required to observe the forms prescribed by the Naval Regulations in regard to official correspondence.

SECOND CLASS.—Themes, once a month.

Composition.—The instructor meets the class once a month and gives out subjects, suggests methods of treatment, and notes books of reference. A part of the time is given to the reading and revision of corrected themes and to commenting upon them. Three subjects are usually given out, differing in aim and scope, of which the cadet may choose any one, and suggestions are made about them with a view to stimulate individual thought. Occasionally cadets are allowed to write on subjects of their own choice; but, as a general rule, the other way is found more satisfactory.*

---

* The following are some of the subjects given for 1875–'76:

November:

1. What good is to come from arctic explorations?
2. The naval hero of the Revolution—his character and career.
3. On leave; being an incident of the vacation.

December:

1. The qualifications of a naval officer.

"None other than a gentleman, as well as a seaman both in theory and practice, is qualified to support the character of a commissioned officer in the Navy; nor is any man fit to command a ship of war who is not also capable of communicating his ideas on paper, in language that becomes his rank." (J. Paul Jones, letter to the Marine Board, 1777.)

FIRST CLASS.—Two hours a week for one term.

Constitution of the United States.—The text of the Constitution is studied by the class, with as full explanation and comment as the time permits.

International law.—The greater part of the term in the hours allotted is occupied with Woolsey's International Law. The leading cases are studied in connection with the text-book, and many original cases, of greater or less complication, involving such principles of international law as may arise in the experience of naval commanders, are given as problems for solution in the recitation-room.

IX. MODERN LANGUAGES.

Professor Girault taught French at the school from 1845 to 1850. At the latter date, the department of modern lan-

---

January:

1. Are standing armies and navies dangerous to civil liberty?

"The relinquishment of privateering would not be a gain to the United States, where a powerful navy is not maintained, on account of its great cost and its danger to civil liberty." (W. L. Marcy, dispatch to Sartiges, July 28, 1856.)

(Captain Luce's answer to Secretary Marcy's statement.)

2. The Anglo-Saxon, the German, and the Celt—three elements in American character and civilization.

February:

1. The Eastern question. (E. A. Freeman in Fortnightly Review, December, 1875.)

2. A narrative version of Shakspeare's Merchant of Venice.

3. What is culture, and how is man to get it?

March:

Subjects chosen by writers.

May:

1. The volunteer-militia system *versus* standing armies.

2. How far is non-professional culture a desirable part of the education of a naval officer?

guages was founded, and included French and Spanish. In November, 1851, the two languages were separated, and Prof. E. A. Roget became head of the department of Spanish, an office which he continued to hold until 1873. Professor Girault remained in charge of the French department till 1866, when he was succeeded by Prof. L. V. Dovilliers. In 1870 Commander E. Y. McCauley became head of the department. In 1873 French and Spanish were again combined in one department, under Commander W. Scott Schley.

PRESENT COURSE.

Cadet-midshipmen and cadet-engineers.

FOURTH CLASS.—Three hours a week.

French.—Fasquelle's Grammar throughout the year.

THIRD CLASS.—First term, two hours a week; second term, three hours a week.

French.—The use of Fasquelle is continued, with Howard's Aid to French Composition, and exercises in composition and dictation.

SECOND CLASS.—First term, four hours a week; second term, three hours a week.

French.—The class read Erckmann-Chatrian's Le Conscrit, continuing the use of Fasquelle, with exercises in composition and dictation. The class also study Prud'homme's French Nautical Phrase-Book.

Spanish.—Spanish is taught through the medium of French, the text-books being Roget's Spanish Manual and Tolon's Reader.

FIRST CLASS.—Two hours a week for one term.

Spanish is continued as before.

In the study of both languages the grammar is used throughout the course, to fix principles of pronunciation and construction, the inflection of verbs and the formation of tenses, and the rules and idiomatic peculiarities of the two languages. When the classes are far enough advanced in the grammar, they have practice in translation into English, and in French and Spanish composition, followed by the analytical study of both languages, and conversations, to educate the ear and tongue.

The instructors in the department are now, and have generally been, natives of France or Spain. Their fitness for the position has always been determined by rigid examination of their qualifications in French, Spanish, and English, the last acquirement being of absolute importance.

The limited time allowed the students stands in the way of their attaining as high proficiency as in the more professional branches, though it serves to fix the knowledge of principles which must be of great use to them in their future intercourse abroad. The immediate object has been to teach them to read and write with correctness, and so to familiarize the ear that, with a little study and opportunity, they will be enabled to use these languages with ease in their official and social intercourse on foreign stations.

X. DRAWING.

The department of drawing was established in 1851, with Prof. Edward Seager in charge. He held the position till 1867. From that time till 1873 it was in charge of line officers of the Navy; and in 1873 Prof. R. S. Smith, previously professor of mathematics, was transferred to this department.

PRESENT COURSE.

Cadet-midshipmen.

FOURTH CLASS.—Two hours a week.

Line-drawing and topography.—The course in the latter branch consists of the representation of ground in detail by the usual conventional methods. The system of contour-lines and that of the line of greatest descent are both taught. Each map is illustrated by a marginal pen-drawing of a coast view, according to the usage of the United States Coast Survey.

THIRD CLASS.—Two hours a week for one term.

Free-hand drawing.—The aim of the instruction in this branch is to attain as high a culture of hand and eye as possible in the student, with special view to its usefulness in the profession. For this purpose, drawings are made altogether from object-models, varying in complexity from a square box to a statue. They comprise groups of boxes, vases, draperies, anchors, blocks, cordage, &c., models of boats and ships, objects used in artillery and ordnance, casts of hands, feet, masks, and of antique statues.

SUMMARY.

First year.

Cadet-midshipmen.

Algebra.
Geometry.
English.
History.
French.
Drawing.

Practical instruction in—

Seamanship.
Naval tactics.
Great-guns.
Infantry-tactics.
Field-artillery.
Boat-howitzers.
Fencing.
Dancing.
Swimming.

Cadet-engineers.

Algebra.
Geometry.
English.
History.
French.
Mechanical drawing.

Practical instruction in—

Use of tools.
Marine engines.
Great-guns.
Infantry-tactics.
Field-artillery.
Fencing.
Dancing.
Swimming.

Second year.

Cadet-midshipmen.	Cadet-engineers.
Trigonometry.	Trigonometry.
Descriptive geometry.	Descriptive geometry.
Analytical geometry.	Analytical geometry.
History.	History.
Rhetoric.	Rhetoric.
Elementary physics.	Elementary physics.
Chemistry.	Chemistry.
French.	French.
Drawing, (free-hand.)	Mechanical drawing.
Practical instruction in—	*Practical instruction in—*
Seamanship.	Use of tools.
Naval tactics.	Marine engines.
Great-guns.	Great-guns.
Infantry-tactics.	Infantry-tactics.
Field-artillery.	Field-artillery.
Boat-howitzers.	Signals.
Signals.	Fencing.
Fencing.	Gymnastics.
Gymnastics.	

Third year.

Cadet-midshipmen.

Seamanship.
Ship-building.
Naval tactics.
Infantry-tactics.
Ordnance instructions.
Astronomy.
Applied mathematics.
Mechanics.
Electricity.
French.
Spanish.
English composition.

Practical instruction in—

Seamanship.
Naval tactics.
Great-guns.
Infantry-tactics.
Field-artillery.
Boat-howitzers.
Signals.
Fencing.
Boxing.

Cadet-engineers.

Marine engines.
Ship-building.
Fabrication and designing of machinery.
Mechanical drawing.
Applied mathematics.
Mechanics.
Electricity.
French.
Spanish.
English composition.

Practical instruction in—

Use of tools.
Marine engines.
Great-guns.
Infantry-tactics.
Field-artillery.
Signals.
Fencing.
Boxing.

Fourth year.

Cadet-midshipmen.	Cadet-engineers.
Seamanship.	Mechanics.
Naval architecture.	Astronomy.
Ordnance and armor.	Mechanical drawing.
Navigation and surveying.	Naval architecture.
Marine engines.	Physical measurements.
Light.	Fabrication and designing of machinery.
Heat.	Marine engines.
Spanish.	Light.
Public law.	Heat.
	Spanish.
	Public law.
Practical instruction in—	*Practical instruction in—*
Seamanship.	Use of tools.
Naval tactics.	Marine engines.
Great-guns.	Great-guns.
Infantry-tactics.	Infantry-tactics.
Field-artillery.	Field-artillery.
Boat-howitzers.	Marine engines.
Mortar-practice.	Signals.
Marine engines.	Fencing.
Signals.	Boxing.
Fencing.	
Boxing.	

CHAPTER IV.

PRACTICE-CRUISES.

The cadets of the newly-formed first and third classes are embarked, immediately after the June examination, on board the practice-ships, to perform such a cruise as the Secretary of the Navy directs.

The practice-ship of the cadet-midshipmen is a sailing vessel, (or vessels,) commanded by the commandant of cadets, and the cruise generally extends along the coast as far north as New Bedford. The cadets are stationed in the watch and station bills with the crew, and perform the same duties; those of the first class being rated as seamen, and those of the third class as ordinary seamen. The cadets of the first class are also detailed to do duty in turn as midshipmen of the forecastle, quarter-deck, and tops, and as mates of decks and hull; and they have frequent opportunities in charge of the deck of working ship and performing evolutions. All the cadets receive special instruction in seamanship and navigation; the latter is more especially given to the first class. This class, during the practice-cruise of 1875, performed the following work, using their own observations in every case: Latitude and longitude by dead-reckoning; course and distance made good; bearing and distance of port; current; longitude, by time-sights, of sun, moon, and star; latitude by meridian-altitude of the same, by observation of the sun off the meridian, by three different methods, and by altitude of * Polaris; determination of deviation by azimuth and by amplitude of sun; determination of time of high water and of sunset; of ship's position, by Sumner's method and by cross-bearings. They also filled in the coast-line between Cape Hatteras and Cape Cod on skeleton charts, and constructed a Mercator's chart of Buzzard's Bay and Vineyard Sound; and plotted the ship's track on the coast-chart, and measured linear distances. Scale-sketches were made of the various anchorages, and descriptions written in their sketch-books.

The third class keep seamanship note-books, in which they describe and illustrate by drawings the fitting and lead of all the rigging of the ship. They are taught to heave the log, get a cast of the lead, and steer, and have frequent exercise aloft. Examinations in seamanship are held, to test their progress.

The practice-ship of the cadet-engineers is a steamer, commanded by an officer detailed from the academic staff. The cadets are divided into watches at stations in the engine and fire rooms. Each cadet is required to keep a rough note and sketch book, in which notes and sketches are made on the spot of all points of interest. The rough notes are carefully rewritten in their journals, and from the rough sketches careful drawings are made in their sketch-books. The general plan of instruction is to familiarize the cadets with the construction, care, and management of the engines of the ship. They are required to make sketches of all the steam and water pipes, and of the different parts of the engines and pumps; and they are constantly on watch with their instructors whenever the ship is under steam. Their stations are frequently changed, in order that each may have an opportunity of learning all the duties required of those in care of the engines, and they are detailed in turn to keep the steam-log.

Upon this cruise the cadet-engineers visit the principal

founderies, rolling-mills, machine-shops, iron-works, and ship yards at the cities on the Atlantic coast. In this way the ship usually visits New York, Philadelphia, Boston, Providence, Chester, and Wilmington; at which places the cadets go ashore, and, in company with an instructor, examine such works and mechanical processes as may be specially pointed out.* The instructor gives explanations, and designates the machinery or process which each is to sketch. The visits to shops on shore are made during four or five days of the week when in port, each visit being four or five hours long. The rest of the time is devoted to writing up journals and making drawings.

Besides the regular officers of each ship, who are taken, as far as possible, from the academic staff, officers are specially detailed to instruct the cadet-midshipmen in navigation, and the cadet-engineers in the principles of steam-engineering.

*About forty such establishments were visited during the practice-cruise of 1875.

As showing how great opportunities of special training in seamanship are afforded by the practice-cruise of the cadet-midshipmen, it may be stated that 380 separate maneuvres were performed during the summer cruise of 1876. The cadets of the first class, numbering 47, had therefore eight maneuvres each, including tacking, wearing, boxhauling, chapelling, getting under way, and anchoring. These movements were directed by the cadet, under the immediate supervision of the commanding or executive officer, or officer of the deck. The cruise in this way gave the cadets practice which they would hardly have got in years of sea-service, though liable at all times during their career to emergencies in which this very experience might be called into requisition.

CHAPTER V.

RELICS AND TROPHIES.

FLAGS.

United States.

Lawrence.—A square red flag, bearing the words "DON'T GIVE UP THE SHIP." The Lawrence was the flag-ship of Commodore Oliver H. Perry in the battle of Lake Erie, September 10, 1813, and upon going into action he displayed this flag at the mast-head. The Lawrence was named after Capt. James Lawrence, commander of the Chesapeake in the action with the Shannon.

American ensign.—This flag was used at the landing of Commodore Matthew C. Perry, at Uraga, near Jedo, in July, 1853, and was the first American flag displayed in Japan.

Great Britain.

Alert.—Sloop of war of 20 guns, commanded by Capt. T. L. P. Laugharne, captured August 13, 1812, by the frigate Essex, 32 guns, Capt. David Porter, in the North Atlantic. The fight lasted eight minutes. The Alert had three men wounded, and was converted into a cartel and sent in. The Essex had no casualties.

Boxer.—Fourteen-gun brig, commanded by Capt. Samuel Blyth. Captured September 5, 1813, off Portland, Me., by the brig Enterprise, 16 guns, Lieutenant-Commanding William Burrows. Both commanders were killed early in the action.

Confiance, Beresford, Chubb, Linnet.—Part of the English fleet captured in the battle of Lake Champlain, off Plattsburg, September 11, 1814, by the fleet under Commodore Thomas McDonough. The English force was commanded by Commodore George Downie, and the Confiance was his flag-ship. He was killed by the dismounting of one of his long 24-pounder guns by a shot from the Saratoga, Commodore McDonough's flag-ship.

Cyane, Levant.—Ships of 20 and 18 guns, respectively, captured off Madeira, February 20, 1815, by the Constitution, 44, under Capt. Charles Stewart. The Cyane was commanded by Capt. Gordon T. Falcon, the Levant by Capt. the Hon. George Douglass.

Detroit, Lady Prevost, Hunter, Little Belt, Chippewa.—Part of the English fleet captured by Commodore O. H. Perry in the battle of Lake Erie, September 10, 1813. The English force was commanded by Commodore R. H. Barclay.

Dominica.—English schooner of 16 guns, captured August 5, 1813, by the privateer schooner Decatur, Captain Diron, of 7 guns.

Duke of Gloucester.—Brig of 14 guns, captured at York, (now Toronto,) Upper Canada, April 27, 1813, by the Lake Ontario squadron, under Commodore Isaac Chauncey. The flag is a royal standard.

Epervier.—Brig of 18 guns, commanded by Capt. R. W. Wales, captured April 29, 1814, off Cape Canaveral, by the Peacock, 22, Master-Commandant Lewis Warrington.

Frolic.—Brig of 22 guns, commanded by Capt. T. Whinyates, captured October 18, 1812, by the Wasp, 18, Capt. Jacob Jones. Both vessels were captured later in the same day by the Poictiers, 74.

Guerriere.—Ship of 38 guns, commanded by Capt. J. R. Dacres, captured August 19, 1812, in lat. 41° 30′ N., long. 55° 30′ W., by the Constitution, 44, Capt. Isaac Hull.

Java.—Ship of 38 guns, commanded by Capt. H. Lambert, captured December 29, 1812, in lat. 13° 6′ N., long. 38° W., by the Constitution, 44, Capt. William Bainbridge.

Macedonian.—Ship of 38 guns, commanded by Capt. John Carden, captured October 25, 1812, in lat. 29° N., long. 29° 39′ W., by the United States, 44, Capt. Stephen Decatur.

Peacock.—Brig of 18 guns, commanded by Capt. William Peake, captured off Demerara, February 24, 1813, after an action of fifteen minutes, by the Hornet, 18, Master-Commandant James Lawrence.

Penguin.—Brig of 18 guns, commanded by Capt. J. Dickenson, captured off Tristan d'Acunha, March 23, 1815, by the Hornet, 18, Master-Commandant James Biddle.

Reindeer.—Ship of 18 guns, commanded by Capt. William Manners, captured June 28, 1814, in lat. 48° 36′ N., long. 11° 15′ W., by the Wasp, 18, Capt. Johnston Blakely.

St. Lawrence.—Schooner of 15 guns, commanded by Lieut. I. E. Gordon, captured February 26, 1815, off Havana, by the privateer schooner Chasseur, 14, Capt. T. Boyle, of Baltimore.

France.

Berceau.—Ship of 24 guns, Captain Senes, captured October 12, 1800, latitude 22° 50′ N. longitude 51° W., by the Boston, 28, Capt. G. Little.

Insurgente.—Ship of 40 guns, commanded by Captain Barreau, captured February 9, 1799, off Basseterre, West Indies, by the Constellation, 36, Commodore Thomas Truxtun.

Algiers.

Estidio.—Brig of 22 guns, captured June 19, 1815, off Cape Palos, by the Guerriere, 44, flag-ship of Commodore Stephen Decatur.

Mezoura.—Ship of 46 guns, captured June 17, 1815, off Cape de Gatt, by the Guerriere, 44.

Mexico.

Flag captured at Mazatlan by a landing-party from the Pacific squadron November 11, 1847. The force was sent from the United States ships Independence, Congress, Cyane, and Erie. The squadron was under the command of Commodore William Branford Shubrick.

Flag captured at Tuspan, April 18, 1847, by a force of seamen and marines from the Gulf squadron, under Commodore Matthew C. Perry. Commander Buchanan took part in this expedition. The town was taken with but little loss to the Americans.

Corea.

Flag of the Corean generalissimo, Fort McKee, Corea, captured June 11, 1871, by Capt. McLane Tilton, United States Marine Corps; Corporal Brown, United States steamer Colorado, and Private Purvis, United States steamer Alaska. Fourteen other Corean flags, captured at about the same time.

JAPANESE BELL.

The Japanese bell suspended in the grounds was presented, July 12, 1854, by the Regent of the Lew-Chew Islands, a dependency of the empire of Japan, to Commodore Matthew C. Perry, at that time the commander-in-chief of the United States squadron in the Asiatic seas, and Minister Plenipotentiary charged with the duty of opening intercourse between the United States and Japan. After the death of the Commodore, March 4, 1858, it was presented to the Naval Academy by his widow, in fulfilment of his wish.

A copy of the Japanese inscription on the bell having been made by a citizen of Japan, Cadet-Midshipman J. G. Kunitomo, now of the second class of the Naval Academy, and transmitted to the Japanese legation at Washington for translation, the following was very kindly furnished:

"In the eighth year of Eiraku and of Kanoye Tora, of the reign of the King of Lew-Chew, Kei-shi-yo-ho-Ho-o offered a prayer of benevolence for the people, and afterward ordered a large bell to be founded. He did this as an act of thanksgiving, and presented it to the temple of Daizen Anji, in the kingdom, in order that the King might reign prosperously and live long, and that the people of the three worlds,—Heaven, Earth, and Hades,—might be saved from infernal doctrines; and therefore it was that he instructed Shokoku Ansai to frame this inscription:

"'This beautiful Bell has been founded, and hung in the tower of the temple. It will awaken dreams of superstition. If one will bear in mind to act rightly and truly, and the Lords and Ministers will do justice in a body, the barbarians will never come to invade. The sound of the bell will convey the virtue of Fushi, and will echo like the song of Tsuirai; and the benevolence of the Lords will continue forever like those echoes.'

"The 20th day, 10th month, 7th year Keitai.*

"SHIU EISHI,

"*Chief Priest of the Temple.*

"EMONNOSKE FUJIWARA KUNIMITO, *Founder of the Bell.*

"YONAFUKU CHIUSEI, *President of the Hanging Ceremonies.*"

FIGURE-HEADS OF VESSELS PLACED IN THE GROUNDS OF THE NAVAL ACADEMY.

Franklin.—Line-of-battle ship, rating 74, and carrying 86 guns. She was built at Philadelphia in 1815, and launched in the same year.

Columbus.—Line-of-battle ship, rating 74, and carrying 80 guns. She was begun in 1816, at Washington, and launched in 1819. She was burned at Norfolk, Va., on the 20th of

* Corresponding to the year 1456.

April, 1861, by order of the Government, to prevent her falling into the hands of the enemy.

Delaware.—Line-of-battle ship, rating 74, and carrying 84 guns. She was begun in 1817, at Gosport, and launched in 1820.

Macedonian.—Ship of 38 guns, captured first from the French by the English, and from the latter by the United States ship United States, as already described. The figure-head belonged to her originally when in the French service.

Constitution.—This vessel, for fifty years the favorite ship of the Navy, was launched at Boston, September 20, 1797, being the third vessel of the newly-organized Navy, in the water. She first went to sea July 20, 1798. She was the flag-ship of Commodore John Barry during the war with France, and of Commodore Edward Preble in the Tripolitan war, in 1804. In the war of 1812 she was victorious in many engagements. Soon after the outbreak of the war she sailed from Annapolis under the command of Capt. Isaac Hull. On the 17th of July she fell in with an English squadron, under Commodore Broke, consisting of the Africa, Shannon, Guerriere, and other vessels, and got away from them after a remarkable chase of three days, which has become famous in naval history. Her exploits later in the war have been already mentioned. After its close she made repeated cruises, and up to the year 1853 she was constantly in commission. Since the war of 1812 she had made twenty-four separate cruises.

The figure-head now in the grounds of the Naval Academy is a representation of President Jackson, and was put on the vessel while she was lying at Boston, under the command of Commodore J. D. Elliot, during the second term of Jackson's administration. It occasioned some demonstration of partisan feeling, and about two months after its attachment to the vessel the head of the figure was cut off and carried away by some person, at the time unknown. A new head was afterward carved and put on in New York. The following extracts from papers of the day give in full the history of the affair—an affair which created much talk and excitement at the time:

Niles's Register for May 17, 1834, (vol. 46, p. 189,) refers to the excitement at Boston on the subject, and states that the figure-head had been placed on the bows of the Constitution "about two or three weeks ago"—*i. e.*, early in May, 1834.

The number for July 12, 1834, says: "Individuals in public employment have no right to force their private preferences on the people's attention. A great excitement had been caused by placing a wooden effigy of President Jackson on the bows of the frigate Constitution. To say the least of that proceeding, it was ill-advised and in bad taste. On the bows of *that* ship the head of no living man should be placed; or, if so, the place belongs to that of the 'Father of the Constitution,' the illustrious Madison."

The same paper quotes from the Boston Courier of July 4, 1834: "It appears that during the night of Wednesday" (*i. e.*, July 2) "the head of this wooden image was sawed off by some person or persons unknown. It is rather a mysterious affair. The Constitution lies at the navy-yard between two seventy-fours, and it is understood that a guard or watch is continually kept on board. It seems impossible that the deed could have been executed without discovery, notwithstanding that the night was dark and rainy. The head, which has been severed from its trunk, it is said, was at least 25 feet above the surface of the water. It is the opinion of several intelligent men who examined the *premises* yesterday that the perpetrators must have gone to their work through the navy-yard.

"It was reported last evening that Commodore Elliot had offered *one thousand dollars* for the discovery of the person or persons who committed the deed."

The number for July 19, 1834, in a short article, says: "There is much feeling on account of the mutilation of the figure-head of the frigate Constitution, and we fear that it may be turned into an important *public* concern, (though probably the uncounseled and unassisted act of a solitary individual, yet unknown,) through the indiscretion of political parties!!! One of these laughs immoderately at the proceeding, and the other is immoderately angry about it; and some are crawling enough to compare it with the personal attack that was made on the President by Ex-Lieutenant *Randolf* of the Navy." It adds: "There is no relation between the two cases; and thousands who would defend the person of the President at the risk of their own lives, see no great harm in sawing off the head of a wooden image. * * *

"No discovery has been made of the head or beheader, whose adroitness and courage was equally remarkable. Rumor, however, says that it was the act of a boy, without counsel or assistance; that he was two hours engaged in the work, during all which he heard the tread of the sentinels, though it rained in torrents; and some particulars are given as to his operations. How were they known?"

It appears that the persons engaged in the affair became afterward known. Volume 53 of Niles's Register for 1837, p. 147, contains the following:

"THE FIGURE-HEAD.—The New York Journal of Commerce contains a report of a trial in one of the courts there of an action for assault and battery, in which Samuel W. Dewey was plaintiff *vs.* Joseph Fay and Edward H. Dixon, defendants. In the course of the evidence one of the witnesses stated that Dewey, who it seems is a captain, informed him on the evening of the assault that he (Dewey) cut off the figure-head of the frigate Constitution. But for a turn the court's proceedings suddenly took, the whole matter would have been exposed. The Boston Sentinel adds: 'There is no doubt that Captain Dewey, who is a native of Cape Cod, cut off the figure-head as stated. It is now in the Navy Department at Washington, where it was lodged by Captain Dewey, the Secretary of the Navy giving him a written obligation that he should never be prosecuted for the offence he had committed.'"

Niles's Register of March 21, 1835, volume 48, page 42, contains this:

"The following is from the New York Daily Advertiser of Monday last," (March 16:)

"'On Saturday forenoon" (March 14) "the head carved by Messrs. Dodge & Sons, of this city, was placed on the trunk representing President Jackson on the bow of the frigate Constitution. The whole affair has been managed with great care and secrecy. It was given out when the frigate came into port that she would remain some five or six weeks, and on Saturday we learn some of her officers were in Philadelphia. When the frigate came up, a few days since, she anchored in the stream, opposite the navy-yard. The head has been carved with great caution, and a few hours after it was put on, two steamboats towed the frigate down the lower bay, where she anchored, some fifteen or twenty miles from the city, so as to be out of the reach of any popular excitement. The manner of placing this head on the frigate appears wholly in character. As the frigate has been provisioned at Boston, there can be no doubt that she came around here for no other object than to accomplish that which could not have been done at Boston. We are exceedingly gratified that, since it has been determined at Washington that the head shall be placed on the bows of this most favored of all other ships in the Navy, that it has been done by stealth. Had the ship been at the wharves of our city, or at any place where the populace could have reached her, we very much fear a riot of the most serious consequences would have followed, the end of which no human being could foretell. So far as we can judge, the opinion is general among all classes of respectable citizens, that neither the head of General Jackson or that of any other living man should be placed on the bow of that of all other frigates, but that she should continue with the same head and appearance with which she has won so many laurels in the wreath of our country's glory. The frigate, however, with whatever block she may have for a head, go where she may, will have the best wishes of every American.'"

OTHER TROPHIES.

Wooden figure of the British lion, crowned, and with one paw resting on the globe. Taken from the quarter-deck of H. B. M. ship Macedonian, after the battle, October 25, 1812, in which she was captured by the United States, Captain Decatur.

Two iron guns, 24-pounders, captured on board the British frigate Confiance, at the battle of Lake Champlain, by Commodore McDonough. These guns are placed vertically one on each side of the entrance of the hall of the department of steam-engineering. One of them is indented on the face of the muzzle by a shot, and slightly cracked; it is the gun which, by its recoil, killed Commodore Downie, the commander of the British fleet. It was identified by Commander Platt, who was in the action, and by Commodore Alexander S. Wadsworth, who saw the guns soon after the fight.*

* Letter from Commodore D. N. Ingraham, Chief of Bureau of Ordnance, to Captain Blake, March 3, 1860.

Two 32-pounder carronades, captured with the British frigate Cyane, by Captain Stewart, in the Constitution. They are placed in the gun-park, in front of the armory.

Eight long brass guns, originally French, captured at the Castle of San Juan d'Ulloa, Vera Cruz, Mexico, which capitulated March 27, 1847. Commodore M. C. Perry was at this time in command of the fleet. The guns are in position in front of the Tripoli monument.

One Whitworth rifled gun, 80-pounder, captured at Morris Island, South Carolina, 1863.

One Armstrong VIII-inch rifled gun, mounted *en barbette*. Built by Sir W. G. Armstrong in 1864, and captured at Fort Fisher. In position in the gun-park.

One Blakely 20-pounder rifled gun, captured at Fort Fisher. In position in gun-park.

One Italian rifled gun, presented to the United States by the Italian government. Gun-park.

One 60-pounder rifled gun, manufactured at Galveston, Tex., from the shaft of the United States steamer Westfield. Gun-park.

One 50-pounder Dahlgren rifled gun.

Two small brass signal-guns, captured from the cruiser Shenandoah. Placed at the entrance of the gunnery-room.

Two suits of Mexican armor, captured in 1847.

Mexican drum, machete, and commander's baton, captured in 1847.

Corean head-piece, breast-piece, and gingals, captured in 1871; and other relics or trophies of various countries and miscellaneous description.

In the library are portraits in oil of John Paul Jones, Decatur,* Preble, Jacob Jones, O. H. Perry, Rodgers, Macdonough, D. Porter, Stewart, J. Biddle, and M. C. Perry. There are

* By Sully.

also large paintings of the battle of Tripoli, of Barney's action in the Delaware with the General Monk, and of the fight between the Constitution and the Guerriere. The original of Barry's commission as senior captain in the Navy, signed by Washington, hangs in the library, in a frame made out of wood of the Constitution.

APPENDIX.

NOTE A.

Extract from Second Annual Report of John Branch, Secretary of the Navy, December* 6, 1830.

As a measure tending to give reputation and efficiency to the Navy, the cultivation of the minds of those who are to compose its active members is a subject of great national interest. It is a fact which will not be questioned that the early education of the officers of the Navy is entirely unequal to the character they have subsequently to sustain.

Few appointments under the Government involve the necessity for more general and scientific attainments. As officers of the Navy, they are required to act as judges of the law and evidence on trials of their brother officers, for offences affecting the lives and character of the accused; as commanders of ships, they should possess not only a practical acquaintance with seamanship, but an accurate knowledge of those branches of mathematics connected with the science of navigation, with astronomy and geography; and as commanders of fleets or squadrons, they must be well-informed on all points of international law, having reference to the rights of neutrals and belligerents, the often-recurring question of the rights of blockade, and other interdictions of intercourse be-

*American State Papers, III, p. 758.

tween powers standing in this relation to each other; to possess an accurate acquaintance with the modern languages, to enable them to enter into discussion on points of difference which may arise with the representatives of foreign states speaking such foreign language; and it may often happen that the communications can only be advantageously made in the language of the party with whom the subject of dispute may exist. The sons of the wealthy may obtain these advantages from the bounty of their parents; but without the aid of public instruction, how are the sons of the less affluent to become qualified to command in the naval service?

It may be further remarked, that while a school on the most liberal and comprehensive plan of instruction has been provided for the military talent of the country, and has been endowed with every attribute for the advancement of the education of the youth who aspire to a share in the toils or the honors of a military life, the only provision which has been authorized by law for the instruction of midshipmen in the Navy is to be found in the allowance of $25 per month to the schoolmasters retained on board the larger vessels of war.

NOTE B.

Report of the Committee on Naval Affairs of the House of Representatives, on making provision for naval schools for midshipmen, communicated January 3, 1834, by Mr. Watmough of the committee.

The Committee on Naval Affairs, taking into consideration the condition of the naval schools as at present established at Boston, New York, and Norfolk, and their inadequacy to effect the object proposed, deem it a duty to present to the House the accompanying bill. It is presumed no one will question the vital importance of these institutions to the service, both as it respects the well-being of the junior officers and their future usefulness to their country.

By the subjoined letter (A) from the Secretary of the Navy, it will be found that there are 450 midshipmen in service. Of these, about one-half are supposed to be at sea; one-fifth on duty at shore-stations; and the remaining 135 are on leave, waiting orders, furlough, or sick. Admitting that of the latter class 35 are sick—and this would seem to be a very large proportion—there still remain 100 youths left entirely to their own guidance, freed from those restraints so essential to their period of life, and subject alone to the influences of their own ardent impulses. The consequences are, in too many instances, fatal. It is believed to be the duty, as it assuredly is within the competency, of Congress to arrest the evils resulting from this state of affairs. The appropriation called for in the bill, under the judicious management of the Secretary, will effect much. The third and fourth sections of the bill, which provide an increase of the pay of the two respective grades of the service, the chaplains and schoolmasters, it is hoped will have the effect to enhance greatly the benefits to be derived from the appropriations; while, in truth, they do no more than fulfill the original intention of Congress in creating those grades, by placing them on a footing consistent with their dignity and usefulness. Their present rate of pay is admitted on all hands to be entirely insufficient. A reference to the annexed letter of the Secretary, (marked "B,") with its accompanying statement, (A,) shows the actual condition of the schools, the amount expended from the contingent fund, but under no law, and the limited number of youths who are enabled to avail themselves of what benefits do result. It is true the Department has lately issued an order requiring all midshipmen, not otherwise employed, to repair to some one of these schools; but as the Government does not feel itself authorized to allow the traveling-expenses incidental to such an order, few will be able to avail themselves of its benefits. The fifth section of the bill is intended to obviate this difficulty. If, however, the whole number should repair as required, it would only afford an additional and paramount obligation to the passage of the bill.

A BILL relative to naval schools.

Be it enacted, &c., That the President of the United States be, and he is hereby, authorized to improve the means of instruction now in operation at New York, Norfolk, and the navy-yard at Charlestown, Mass.

SEC. 2. That the sum of $10,000 be, and the same is hereby, annually appropriated, until otherwise ordered by law, out of any moneys not otherwise appropriated, to carry into effect the provisions of this act.

SEC. 3. That from and after the passage of this act, the pay of chaplains in the Navy shall be $1,200 per annum, and that, in addition to the duties now imposed upon them, they shall be required to instruct the junior officers in mathematics, in natural and moral philosophy, in history, and in such other branches of science as may be deemed by the Secretary of the Navy best calculated to advance the interests and elevate the character of the service.

SEC. 4. That from and after the passage of this act, the pay of schoolmasters in the Navy of the United States shall be $1,200 per annum, and it shall be the duty of the Secretary of the Navy to see that no individual shall be appointed to said station unless his application be accompanied by the most satisfactory testimonials of intellectual and moral attainments.

SEC. 5. That each midshipman or junior officer, when not under orders, or furloughed by competent authority, shall be directed by the Secretary of the Navy to attend at such one of the schools as may be designated by the Secretary, and diligently to submit himself to instruction, and while there shall be subject to all the rules and regulations for the better government of the Navy, as though actually engaged in service on shipboard; and the order of the Secretary of the Navy, or of any superior officer competent to give the same, to any midshipman to repair to said schools, shall be deemed a sufficient voucher to entitle said midshipman to the full amount of his transportation.

SEC. 6. That the Secretary of the Navy shall prepare, or cause to be prepared, such rules and regulations as may be deemed necessary for the good order, sound government, and direction of the said schools.

SEC. 7. That the pay specified above for the chaplains and schoolmasters shall be in lieu of and in full of all compensations and allowances whatever at present made.*

* Three communications from the Secretary of the Navy accompany this report; the substance of the first is given in the text; the second will be found in the note, and the third contains a faint commendation of the proposed bill. The whole may be found in the American State Papers, Naval Affairs, IV, p. 484.

NOTE C.

Extract from the report of Mahlon Dickerson, Secretary of the Navy, December 8, 1835.*

The compensation to be given by the late pay-bill to professors of mathematics is such as to command the services of those who are every way competent to perform the duties of this station. A regulation is adopted to appoint none to this station who shall not receive a certificate of competency after submitting to a rigid examination by scientific gentlemen who shall be appointed for that purpose. This will be of great advantage to the young officers of the Navy; and if a large portion of them should be called into active service by employing an additional naval force for the protection of our commerce, they will be enabled to perfect themselves in seamanship, the most important part of their education, and which can be acquired only at sea; but to make them accomplished officers, something more is required than can probably be derived from those sources. A knowledge of military tactics, of engineering and drawing, is deemed indispensable in the education of an officer of the Army, and which ought to be deemed equally so in the education of a naval officer. So much of chemistry, geology, and natural history as is taught at the Military Academy, although not absolutely essential to the military or naval officer, yet is decidedly more important to the latter than to the former.

* American State Papers, Naval Affairs, IV, 732.

If provision should be made for the admission of a class of one hundred midshipmen at a time at the Academy at West Point, to pursue such studies as should be prescribed by the Navy Department, and to be succeeded at the end of one or two years by another class, all in their turn might receive the advantage of this course of studies, highly necessary to their education as accomplished officers of the Navy, and at a small expense; as the midshipmen, while at the Academy, would receive no more pay than if attending the schools at the navy-yards, or if waiting orders.

NOTE D.

Report of the Committee on Naval Affairs on the expediency of the establishment of a naval school; communicated to the Senate May 14, 1836.

Mr. Southard, from the Committee on Naval Affairs, reported a bill to establish a naval academy; which was read, and ordered to a second reading. The report is as follows:

"The Naval Committee, to whom were referred the resolutions of sundry officers of the Navy in relation to a naval school, report:

* * * * * * *

"They have directed their chairman to report a bill for a naval school.

"At the last session of the Senate a bill was introduced for this object, and subsequently reported by the committee, but was not finally acted upon. In again presenting it to the Senate, the committee are influenced by a strong and decided conviction of its indispensable necessity to the public interests and to the efficiency of the Navy.

"Our Navy visits every land and every ocean. It protects a commerce at this moment as valuable as that of any other nation, though less than one other in amount of men and tonnage, scattered over the whole habitable globe and exposed to dangers of every possible description. In the protection of this commerce our naval officers are often brought in contact with the governments and official agents of every civilized nation, and are often obliged to have intercourse with them upon subjects which can only be properly treated by well-educated and well-informed men. They are, indeed, our national representatives in all other countries, and from them much of the estimate of us, as to our manners, intelligence, and character as a nation, must be drawn. It is not possible that their duties can be performed in the manner in which we should desire without science, intelligence, and knowledge. Besides, we are a growing nation, and it is our interest and our duty to draw from every other region every species of knowledge which can be useful to us. This can be more effectually and usefully accomplished by this than by any other class of our citizens. But how can all these be accomplished by them without proper practical and useful education? And where are they to receive this education? They are appointed when mere boys—generally between the ages of fourteen and seventeen—when it is not possible that they should be well-informed and disciplined scholars. Their situation and duties in the service render it equally impossible that they should make extensive literary or scientific acquirements beyond the mere practical duties of the seaman. They have not pay enough at that period of their service to purchase the means of instruction, nor time enough to acquire it.

"The only mode by which it can be secured is by the establishment of a school which shall combine literary and scientific instruction with the practical performance of a portion of their duties; and this may be accomplished by competent teachers, and by connecting with the school one or more small vessels, in which they may be compelled, under proper guidance, to perform in turn all the services of the common sailor with those also which belong to office and command." (Gales & Seaton's Register of Debates, 12, p. 1453.

NOTE E.

Rules and regulations for the government of the United States Naval School at Fort Severn, Annapolis.

ARTICLE 1. The laws and regulations for the government of the Navy of the United States are to be strictly observed by every person attached to the school.

ART. 2. All regulations for the discipline and government of the school issued from time to time by the Superintendent must be strictly obeyed.

ART. 3. All officers are required to observe toward each other a courteous deportment, and to conduct themselves on all occasions with propriety and decorum.

ART. 4. Officers having cause of complaint against any person connected with the school will make known such cause to the Superintendent.

ART. 5. The professors will be held responsible for the regular and orderly conduct of their respective classes while under their immediate instruction.

ART. 6. As obedience and subordination are essential to the purposes of the school, all midshipmen are required to obey the commands of the professors. The strictest attention to order and study is required in the recitation-halls; and no midshipman will be allowed to absent himself from them without permission from a professor.

ART. 7. No person will be excused from the performance of his duties on the plea of sickness, unless so excused by the surgeon; and no officer whose name is on the sick-list will be permitted to leave the bounds of the institution unless it is recommended by the surgeon.

ART. 8. The professors are required to keep records of all the recitations, and report weekly to the Superintendent the progress and relative merit of the students, and their absences and all other delinquencies. From these weekly reports the Superintendent will make a quarterly report to the Secretary of the Navy.

ART. 9. The professors are not permitted to exercise any discretionary power in excusing the students for absence from recitation or for tardiness, but must report all such cases to the Superintendent.

ART. 10. During the hours appropriated to study, previous to recitations, the midshipmen are directed to confine themselves to their rooms for that purpose, and are not permitted to lounge or promenade about the grounds of the institution.

ART. 11. A conduct-roll will be kept by the Superintendent, to be laid before the board of examiners, to embrace all improprieties committed at the school—such as neglect of duty, insubordination, disobedience of orders, inattention to studies, tardiness at recitations, breaking liberty, incorrect deportment at recitation, indecorous conduct at the mess-table or elsewhere, irregularity at meal-hours. All serious offences will be reported to the Secretary of the Navy for his action.

ART. 12. As one of the objects of the Government in retaining "acting midshipmen" at the school previous to their being sent to sea is to ascertain whether their qualifications and deportment are calculated to reflect credit upon the Navy if retained in it, there will be a semi-annual examination of the junior class of acting midshipmen in all the branches taught them since joining the school.

ART. 13. No midshipman is permitted to go beyond the

limits of the institution without permission from the Superintendent or officer in charge.

ART. 14. One midshipman from each room occupied by the students will perform the duties of superintendent of the room for one week; and he will be held responsible for the cleanliness and general neat arrangement of the room.

ART. 15. No midshipman shall remove from the room assigned to him without permission from the Superintendent.

ART. 16. No midshipman shall bring, or cause to be brought, within the limits of the institution, any wine, porter, or other intoxicating or spirituous liquors.

ART. 17. No midshipman shall cook or prepare food in his room, or give any entertainment, without permission from the Superintendent.

ART. 18. No meals are to be furnished to midshipmen in their rooms except in cases of sickness, and then only by the surgeon's orders.

ART. 19. Smoking cigars is prohibited in any of the midshipmen's rooms, recitation-halls, or mess-room. Chewing tobacco in the mess and recitation rooms is positively prohibited; and no acting midshipman will be permitted to chew or smoke tobacco.

ART. 20. The students are cautioned and enjoined not to mark, cut, or in any manner deface or injure the public buildings or property of any kind.

ART. 21. The midshipmen must prepare their clothes for the washerwoman before recitation-hours on Monday morning.

ART. 22. A midshipman shall be detailed as "officer of the day," whose duty it shall be to carry into effect any orders he may receive from the Superintendent. His duties will commence at 8 a. m. and continue until 10.30 p. m. He will occupy office No. 1, at the gate, and not absent himself from there longer than his duties render it necessary. He will, when applied to by visitors and strangers, give any information required respecting the institution or persons connected with it. The watchmen will be under his orders, and assist him in executing the orders of the Superintendent. He will occasionally walk through the yard and see that no improprieties are committed by any one. He is not to visit any of the midshipmen's rooms, except on duty. He will, at 10.30 p. m., see all lights and fires extinguished in the recitation-halls, mess-room, kitchen, and midshipmen's rooms, and report to the Superintendent. The watchman will accompany him to extinguish the fires and lights. He will keep a record of the weather, height of the barometer and thermometer at the hours of 8 a. m., meridian, and 8 p. m. He will record the arrival or departure of any officer attached to the school, mention in the record-book the number of mechanics and others employed from day to day, and insert the names of all visitors to the institution in the visitors' register. A watchman will remain at the gate during the meal-hours of the officer of the day. The meal-hours are as follows: Breakfast at 8 a. m., dinner at 1.30 p. m., and supper at 6 p. m.

ART. 23. The midshipmen who wish permission to visit the city of Annapolis, or go beyond the bounds of the institution, will record their names in the liberty-book by 4 o'clock p. m. of each day. The "officer of the day" will take charge of the liberty-book, and submit the list of applicants at that hour to the Superintendent, or officer in charge during his absence, for his approval. Permission to be absent will be granted only after the regular hours appropriated to recitations and study during the day, and extend only until 10 o'clock p. m., unless by special permission to exceed that hour. All midshipmen must report their return to the officer of the day, who is directed to note the time of such return in the liberty-book, for the inspection of the Superintendent or commanding officer at 9 o'clock the following morning. In the absence of the officer of the day from his office, officers will note the time of their return opposite their names. Any officer who is on the surgeon's report, desiring liberty, will, after obtaining his consent, insert opposite his name "doctor's consent."

The liberty-book is to be regarded as an official record, exhibiting faithfully each officer's return to the institution; and all entries must be made in ink.

Approved:

GEORGE BANCROFT.

NAVY DEPARTMENT, *August* 28, 1846.

NOTE F.

DETERMINATION OF THE WAVE-LENGTH OF A RAY OF LIGHT.

BY CADET-MIDSHIPMAN S. J. BROWN, FIRST CLASS, 1876.

This determination was made by means of an improvised spectrometer. A large Duboscq spectroscope was used, by removing the prisms from the table, and placing in the centre of the table the rulings on glass, which were to produce the diffraction-spectra.

In order to find the number of rulings on the glass, and their distance apart, placed the ruled side of the glass in contact with a steel scale graduated to $.2^{mm}$. Placed both under a microscope, with the right edge of the rulings over the centre of a division of the scale; then counted the rulings and the divisions of the scale as they moved past a black spot on the eye-piece of the microscope. I counted 294 spaces on the glass, the 289th line coming exactly on the 25th division of the scale, leaving 6 lines over. The number of rulings to a scale-division is equal to $288 \div 25 = 11\frac{13}{25}$. Hence, 6 lines would be $\frac{6}{11.52} = .5208$ divisions of the scale; the whole distance 25.5208; and consequently the rulings are $.017361^{mm}$ apart, a distance too great to secure the most accurate result. These measurements were repeated many times.

To get the glass in truly perpendicular position to the spectroscope-table, I imbedded it in a piece of cork, placing the rulings vertical or parallel to the face of the telescope and parallel to the slit. Placed the second telescope 180° from the other, so that their axes coincided, which was known by the position of the image of the slit on cross-hairs. I found that six turns of the micrometer-screw moved the second telescope through one degree. There were fifty divisions on the micrometer-head, or one division = 12″.

Placed metallic sodium in the flame, and measured from right-hand edge of central band to right-hand edge of the second diffraction-band on the right; then reversed the screw, and read from right-hand edge of second diffraction-band on the right, to the same edge of second band on the left. The mean of the several angles taken was 1° 56′ 1″.2. The wave-length of the ray is $l \sin \varphi$, where—

$\varphi = 1° \; 56' \; 1''.2$, and l = distance of rulings apart.

$l = .017631$ .... log 8.2462769

$\varphi = 1° \; 56' \; 1''.2$ .... log sin 8.5281641

Wave-length = .0005948^{mm} .... log 6.7744410

This is for the D_2 line of the solar spectrum.

DETERMINATION OF SPECIFIC HEAT OF LEAD.

BY CADET-MIDSHIPMAN H. C. GEARING, FIRST CLASS, 1876.

The method employed was that of mixture, by mixing lead of known weight with a known weight of water, and from the weights and rise of temperature computing the specific heat. Two thermometers were used in the experiment: one marked "Celsius" and the other "C." Thermometer marked "Celsius" when placed in melting ice read 0°.8; in steam of boiling water, 100°.3. Thermometer marked "C," in melting ice, read 0°.6; in steam of boiling water, 100°.4. The barometer read at the time 30.20 inches; attached thermometer,

73° F.=22°.77 C. The barometric height corrected for temperature=$h-0.000181\ h\ .\ t$, where h is the observed height and t is the temperature centigrade, and 0.000181 is the coefficient of expansion of mercury. The true height of barometer was found by this formula to be 30.08 inches. The boiling-point of water corresponding to this height, given in standard tables, is 100°.15. The change in error of Celsius for 100° is 0°.65; of C, 0°.35. If the changes in the errors of the thermometers be taken as uniform, change in error for Celsius in 1°=0°.0065; in C, 0°.0035.

The water was placed in a small glass vessel, which was itself placed in a larger vessel, the contact being prevented by wrappings of cotton yarn about the smaller vessel. This was to prevent loss of heat by radiation or conduction. Obtained the weight of the specimen of lead (pure), smaller glass vessel, and water (distilled), by method of double weighing. Suspended the lead by a silk thread in a vessel whose temperature was maintained constant by being surrounded by steam, and obtained the temperature to which it was raised by thermometer Celsius. When reading of thermometer became stationary, quickly removed the lead and placed it in the water, whose temperature was previously ascertained by thermometer C. Kept stirring the lead and water well until the highest reading of thermometer C had been obtained. If M is the mass or weight of the specimen of lead, c its specific heat, T the temperature of the lead, m the weight of water, m_1 that of the smaller glass vessel, c_1 the specific heat of glass, θ the final temperature of lead and water, t the original temperature of water, we have the formula:

$$M\,c\,(T-\theta) = m\,(\theta - t) + m_1 c_1\,(\theta - t)$$

$$c = \frac{(m + m_1 c_1)\,(\theta - t)}{M\,(T-\theta)}$$

In the experiment—

M =.41405 lbs., m=.44422 lbs., m_1 = .13318 lbs., c_1=.19768

Temp. of lead, by Celsius, = 97°, corrected = 96°.83 = T

Temp. of water, by C, = 23°, corrected = 22°.48 = t

Final temp., by C, = 25°, corrected = 24°.49 = θ.

These values substituted in the above equation give—

$$c = \frac{(.44422 + .02611) \times 2.01}{.41405 \times 72.34} = \frac{.9453633}{29.9524}$$

c = 0.03156, the specific heat of lead.

DETERMINATION OF THE SPECIFIC HEAT OF CADMIUM.

BY CADET-MIDSHIPMAN E. M. KATZ, FIRST CLASS, 1876.

The experiments were conducted according to the "method of mixtures." When two bodies of unequal temperature are brought together, the hotter gives off heat to the colder until their temperatures are equal. The increase or decrease in temperature will be inversely as the capacity of the body for heat. Referring the capacity thus found to a unit mass, we obtain the specific heat of the body.

In the experiments, a hot piece of cadmium was plunged into a mass of distilled water; the original and resulting temperatures being observed both for the metal and water. To heat the cadmium, it was placed in an air-space surrounded by steam at 100° C. In this space, a thermometer was also placed. The water was contained in a beaker placed inside of a larger beaker, the two being kept apart by a cotton skein wrapped about the top of the inner one. This prevented most of the loss of heat by radiation and conduction. In recording temperatures, two thermometers were used; one being marked "Celsius," the other marked "C." The following comparisons were taken:

	In melting ice.	In steam of boiling water.
Celsius	00°.8	100°.3
C	00°.6	100°.4

Barometer, 30''.2; thermometer attached, 73° F = 22.77° C.

Reducing the barometer to what it would have been at 0° C., $b = 30''.2 - 0.000181 \times 30''.2 \times 22.77 = 30''.08 = 764^{mm}$.

Under a pressure of 764^{mm}, the boiling-point of water is 100°.15 C.

To correct the readings of each thermometer for a reading a, we therefore have—

For Celsius, $a + .8 - .0065\, a$

For C, $a + .6 - .0035\, a$

Used "double weighings," viz: first weighed the body against a counter-weight, and then removed the body and put weights in its place. This eliminated errors of the balance.

Record of the two measurements.

Weight of cadmium,	.16988 lb.		.16955 lb.*
Weight of water,	.94460 lb.		.6176 lb.
Weight of inner beaker,	.20668 lb.		.1358 lb.
Temperature of cadmium,	95°	[thermometer Celsius]	98°
Temperature of water,	19°.2	[thermometer C]	22°.6
Resulting temperature,	20°	[thermometer C]	23°.8

Thermometer-reductions.

95°	[Celsius]	= 95°.18 C.	98°	[Celsius]	= 98°.2 C.
19°.2	[C]	= 19°.73 C.	22°.6	[C]	= 23°.1 C.
20°	[C]	= 20°.53 C.	23°.8	[C]	= 24°.3 C.

* This loss of weight was occasioned by the cadmium dissolving in the water during the interval between the experiments, thereby, also, rendering scraping necessary.

	First measurement.	Second measurement.
Cadmium fell in temperature,	74°.65 C.	73°.96 C.
Water and glass rose in temperature,	00°.8 C.	1°.2 C.
Mean temperature of water,	20°.13 C.	23°.7 C.
Mean specific heat of water,	1.0012162	1.00153

Formula.

$$M\,T\,C = m\,t\,c + m'\,t'\,c'$$

M = mass of cadmium.
m = mass of water.
m' = mass of glass.
T = range of temp. through which cadmium fell.
t = range of temp. through which water rose.
t' = range of temp. through which glass rose.
C = specific heat of cadmium.
c = specific heat of water.
c' = specific heat of glass.

First measurement.

$.16988 \times 74.65\,x = .9446 \times .8 \times 1.00122 + .20668 \times .8 \times .19768$

.16988..log = 9.23014–10 0.9446 ..log = 9.97525–10 0.20668 ..log = 9.31530–10
74.65 ..log = 1.87303 0.8 ..log = 9.90309–10 0.8 ..log = 9.90309–10
1.00122..log = 0.00052 0.19768 ..log = 9.29597–10
1.10317
0.75659..log = 9.87886–10 0.032686..log = 8.51436–10
0.03268
0.78927..log = 9.89723–10
log = 1.10317

No. Corr. = .062239 = specific heat. log = 8.79406–10

Second measurement.

$.16955 \times 73.9\,x = .6176 \times 1.2 \times 1.00153 + .1358 \times 1.2 \times .19768$

.16955..log = 9.22930–10 0.6176 ..log = 9.79071–10 0.1358 ..log = 9.13290–10
73.9 ..log = 1.86864 1.2 ..log = 0.07918–10 1.2 ..log = 0.07918–10
1.00153..log = 0.00065 0.19768 ..log = 9.29597–10
1.09794
0.74223..log = 9.87054–10 0.03222..log = 8.50805–10
0.03222
0.77445..log = 9.88890–10
log = 1.07994

No. Corr. = .061795 = specific heat. log = 8.79096–10

Mean result = .062017.

Atomic weight = 112. Atomic heat = 122 × .062017 = 6.9.

THE DETERMINATION OF THE LATENT HEAT OF STEAM.

By Cadet-Midshipman Walter McLean, First Class, 1876.

The thermometer marked "Celsius" was used in this determination. This thermometer, placed in melting ice, read $0^\circ.8$, and, in the vapor of boiling water, $100^\circ.3$. The water was boiled under the following conditions: bar. $30^{in}.2 = 767^{mm}.0661$; att. ther. 73° F. $= 22^\circ.777$ C. The height of bar. was corrected by the formula $b = l - .000181\, lt$, where $b =$ corrected height of bar., $l =$ height of bar. as read $= 767^{mm}.0661$., $t =$ att. ther. $= 22^\circ.777$, and $.000181 =$ coef. of expansion of mercury, $b = 763^{mm}.75182$. The temperature of steam, under above conditions, as determined by Regnault, $= 100^\circ.142$. The temp. of steam, as marked by ther. used, $= 100^\circ.3$ $\therefore$ correction to be applied to ther. $= -0^\circ.158$. The temp. of freezing by ther. $= 0^\circ.8$ $\therefore$ correction to ther. $= -0^\circ.8$. Hence, $-0^\circ.642 =$ change in correction of ther. between boiling and freezing points, and $-0^\circ.00642 =$ correction to be applied to reading of ther. for each degree. To determine the "water-equivalent" of the ther. used, weighed a quantity of water in a test-tube, read its temp. by ther., and then heated ther., and placed it in the water and noted the rise in temp. Then

$$mc(T - \theta) = m'(\theta - t) + m''c'(\theta - t)$$

where $m =$ wt. of ther., $T =$ temp. ther. was raised to, $\theta =$ temp. of water after the ther. was introduced, $m' =$ wt. of water, $t =$ temp. of water at first, $m'' =$ wt. of tube, and $c' =$ sp. heat of glass in tube. The amount of water taken $= .01$ lb., wt. of tube $= .04188$ lb., temp. of water at commencement $= 23^\circ$ (per ther.) $= 22^\circ.853$, heated ther. to $90^\circ = 89^\circ.422$, and temp. of water after ther. was introduced was $25^\circ = 24^\circ.84$.

$$\therefore m\,c\,(89^\circ.422 - 24^\circ.84) = m'\,(24^\circ.84 - 22^\circ.853) + .04188 \times .198 \times (24^\circ.84 - 22^\circ.853)$$

$$\therefore m\,c = \frac{.0183 \times 1.987}{64.582} = .00056 \text{ lb.} = u$$

I then made a calorimeter by taking two glass beakers, one being considerably larger than the other. Around the top of the smaller one placed a grommet of cotton yarn, and then placed it in the larger one, the grommet preventing contact, and forming a non-conducting jacket of air between the two. A glass retort was filled with water, the end of the neck being fitted with a small tube bent at right angles. The water in the retort was made to boil, the steam escaping by the small tube. While the water was boiling, noted the bar. $29^{in}.82$ and att. ther. 78° F., and, as before, determined the temp. of steam under these conditions to be 99°.786. While the water was still boiling, and steam was emitted from the tube, the tube was introduced into the calorimeter and steam condensed. Care was taken to prevent the steam from condensing before it reached the calorimeter by keeping the neck heated, as it was necessary that the water in the calorimeter should receive heat from the steam alone. The distance that the end of the tube was immersed below the water in the calorimeter was measured, and the increase in temp. of steam calculated, and found to be 0°.004, so that the temp. of steam, as it entered the calorimeter, was 99°.79. Before introducing the steam into the calorimeter, the small beaker containing water was weighed, its weight being .67203 lb. The beaker alone weighed .13583 lb., so that the water weighed .5362 lb. Immediately before introducing the steam, the temp. of the water was noted, and found to be 26° = 25°.833; and the supply of steam was stopped when the temp. had risen to 52° = 51°.667. Then the beaker and water were again weighed, the wt. being .69693, giving .0249 lb. of condensed steam. Having obtained these data I was prepared to calculate the latent heat of steam. From the principle that the amount of heat taken up by the water in the calorimeter, the ther., and the calorimeter itself, is equal to the amount of heat given up by the steam in condensing, we are enabled, with the data obtained, to form an equation from which we may easily determine the latent heat required.

Letting $M =$ wt. of steam condensed,
$m =$ wt. of water,
$m' =$ wt. of beaker,
$c' =$ specific heat of glass in beaker,
$u =$ water-equivalent of thermometer,
$T =$ temp. of steam,
$t =$ temp. of water at beginning,
$\theta =$ temp. of water at end,
$x =$ latent heat of steam,

we see that

$$Mx + M(T - \theta) = (m + u + m'c')(\theta - t)$$

$$\therefore Mx = (m + u + m'c')(\theta - t) - M(T - \theta)$$

$m' = .13583$ .... log 9.13300
$c' = .1976$ .... log 9.29579

$m'c' = .02684$ .... log 8.42879
$m = .5362$
$u = .00056$
$m'c' + m + u = .5636$ ...... log 9.75097
$\theta = 51^\circ.667$
$t = 25^\circ.833$
$\theta - t = 25^\circ.834$ .... log 1.41202

$(m'c' + m + u)(\theta - t) = 14.554$ .. log 1.16299

$$
\begin{aligned}
M &= \ .0249 \ \ldots\ldots\ \log 8.39620 \ldots\ldots \log 8.39620 \\
T &= 99^{\circ}.79 \\
T - \theta &= 48^{\circ}.123 \ \ldots\ldots\ \log 1.68236 \\
M\,(T-\theta) &= 1.1983 \ldots\ldots\ \log 0.07856 \\
(m'\,c' + u + m)\,(\theta - t) - M\,(T-\theta) &= 13.3557 \ldots \log 1.12568 \\
x &= 536.39 \ldots\ldots\ldots \log 2.72948
\end{aligned}
$$

DETERMINATION OF THE HORIZONTAL COMPONENT OF THE EARTH'S MAGNETISM AT ANNAPOLIS, MD.

BY CADET-MIDSHIPMEN A. JEFFRIES AND H. M. WITZEL, SECOND CLASS, 1876.

The magnetometer used is supported by a tripod. The box is leveled by means of three foot-screws; and the stand upon which it rests can be turned horizontally about an axis through its centre. The telescope is set upon the stand in the prolongation of the axis of the magnet. An azimuth-circle is used, in connection with the telescope, for determining the value of a division of the scale, which shows the deflections of the magnet to the right or left, and serves to measure the declination. This scale is engraved upon a plate of glass in the north end of the magnet, and is read by means of a lens in the south end. It is numbered from 0 to 16, each numbered division being divided into ten equal parts. The magnet, which is in the shape of a hollow cylinder, is carried by a stirrup connected with the torsion-head by means of several fibers of cocoon-silk. The torsion-head is used to get the torsion out of the silk fibers. To do this, a hollow cylinder of brass, of the same weight as the magnet to be used, is placed in the stirrup and allowed to come to rest. If its axis does not coincide with the magnetic meridian, it is made to do so by turning the torsion-head to the right or left.

In connection with the box of the instrument is a deflecting-bar, which extends to about thirty inches on each side; it is placed at right angles to the box, so as to be in the plane of the magnetic prime vertical when the box is in the magnetic meridian. It supports two long semi-cylinders of brass, which are graduated to tenths of a foot, and of such a height that when the deflecting-magnet is placed in them, the axes of the two magnets are at the same level. The bar is graduated in order to show the distance between the centers of the magnets.

In making the experiments, the two magnets used are of different lengths; the short one being 3.3 inches long, and the long one 3.9 inches. The short* magnet is used as the oscillating and deflecting magnet in determining M H and $\frac{M}{H}$ respectively. To obtain the values of deflections, it is necessary to determine the value of a scale-division and the magnetic axis of the magnet; these were obtained from the following observations made by Cadet-Midshipmen Winterhalter and Taylor. To determine the magnetic axis of either magnet, it is placed in the stirrup, and made to vibrate through a small arc, and the extreme right and left readings are noted by means of the telescope; this is repeated after the magnet has been turned 180° in the stirrup. In the first case, the figures of the scale are erect, while in the second case they are inverted.

* The long magnet should have been used.—W. T. S.

Axis of magnet T. V. 14.

Magnet.	Scale-reading.		Mean.	Means of 1 and 3, 2 and 4.	Axis.
	Left.	Right.			
E.	2.8	7.8	5.3		
I.	13.0	2.65	7.82	5.3	6.55
E.	2.7	7.9	5.3	7.81	
I.	9.5	6.1	7.8		

Axis of magnet T. V. 13.

Magnet.	Scale-reading.		Mean.	Means of 1 and 3, 2 and 4.	Axis.
	Left.	Right.			
I.	15.05	14.9	14.97		
E.	13.2	13.8	13.5	14.89	14.225
I.	15.3	14.3	14.8	13.56	
E.	15.5	11.75	13.62		

To determine the value of a scale-division, the magnet is stationary and the cross-wires of the telescope made to coincide with 0 on the scale; at the same time, the reading of the azimuth-circle is taken. The cross-wires are then brought to 1, 2, 3, 4, &c., up to the end of the scale, the reading of the azimuth-circle being taken at each number. The readings are then taken in the reverse order, and the mean of the two readings for each division is noted. The mean of all these means will be the value of a scale-division.

Value of scale-division of magnet T. V. 13.

Division.	Mean of two readings.	Value of 80 divisions.
	° ′ ″	° ′ ″
10	235 42 30	
20	235 21 00	
30	234 56 30	
40	234 33 00	
50	234 10 30	
60	233 48 30	
70	233 25 00	
80	233 02 30	
90	232 40 00	3 02 30
100	232 18 30	3 02 30
110	231 54 00	3 02 30
120	231 31 00	3 02 00
130	231 08 00	3 02 30
140	230 45 30	3 03 00
150	230 22 30	3 02 30
160	230 00 00	3 02 30
Mean................		3 02 30
Value of 1 division...		2′.281

OBSERVATIONS FOR $\frac{M}{H}$.

In determining $\frac{M}{H}$, the long magnet was placed in the stirrup and the short one used as the deflecting-magnet. The time was taken for one hundred oscillations in sets of ten, the time being noted at the end of each set. The oscillations were counted as the magnetic axis of the magnet passed over the cross-wires of the telescope from *left* to *right.* The extreme scale-readings were also taken, but do not appear in the work. The deflecting-magnet was placed on the east and west ends of the deflecting-bar, with its north end east; and, after the scale-readings and times were noted, the north end was shifted so as to point to the west, and the same readings were taken.

OBSERVATIONS FOR M H.

To determine the moment of inertia of short magnet: Suspend the magnet by itself, and afterward in connection with a ring of known moment of inertia, and note the times of one hundred oscillations, in sets of ten each, in both cases. Then

$$K = K_1 \frac{t^2}{t^2 - t_1^2}$$

in which K is the moment of inertia of magnet, K_1 that of the ring, and t and t_1 the times of oscillation.

Suspend the small magnet, and cause it to oscillate. Note the times of one hundred oscillations, as before.

Observations for $\frac{M}{H}$.

Deflecting-magnet in magnetic prime vertical.—Magnet T. V. 14 deflecting.

Magnet.	N. end.	Time.	Temp.	Scale-readings.	Alternate means.	Differences.	Distance.
		h. m.	°				
West.	W.	11 45	67	125.2			
	E.			160.5	125.2	35.3	
	W.	12 10	67.5	125.0	160.0	35.0	
	E.			159.5			
		11 57.5	67.5			35.1	2.2 feet.
East.	E.	11 50	67	160.0			
	W.			125.5	159.6	34.1	
	E.	12 15	68	159.2	125.3	33.9	
	W.			125.2			
		12 25	67.5			34.0	
Means.......		12 0	67.4			$2\mu = 34.6$	

One scale-division = 2′.281 } Taylor and Winterhalter.
$1 + \frac{h}{f}$.... log 0.00110 }

$$\frac{M}{H} = \tfrac{1}{2}\, r^3 \tan \mu \left(1 - \frac{P}{r^2}\right)$$

$$P = \frac{A - A'}{\frac{A}{r^2} - \frac{A'}{r_1^2}}$$

Magnet.	N. end.	Time.	Temp.	Scale readings.	Alternate means.	Differences.	Distance.
		h. m.	°				
West.	W.	12 03	67.5	131.9			2.6 feet.
	E.			153.0	131.5	21.5	
	W.	12 25	69	131.2	152.9	21.7	
	E.			152.7			
		12 11	68.5			21.6	
East.	E.	11 56	67	153.0			
	W.			132.0	152.3	20.3	
	E.	12 17	69	152.3	131.9	20.4	
	W.			131.8			
		12 6.5	68			20.3	
Means........		12 8.7	68.1			$2\mu' = 20.9$	

$\mu = 17^d.3$.......log 1.23805
$1^d = 2'.281$......log 0.35813
$1+\frac{h}{f}$ ....log 0.00110

$\mu = 39'.562$ .....log 1.59728

μ...........log tan 8.06099
r^3..............log 1.02726
½..............log 9.69897

A = .061266....log 8.78722

A..............log 8.78722
r^2............colog 9.31516

.012658....log 8.10238

$\mu' = 10^d.45$......log 1.01912
$1^d = 2'.281$......log 0.35813
$1+\frac{h}{f}$ ....log 0.00110

$\mu' = 23'.897$.....log 1.37835

u′..........log tan 7.84203
r_1^3.............log 1.24491
½..............log 9.69897

A′ = .061082....log 8.78591

A′..............log 8.78591
r_1^2...........colog 9.17006

.009036....log 7.95597

Magnet T. V. 14 suspended with ring No. 7.—8 fibers.

No. of vibrations.	Time.	Temp.	Time of 50 vibrations.
	h. m. s.	°	*m. s.*
0	1 26 09	72.5	
10	28 28		
20	30 47.5		
30	33 07		
40	35 26		
50	37 45		11 36
60	40 04.5	72.5	11 36 5
70	42 24		11 36.5
80	44 43		11 36
90	47 03		11 37
100	49 22	73	11 37
Mean............................			11 36.5
			$t_1 = 13.93$

Magnet T. V. 14 suspended.—8 fibers.

No. of vibrations.	Time.	Temp.	Time of 52 vibrations.
	h. m. s.	°	*m. s.*
0	1 57 1.5	72.25	
10	58 34		
20	2 0 06		
30	1 37.5		
40	3 09		
50	4 41		
52	4 59.5		7 58
62	6 31.5		7 57.5
72	8 03		7 57
82	9 34		7 56.5
92	11 07		7 58
102	12 38.5	72.5	7 57.5
Mean............................			7 57.4
			$t = 9.181$

$$\frac{A}{r^2}-\frac{A'}{r_1^2}= .003622..\text{colog } 2.44105$$
$$A-A' = .000184 \ldots.\text{log } 6.26482$$
$$r^2 ..\text{colog } 9.31516$$

$$\frac{P}{r^2}= .010496 \ldots \text{log } 8.02103$$

$$1-\frac{P}{r^2} = .989504 \ldots.\text{log } 9.99542$$
$$A \ldots.\text{log } 8.78722$$

$$\frac{H}{M} \ldots.\text{log } 8.78264$$

To determine M H.

$$M H = \frac{\pi^2 K}{T^2} \qquad K = K_1\frac{t^2}{t_1^2-t^2} \qquad K_1 = \tfrac{1}{2}\,(r^2+r_1^2)\,W$$

$$\therefore M H = \frac{\pi^2 \times \tfrac{1}{2}\,(r^2+r_1^2)\,W \times \dfrac{t^2}{t_1^2-t^2}}{T^2}$$

$r = .10801$ ft. $r_1 = .0832$ ft. $W = 89.839$ grams.

Magnet T. V. 14 suspended by four fibers.

No. of vibrations.	Time.	Temp.	Time of 50 vibrations.
	h. m. s.	°	*m. s.*
0	9 24 38		
10	26 09		
20	27 40	68.75	
30	29 11.5		
40	30 44		
50	32 15		7 37
60	33 46.5		7 37.5
70	35 16.5		7 36.5
80	36 49.5		7 38
90	38 20.5		7 36.5
100	39 51.5		7 36.5
Mean			7 37
			T = 9.14

π^2..........log 0.99430
½..........log 9.69897
$(r^2+r_1^2)$.... log 8.26903
$1+\frac{h}{f}$.......log 0.00022
W........., log 1.95347
1.18843
t^2..........log 1.92578
$(t_1^2-t^2)$...colog 7.95960
T^2.......colog 8.07810

M H.......log 0.06790
$\frac{M}{H}$........colog 1.21736

2)1.28526

H=4.3917..log 0.64263

NOTE.—This value of H is in the foot-grain system; to convert it into the centimetre-gramme system, add the logarithm 8.66378 to the log of H given above.

H = .2025 in centimetre-gramme system.

In combining M H with $\frac{M}{H}$, no correction for temperature is introduced, because the difference of temperature was so small that the correction would be nearly inappreciable. The dimensions of the inertia-ring from which the above dimensions were obtained were taken at 86° F.

DETERMINATION OF THE DIP OF THE MAGNETIC NEEDLE AND TOTAL INTENSITY OF EARTH'S MAGNETISM.

BY CADET-MIDSHIPMAN J. K. BRICE, SECOND CLASS, 1876.

The construction of the dipping-needle, by which this was

determined, made it necessary to determine the magnetic prime vertical, and from it the meridian. The instrument had one needle, moving in a vertical plane; the angle from the horizon was measured by a circle graduated to twenty minutes. The motion of the instrument in azimuth was read by means of a circle graduated to read to one minute by means of a vernier. To determine the prime vertical, the azimuth-circle was read when the needle was vertical. The following readings were taken:

Prime vertical.

Circle south.		Circle north.	
Face south.	Face north.	Face north.	Face south.
71° 30′	76° 59′	77° 16′	72° 28′
Mean 74° 14′.5		Mean 74° 52′	
Mean 74° 33′ 15″			

The instrument was then turned + 90° and — 90° in azimuth, and the following readings of the dip taken:

Circle east.				Circle west.			
Face east.		Face west.		Face east.		Face west.	
N.	S.	N.	S.	N.	S.	N.	S.
71°	71° 40′	69° 30′	69° 25′	71° 25′	71° 30′	69° 50′	69° 40′
Mean 70° 23′ 45″				Mean 70° 36′ 15″			
Mean dip 70° 30′							

The magnetism of the needle was then reversed by stroking it with bar-magnets, and the observations repeated:

Prime vertical.

Circle north.		Circle south.	
Face south.	Face north.	Face north.	Face south.
27° 00′	20° 33′	19° 57′	26° 00′
Mean 23° 46′ 30″		Mean 22° 58′ 30″	
Mean 23° 22′ 30″			

Meridian.

Circle east.				Circle west.			
Face east.		Face west.		Face east.		Face west.	
N.	S.	N.	S.	N.	S.	N.	S.
70° 10′	70°	71° 40′	72°	70° 40′	70°	71° 50′	71° 50′
Mean 70° 57′ 30″				Mean 71° 5′			
Mean dip 71° 1′ 15″							

Mean of two observations 70° 45′ 37.5″, dip.

The total intensity is found by dividing H, the horizontal intensity, by the cosine of the dip:

$$R = \frac{H}{\cos\theta}$$

$$H = 4.357$$

H .... log 0.63918
θ .... log cos 9.51789

13.22 ....log 1.12129

MEASUREMENT OF RESISTANCE OF YARD-TELEGRAPH.

By Cadet-Midshipmen David and Orchard.

Annapolis, *June*, 1876.

This line is a short one, used for sending messages between distant points of the yard.

The battery is placed in the battery-room of the laboratory, and consists of six gravitation-cells set up in series. These cells are used because they will produce a steady current for a long time in a closed circuit. From the laboratory there are two branches of the line: one extending to the new buildings, connecting with a sounder, then connecting with the earth; the other leads to the office of the officer in charge, old buildings, then to the Superintendent's office, and lastly to the commandant's house, where connection is made with the earth. At each of these stations, connection is made with a sounder for receiving messages. In the measurement, a Wheatstone's bridge, a single needle galvanometer, and three gravitation-cells were used.

Call resistance of line to new building A, and of other branch B.

First. To measure A or B, make connections for battery and galvanometer as usual; connected end of line to be measured between r and battery; connected end of R′ with the earth. Took $\frac{r}{R}=\frac{1}{10}$, distant end of line to earth.

Second. To measure A+B, connections as before except that end of other branch of line was connected between R′ and battery. Both ends of line to earth.

Third. To measure insulation resistance, insulate both ends of the line and make connections as in second case.

Fourth. To measure resistance of both branches in multiple arc, connect both branches between r and battery; the other ends being to earth. Connect R′ and galvanometer with the earth.

The following were the results obtained:

Resistance of A................ 8.63 ohms.
Resistance of B................17.20 ohms.
Resistance of A+B ....25.83 ohms.
Resistance in multiple arc........ 5.74 ohms as measured.

$$\text{Resistance in mult. arc} = \frac{A\,B}{A+B} = 5.74 \text{ ohms as computed.}$$

Insulation resistance of whole line, 800,000 ohms.

TO DETERMINE THE ELECTRO-CHEMICAL EQUIVALENTS OF COPPER, ZINC, HYDROGEN, AND OXYGEN.

BY CADET-MIDSHIPMEN J. K. BRICE AND O. G. DODGE, SECOND CLASS, 1876.

The object of determining the electro-chemical equivalents of these elements is that, by knowing them, we may be able to measure the strength of a current of electricity passing through any of their electrolytic compounds, by observing the quantity of the element decomposed in a given time; or, knowing the current, we may find the weight of the element it will deposit in a given time.

To determine these quantities, three decomposing-cells, containing copper sulphate, copper nitrate, and zinc sulphate, and a voltameter containing acidulated water, were placed in the circuit, and a current was sent through them from five Grove's cells. The platinum electrodes immersed in the decomposing-cells, each positive one having first been coated with the metal contained in the electrolyte, were carefully weighed before and after the current was passed. From these weighings, the exact weight of the metallic element deposited on each negative electrode and that taken from each positive one was obtained. Having noted the whole time that the current was passing, the amount deposited per second was readily found from the whole amount deposited.

The current was passed through the voltameter for a short time before beginning the experiment to saturate the water with the gases; so the difference between the readings of the voltameter at the beginning and end gave the whole volume of the gases decomposed. These volumes had to be corrected for temperature and pressure and tension of the aqueous vapor that was mixed with them. Since eight parts, by weight, of oxygen were liberated for every one part of hydrogen, it was unnecessary to work out the electro-chemical equivalent of more than one of the gases from its observed volume.

In order to find the strength of the current, it was assumed that the measurements were correct, and it was deduced from the copper nitrate by dividing the weight of copper deposited per second by its electro-chemical equivalent, as taken from Jenkin's Electricity.

COPPER NITRATE.

	Grams.
Weight of positive electrode before experiment...	1.6590
Weight of positive electrode after experiment	1.5825
Weight of negative electrode after experiment	1.32475
Weight of negative electrode before experiment ...	1.24730
Weight deposited on negative electrode..........	.07745
Weight dissolved from positive electrode	.0765

Time current was passing, 45 m. = 45 × 60 sec.

Electro-chemical equivalent of copper, .00324 grams.

$$C = \frac{.07745}{45 \times 60 \times .00324}$$

.07745 . . . . log 8.88902 − 10
45 . . . . log 1.65321
60 . . . . log 1.77815
.00324 . . . . log 7.51055
——— 0.94191

C . . . . log 7.94711

COPPER SULPHATE.

	Grams.
Weight of positive electrode before experiment. . . .	1.4506
Weight of positive electrode after experiment	1.3895
Weight of negative electrode after experiment	1.385
Weight of negative electrode before experiment . . .	1.309
Weight deposited on negative electrode	.076
Weight dissolved from positive electrode	.0611

Unfortunately, the copper on the positive electrode was all dissolved before the experiment was completed, which accounts for the great difference between the amount deposited and that dissolved. As soon as the copper was all off of the positive electrode, the solution, semi-saturated at first, began to get weaker. Furthermore, the sulphuric acid set free attacked the deposited copper. So the deposit must have been too small, and, in consequence, the electro-chemical equivalent also.

$$\text{Electro-chemical equivalent} = \frac{.076}{60 \times 45 \times C}$$

.076 . . . . log 8.88081 − 10
60 . . . . log 1.77815
45 . . . . log 1.65321
C . . . . log 7.94711
——— 1.37847

Electro-chemical equivalent = .00318 . . . . . log 7.50234

ZINC SULPHATE.

	Grams.
Weight of positive electrode before experiment.....	1.2734
Weight of positive electrode after experiment......	1.1842
Weight of negative electrode after experiment	1.3562
Weight of negative electrode before experiment	1.2750
Weight deposited on negative electrode............	.0812
Weight dissolved from positive electrode...........	.0892

$$\text{Electro-chemical equivalent of zinc} = \frac{.0812}{60 \times 45 \times C}$$

.0812..............................	log 8.90956 − 10
$60 \times 45 \times C$	log 1.37847
Electro-chemical equivalent = .0033968...	log 7.53108

HYDROGEN.

Corrected barometer, 76.611^{cm}.

Thermometer, 17.778 C.

Height of column of water in voltameter, 43.3^{cm}.

Specific gravity of the acidulated water, 1.053.

Specific gravity of mercury, 13.5592.

Height of an equivalent column of mercury:

$$\frac{43.3 \times 1.053}{13.5592} = 3.3634^{cm}$$

Tension of aqueous vapor in gas, 1.5170.

$76.611 + 1.517 - 3.3634 = \text{pressure on gas} = 74.765^{cm}$

By Charles's law:

$$29.6 : V' = 273 + 17.773 : 273$$

$$V' = \frac{29.6 \times 273}{290.778}$$

By Mariotte's law:

$$V' : V = 76 : 74.765$$

$$V = \frac{74.765 \times V'}{76} = \frac{74.765 \times 29.6 \times 273}{290.778 \times 76}$$

74.765 .... log 1.87370
29.6 .... log 1.47129
273 .... log 2.43616

5.78115

290.778 .... log 2.46356
76 .... log 1.88081
4.34437

V = corrected volume of gas .... log 1.43678

Specific gravity of hydrogen = .0012932 × .0693.

Weight of hydrogen in grams = V × .0012932 × .0693.

$$\text{Electro-chemical equivalent} = \frac{V \times .0012932 \times .0693}{60 \times 45 \times C}$$

V .... log 1.43678
.0012932 .... log 7.11167—10
.0693 .... log 8.84073—10

7.38918—10

60 × 45 × C .... log 1.37847

Electro-chemical equivalent = .0001025 ...... 6.01071—10

OXYGEN.

Electro-chemical equivalent = .0001025 × 8 = .00082

BRADLEY'S TANGENT GALVANOMETER COIL No. 2.

METHOD OF FINDING THE CONSTANT.

BY CADET-MIDSHIPMAN O. G. DODGE, SECOND CLASS, 1876.

The construction of this instrument makes it impossible to measure the size of the coil or count the turns. It is therefore necessary to determine the constant by comparison with a standard, or by electrolysis, the method here employed.

The galvanometer, a eudiometer containing acidulated water, a decomposing-cell containing neutral copper sulphate semi-saturated, were placed in circuit with three cells of a Grove's battery. The eudiometer used was so made that both the oxygen and hydrogen were collected in the same tube, which had been carefully calibrated. Two strips of platinum, carefully cleaned, were selected as electrodes for the copper sulphate. Upon one of these, a reguline deposit of copper was formed to act as the positive electrode. The following weighings and observations were made:

	Grams.
Positive electrode with copper deposited..........	1.6916
Negative electrode..............................	1.2768

The circuit was then closed, the time being noted. The deflections of the galvanometer and the readings of the eudiometer were taken at intervals of five minutes. When the circuit was broken, the barometer and thermometer were read.

Time.	Galvan.	Eudiometer.	Bar.	Ther.
h. m.	°	*mm.*	*inches.*	°
3 00	82.75	0		
05	82.75	23		
10	82.00	45		
15	82.00	66		
20	81.50	87		
25	81.25	107		
30	81.25	127		
35	80.75	146		
40	80.50	164		
45	80.00	182	30.01	68.303 F.

Interval = 45^{m}.

Mean deflection = $81^\circ\ 28'\ 30''$.

Volume of gases = 31.89 $cm.^3$.

Positive electrode.......................... 1.6349 grams.
Negative electrode.. 1.3309 grams.

Deposited...... .0541 " Dissolved.. .0567 "

Mean .... .0554 "

$$.00324 : 10 \text{ webers} :: \frac{.0554}{60 \times 45} : x \text{ webers}$$

$$\therefore x = \frac{.554}{60 \times 45 \times .00324}$$

$$C = \text{constant} = \frac{x}{\tan D}$$

$$\therefore C = \frac{.564}{60 \times 45 \times .00324 \times \tan D}$$

.554		log 9.74351
60	log 1.77815	
45	log 1.65321	
.00324	log 7.51055	
81° 28′ 30″	log tan .82421	
		1.76612
C		log 7.97739

$$C = .009492$$

32.8^{cm}=column of water in eudiometer.
2.4131^{cm}=equivalent column of mercury.
1.76^{cm}=tension of vapor in eudiometer.
75.945^{cm}=corrected height of barometer.

$\therefore 75.945 + 1.76 - 2.4131 = 75.292^{cm}$ pressure on gases.

$$68.^\circ303 \text{ F.} = 20.^\circ185 \text{ C}$$

By the laws of Boyle and Charles, we have:

$$31.89 \text{ cm.}^3 : V_1 :: 293.185 : 273$$

$$\therefore V_1 = \frac{31.89 \times 273}{293.185}$$

$$V_1 : V_2 :: 76 : 75.292$$

$$\therefore V_2 = \frac{31.89 \times 273 \times 75.292}{76 \times 293.185}$$

$$V = \text{volume formed per second} = \frac{31.89 \times 273 \times 75.292}{76 \times 293.185 \times 60 \times 45}$$

$$.1721 : 1 \text{ weber} :: V : x \text{ webers}$$

$$\therefore x = \frac{V}{.1721}$$

$$C = \text{constant} = \frac{x}{\tan D} = \frac{V}{.1721 \times \tan D}$$

$$\therefore C = \frac{31.89 \times 273 \times 75.292}{76 \times 60 \times 45 \times 293.185 \times .1721 \times \tan D}$$

31.89	log 1.50365	
273	log 2.43616	
75.292	log 1.87675	
		5.81656
76	log 1.88081	
60	log 1.77815	
45	log 1.65321	
293.185	log 2.46715	
.1721	log 9.23578	
81° 28′ 30″	log tan .82421	
		7.83931
C	log	7.97725

C=.009489

NITRO-GLYCERINE.

By Cadet-Midshipman Frank J. Sprague, Third Class, 1876.

The germ of that numerous group, nitro substitution compounds, may be deemed to have started with Professor Callan proposition to add sulphuric acid to the nitric acid of Grove's battery. The German philosopher Schönbein investigated this remarkable mixture, and discovered ozone and gun-cotton, the last of which was patented by him in 1846.

Numerous controversies arose as to the nature of the changes which the cotton had undergone, and, aroused by these, Ascague Sobrero, a pupil of Pelouze, in Paris, and now professor of chemistry in the University of Turin, made a series of experiments. Walter Crum having stated that "pure gun-cotton was lignine, in which three atoms of water were replaced by three atoms of nitric acid," Sobrero made similar compounds with gum, sugar, dextrine, manna, and finally glycerine, where it was evident that there could be no absorption, as stated by some of the writers on gun-cotton. He was rewarded by the discovery of nitro-glycerine. This was in 1847 or 1848. The discovery remained dormant until the Crimean war, when it was rumored that Admiral Napier was prevented from taking Cronstadt from fear of torpedoes charged with nitro-glycerine by Professor Jacobi, as well as by the difficulties of navigation. In 1864, eighteen years after its discovery, Alfred Nobel, a Swedish engineer, obtained a patent for its application to blasting purposes. So little was nitro-glycerine then known that he has been credited with its discovery.

Nobel also attempted to control its use in the United States, but finally failed.

Soon after its introduction into this country, three startling accidents occurred, which threw this new explosive into public disfavor. The first was in 1865, when an explosion occurred in Greenwich street, New York, opposite the Wyoming Hotel, caused by throwing a box of "glonoin" into the street, which had been left by a German as security for his board. The next was that on board the steamer European, at Aspinwall, in 1866. Forty-seven persons were killed or mortally injured; the vessel, pier, and adjacent warehouses were destroyed, the loss amounting to over $1,000,000. Immediately succeeding this was an explosion in the office of Wells, Fargo & Co., San Francisco. Eight persons lost their lives, and property to the amount of $250,000 was destroyed. Noting these accidents, George M. Mowbray, then of Titusville, Pa., undertook the preparation and qualitative examination of nitro-glycerine, and shortly afterward advertised to manufacture it for miners and others.

In 1867, at the invitation of Chief Engineer Doane, Mr. Mowbray arrived in North Adams, and undertook to furnish the Hoosac Tunnel with nitro-glycerine. Since then he has almost steadily been manufacturing this explosive, and during the eight years since he began he has had but three accidents at the manufactory, having made over one million pounds in this time. The first accident was on December 23, 1870, when a magazine exploded, supposed to have been caused by the accidental starting of a flame. The fore man was killed.

March 12, 1871, another explosion of a magazine took place, caused by continuous overheating. Sixteen hundred pounds were in the magazine at the time, and 600 pounds of congealed nitro-glycerine within 12 feet of the magazine. This last did not explode, although battered and bruised, and no one was hurt.

The third was the explosion of the works, two men being killed and one slightly injured. This was January 26, 1876. The works are now rebuilt and running.

So nitro-glycerine has been known but about ten or twelve years in the United States as a blasting agent, and has been known to chemists but twenty eight or nine years. Among the more prominent of those who have investigated, written upon, and used it, are Railton, Girard, De Vrij, Millott, Vogt, Nobel, Papillon, and Berthollet on the continent, and Mowbray and Hill in this country.

Such is a brief and partial *résumé* of the history of nitro-glycerine. In following out a more detailed account, we are surprised by the various names given to it, and the conflicting statements of its properties and composition.

For synonyms we find the following: Nitrate of oxide of lipyl, [glycerine,] (Berzelius;) glonoin, mono-, di-, and tri-nitro-glycerine, (Liecke;) glonoine, (Gmélin;) fulminating oil, nitroleum, tri-nitrin, glyceryl nitrate, (from Wagner.)

Its formula is $C_3\,H_5\,(NO_2)_3\,O_3$, though it may be written differently in conforming to different theories.

Modern researches have shown that there are three nitrins, mono-, di-, and tri-nitrin, whose formulæ are as below.

Nitro-glycerine is made from glycerine and nitric acid, sulphuric being mixed with the nitric to absorb the water formed during the process, and thus keep the nitric acid of the required strength. In the chemical action that takes place, the radical nitryl (NO_2) of the nitric acid takes the place of one, two, or three atoms of hydrogen in the glycerine, according as one, two, or three molecules of nitric acid unite with one of glycerine. The products are mono-, di-, and tri-nitro-glycerine, and the reactions are as follows:

$$(1)\qquad \left.\begin{matrix}H\\NO_2\end{matrix}\right\}O+\left.\begin{matrix}C_3\,H_5\\H_3\end{matrix}\right\}O_3=\left.\begin{matrix}C_3\,H_5\\H^2\\NO_2\end{matrix}\right\}\quad+\left.\begin{matrix}H\\H\end{matrix}\right\}O$$

$$(2)\qquad 2\left(\left.\begin{matrix}H\\NO_2\end{matrix}\right\}O\right)+\left.\begin{matrix}C_3\,H_5\\H_3\end{matrix}\right\}O_3=\left.\begin{matrix}C_3\,H_5\\H\\(NO_2)_2\end{matrix}\right\}O_3+2\left(\left.\begin{matrix}H\\H\end{matrix}\right\}O\right)$$

$$(3)\qquad 3\left(\left.\begin{matrix}H\\NO_2\end{matrix}\right\}O\right)+\left.\begin{matrix}C_3\,H_5\\H_3\end{matrix}\right\}O_3=\left.\begin{matrix}C_3\,H_5\\(NO_2)_3\end{matrix}\right\}O_3+3\left(\left.\begin{matrix}H\\H\end{matrix}\right\}O\right)$$

where the first gives mono-nitro-glycerine, $H_2\,C_3\,H_5\,(NO_2)\,O_3$; the second, di-nitro-glycerine, $H\,C_3\,H_5\,(NO_2)_2\,O_3$; and the third, tri-nitro-glycerine, $C_3\,H_5\,(NO_2)_3\,O_3$.

The tri-nitro-glycerine is the only one of these compounds which has yet been successfully prepared, and is the one which is employed in blasting and for torpedoes; hence the rest of the paper will be devoted to this compound.

We have, then, the formula for tri-nitro-glycerine, $C_3\ H_5\ (NO_2)_3\ O_3$, which, written on the triple type of water, is $\left.\begin{matrix}C_3H_5\\(NO_2)_3\end{matrix}\right\}O_3$, where the radical NO_2 is univalent, and $C_3\ H_5$ trivalent, as before in glycerine. Written graphically, it is:

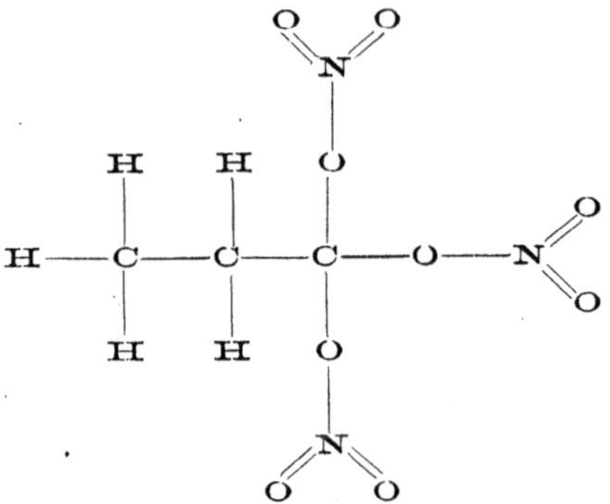

That of glycerine being:

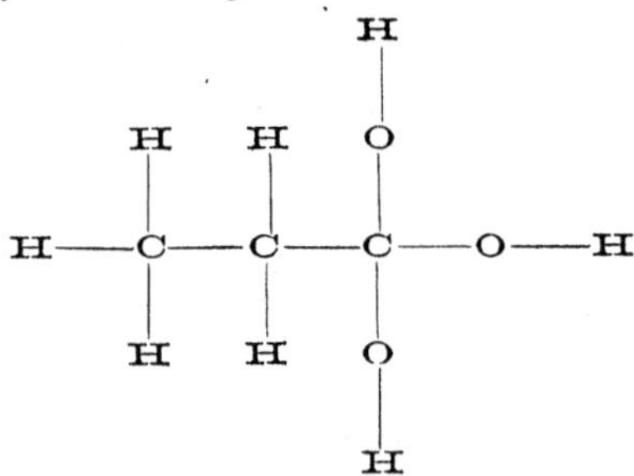

Comparing, we see that the formula for tri-nitro-glycerine may be written by substituting one atom of NO_2 for an atom of hydroxyl, HO, in glycerine; and this is perhaps the best way to show the similarity and difference between the molecules of these two substances.

The formula for manufacture, written graphically, would be:

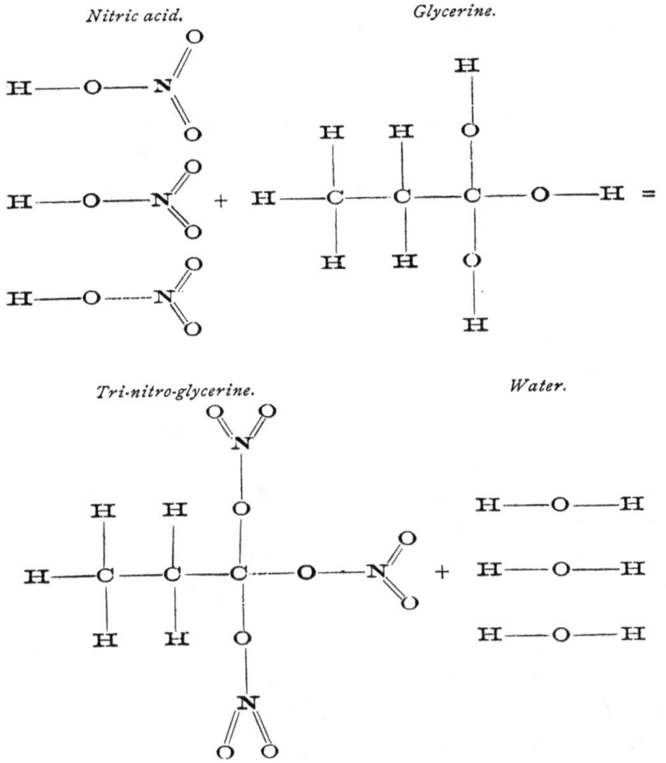

Nitric acid. + *Glycerine.* =

Tri-nitro-glycerine. + *Water.*

The composition is as follows:

			Centesimally
C.—Carbon....	3 atoms..	36 micro-criths..	15.859 +
O.—Oxygen ...	9 " ..	144 " ..	63.436 +
N.—Nitrogen ..	3 " ..	42 " ..	18.502 +
H.—Hydrogen.	5 " ..	5 " ..	2.203 —
One molecule =	20 " ..	227 " ..	100.000

A brief description of the method of manufacture by Mr. Mowbray, which differs but little from that employed by Mr. Walter N. Hill at the Torpedo Station, will be given.

Fresh nitric acid (sp. gr. 1.45) direct from the stills is taken up by sulphuric acid.

The acids are afterward thoroughly mixed and nitrous fumes expelled by a current of air furnished by blowers. The acid mixture is now distributed in stone pitchers arranged in troughs. The troughs are filled with ice-cold water, or ice and salt, to within four inches of the top of the jars. From glass jars arranged on a shelf above the pitchers, chemically pure glycerine is allowed to fall, drop by drop, by means of a siphon with a rubber tube attached, into the mixture of nitric and sulphuric acids.

A current of air is forced through each pitcher by a rubber and glass tube while the acids and glycerine are mixing.

During the one and a half to two hours required for this operation, great care and close attention are necessary. Nitrous fumes are given off. If too freely, the mixture is stirred with the glass tube already mentioned. Sometimes this is caused by the glycerine running too fast, which fires the mixture, wastes the glycerine, forming oxalic acid, and giving off abundant fumes.

If such is the case, the flow of glycerine is stopped and the mixture stirred. If the current of air is stopped, the mixture will take fire. When the action is complete, no more fumes being given off, the nitro-glycerine is dumped into a large tank of water at 21°.1 C., where it sinks to the bottom.

After remaining about fifteen minutes, the water is drawn off the top, and the nitro-glycerine run off into a large swinging wooden tub, where it is washed three times with water and twice with soda, a current of air working through it meanwhile. It is then removed to the magazine and poured into "crocks," (earthenware jars, holding sixty pounds.) These are immersed to within six inches of the top in water at 21°.1 C., where they remain about seventy-two hours, during which time any impurities rise to the surface as scum. The nitro-glycerine is then chemically pure and ready for packing. It is put in tin cans lined with paraffine and frozen, in which state it is stored away.

It takes one and a half or two hours to make it, seventy-two to purify it, and forty-eight to congeal it.

When pure, nitro-glycerine is nearly colorless, but ordinarily has a light lemon tint, owing to coloring matter in the glycerine used, (Mowbray.)

When freshly made, it is creamy-white and opaque, but clears on standing, (Hill.) It is an oily, odorless liquid, but has a sweet, pungent, aromatic taste; is very poisonous, and handling at first, or tasting from the point of a pin for the first time, gives one a persistent, throbbing headache, but persons lose this sensitiveness to its effects after using it some time. It is a powerful refractor of light, (Mowbray,) and is inflammable, lighting with a flame, and burning without explosion, yielding a light ethereal flame of considerable volume, (Mowbray.)

Freezing-point, when fresh, is — 16°.1 to — 15° C.; cleared, 3°.9 to 4°.4 C., (Hill.) It freezes at 7°.2 C., and contracts one-twelfth of its bulk, (Mowbray.)

Freezes to a white crystalline mass, and when frozen is very difficult to explode, even with a heavy charge of fulminate. In the air, when pure, it may be kept a long time without change.

It decomposes at 160° C., giving off red fumes, (Mowbray.) Easily decomposes by drying in a warm room with rarefied air, (Williamson.) It is instantly decomposed when dissolved in alcohol, (Mowbray.)

When impure, it rapidly changes, becoming orange-yellow,

and evolving fumes; its freezing-point is lowered, and it is then liable to be exploded by any jar. The impurity of the article has been in all probability the cause of many explosions. In some cases, the pressure exerted by gas formed in closed vessels may have had some influence on it, and, in view of this, N. K. List has proposed to use loosely-stoppered vessels, or have them fitted with a safety-valve. In treating of the explosion of nitro-glycerine, some general principles may be given, (from Hill:)

"The explosive effect is dependent upon—

"1st. The great change of state produced; that is, the formation of gas very much greater in volume than is the substance from which it is derived, and which is still more expanded by the heat evolved;

"2d. The shortness of time required for the change to take place."

"The circumstances of explosion may be generally considered under—

"1st. The physical or mechanical condition of the substance itself;

"2d. External condition;

"3d. Mode of firing."

"The explosive effect is dependent also on these.

"Roux and Sarran divide explosions into two kinds:

"First order, or detonation;

"Second order, or simple explosion.

"Detonation is the instantaneous explosion of a body.

"The following comparison is given:

	Second order.	First order.
Gunpowder	1.00	4.34
Gun-cotton	3.00	6.46
Nitro-glycerine	4.80	10.13"

(Hill, Notes on Explosives.)

If lighted, nitro-glycerine produces an explosion of the second order; if detonated, of the first.

To fully develop its power, it must receive a peculiar vibratory shock, which breaks up the molecule. This may be imparted by a concussion, either immediate or remote, and it has been done by a note from a violin.

But it does not always explode by concussion, probably because the conditions are not fully complied with. An exploder suspended over the glycerine in a partially-filled cartridge has been exploded without affecting the glycerine.

Containing-bottles have been smashed, and no further injury resulted.

When nitro-glycerine is allowed to drop on a hot plate, we have the following actions:

If the plate is moderately hot, it volatilizes quietly.

If red-hot, it volatilizes instantly.

If just hot enough to cause the nitro-glycerine to boil, it explodes violently, or detonates.

The best method of exploding is to fire an exploder immersed in the liquid nitro-glycerine by electricity. The exploder should be charged with a fulminate.

The products of decomposition are given differently. The Engineering Journal (November 17, 1871) gives this:

One grm. nitro-glycerine gives 284 c. c. of the following gases at 0° C. and 29.7 inches (75.5^{cm}) barometrical pressure:

Carbonic acid	45.72	volume.
Binoxide of nitrogen	20.36	
Nitrogen	33.92	
	100.00	

Wagner gives this:

Water, (steam)	20.00	
Carbonic acid	58.00	
Oxygen	3.50	
Nitrogen	18.50	
	100.00	parts.

According to experiments made in Belgium, the combustion of nitro-glycerine does not yield free oxygen, but a large quantity of nitrogen suboxide, according to the formula

$$2\,(C_3\,H_5\,N_3\,O_9) = 6\,CO_2 + 5\,H_2O + N_2O + 4\,N$$

When fully exploded, no poisonous gases are given off; but when imperfectly, oxides of nitrogen are formed, and the whole quantity of gas will be lessened. (Hill.)

Its firing-point has been given as 180° C. M. P. Champion did not find this to be the case. M. Leygue designed an apparatus by means of which M. Champion prepared the following table, giving the various changes at different temperatures to which nitro-glycerine may be subjected:

365° F., boils, volatilizes with disengagement of yellow vapor.
381° F., evaporates slowly.
392° F., evaporates rapidly.
422° F., deflagrates violently.
442° F., deflagrates lively.
465° F., detonates with difficulty.
494° F., detonates very perfectly and violently.
512° F., detonates feebly.
548° F., detonates feebly with flame.

Mowbray, Appendix.

At a dark-red heat, nitro-glycerine assumes the spheroidal state, and evaporates without explosion.

The following table gives the temperature at which certain explosive substances burn or detonate:

	Degrees F.
Powder used in the Chassepôt rifle	380
Fulminate of mercury	392
Mixture of equal parts of sulpuur and K Cl O	392
Abel's gun-cotton, compressed	400
Gun-cotton, loose	428

Sulphur burns in air	475
Nitro-glycerine explodes	493
Sulphuret of antimony 1 part, chlorate of potash 1 part, explodes	536
Sporting-gunpowder	540
Cannon-powder	563
Picrate of mercury, of lead, of iron	565
Designolle's torpedo-powder, (picrate;) artificial saffron	600
Picric acid, picrates of magnesia, of ammonia, of potash	605
Musket picrate powder	610
Cannon-powder, quickened with picrate	716

Various methods have been devised whereby nitro-glycerine may be rendered safer to use. (Mowbray, Appendix.)

Mowbray has made the following:

Nitro-glycerine, 30 pts.
Nitro-toluol, 10 pts.

This will not explode by blows, burns when thrown on a fire, and explodes only with a very heavy charge of fulminate, fifteen or twenty grains.

The chief drawback is that it does not solidify at a moderate temperature, and is thus liable to evaporate, leaving the glycerine unprotected.

Nobel dissolves it in wood-spirit, and separates it by adding water. Seeley says of this:

(1) Wood-spirit is expensive, and is lost in the large amount of water used to wash it away;

(2) It may evaporate, being volatile, and leave the nitro-glycerine unprotected;

(3) Chemical action takes place between these two bodies;

(4) Vapor of wood-spirit is very volatile, and forms with air an explosive mixture.

The most common method is to mix the nitro-glycerine

with moist matter. The principal of these mixtures used for blasting are the following:

Dynamite.—Is a mixture of nitro-glycerine with siliceous earth, infusoria, tripoli, rotten-stone, &c. These are very good absorbents, taking up two or three times their own weight of the explosive. When frozen solid, it is inexplosive; but, if in grains, it can be exploded. It is not very sensitive to friction or percussion. With 75% of nitro-glycerine, it is about six times as strong as powder. It should be dry. It is liable to exudation.

Giant-powder—Dynamite No. 2.—This is dynamite mixed with nitrate of potash or soda, with perhaps a little paraffine and charcoal.

Lithofracteur, or "*Rend-rock.*"—Nitro-glycerine and finely-divided powder, or nitro-glycerine, kieselguhr, coal, sulphur, and potassium or sodium nitrate.

Dualin.—Sawdust and nitro-glycerine, containing sometimes a little saltpeter; the best is about half as strong as nitro-glycerine alone.

Porifera nitroleum.—Nitro-glycerine and sponge, or other vegetable fiber.

Metalline nitroleum.—Nitro-glycerine and red lead or other metallic powder.

Selenitic powder.—Nitro-glycerine and plaster of Paris.

Titanite.—Granulated gun-cotton and nitro-glycerine.

Vulcanite.—Rifle-powder and nitro-glycerine.

Mica-powder.—Mica scales coated with nitro-glycerine. This congeals at about the same temperature as nitro-glycerine. In this condition, a lump burns like saltpeter. It is nearly as powerful as nitro-glycerine. It is unlike dynamite in being coated, while, in the latter, the nitro-glycerine is absorbed. Infusorial silica, being so great an absorbent, has come into use to quite an extent, and may be taken as one of the best representatives of the class of absorbents, so that dynamite may be compared with mica-powder. To show the difference, I have the following direct from Mr. Mowbray:

" { 50% of nitro-glycerine.
{ 50% of infusoria, (rotten-stone burned to a red heat.)

"This mixture will not explode, nor will it burn when flame is applied to it.

" { 12% of nitro-glycerine.
{ 88% of mica scales.

"This will explode violently, and burns when lighted.

"Evidently, the explosive power of nitro-glycerine is partly lost when mixed with infusoria. Only when there is a percentage of 66–75 parts of nitro-glycerine to 34–25 parts of infusoria, does it make a good explosive.

"Again,

" 50% of nitro-glycerine " 50% of *powdered* mica	is not as good as	50% of nitro-glycerine, 50% of mica *scales*.

"Fifty per cent. of nitro-glycerine with mica scales was much more effective than 77% of infusoria with nitro-glycerine in artificial blocks of stone. In fact, whenever nitro-glycerine is absorbed, instead of being superficially coated over inert matter, there is a considerable loss of force."

This is further evident when we compare the relative force of the two with nitro-glycerine.

Theoretically, calling nitro-glycerine ten times as strong as powder, dynamite containing 75% should be seven and a half times as strong. Mica-powder is nearly as strong as the explosive itself. The latter can be fired after being in water; the former cannot, which is a very important consideration in wet ledges and submarine work.

The following table gives various mixtures of nitro-glycerine with other substances, together with their sensitiveness:

Table of explosive mixtures, by Messrs. Chas. Girard, Millott, and Charles Vogt, Paris, (Comptes-Rendus de l'Académie, t. lxxi, No. 20.)

Composition.		Beneath a weight of ten and one-half pounds avoirdupois, falling from a distance of—			Observations.
		65 inches.	40 inches.	20 inches.	
Pure silica; Nitro-glycerine	3.00; 1.00	Explodes with difficulty.	Explodes still more difficultly.	Explodes still more so.	These proportions give a powder perfectly dry.
Silica; Nitro-glycerine	3.00; 3.00	Explodes well	Explodes easily	Explodes	Pulverulent, but moistens paper.
Silica; Nitro-glycerine	0.40; 3.62	Explodes promptly.	Explodes well	do	Very damp and saturates paper.
Silica, (residue from alum-factories.); Nitro-glycerine	2.70; 3.00	Explodes well	Explodes well but partially.	Explodes with difficulty.	A pasty mass and saturates paper.
Alumina; Nitro-glycerine	1.20; 1.00	do	Explodes rather difficultly.	Explodes with great difficulty.	Semi-pulverulent, moistens paper.
Alumina; Nitro-glycerine	3.00; 1.00	Explodes with difficulty.	Explodes; requires several blows.	Explodes slightly	Dry powder, not moistening paper.
Kaolin, washed and ground; Nitro-glycerine	5.40; 3.40	Explodes well	Explodes	Explodes with difficulty.	Moistens paper.
Tripoli, washed; Nitro-glycerine	2.11; 2.68	do	do	do	Do.

Clay, ground Nitro-glycerine	2.25 2.05	....do	Explodes well	Explodes	Pasty mass, saturates paper.
Gypsum, ground Nitro-glycerine	8.50 3.68	....do	Explodes in portions.	Explodes still in portions.	Pasty mass, moistens paper.
Bricks, ground Nitro-glycerine	8.00 4.15	....do	Explodes	Explodes with difficulty.	Moistens paper by compression.
Ethal Nitro-glycerine	0.50 1.00	Explodes with difficulty.	....do	......do	Very moist pasty mixture.
Ethal Nitro-glycerine	1.00 1.00	Explodes with great difficulty.	....do	Does not explode	Powder almost dry, moistening paper slightly.
Sugar, powdered Nitro-glycerine	0.50 1.00	Explodes in close cartridges, but not alone.	Explodes with difficulty.	....do	Almost liquid.
Sugar, powdered Nitro-glycerine	1.00 1.00	Explodes with difficulty.	Explodes with great difficulty.	....do	Very thick liquid with crystals of sugar.
Sugar, powdered Nitro-glycerine	3.00 5.00	Explodes very badly	Does not explode	......do	Powder almost dry, moistening paper.
Sugar, in lumps Nitro-glycerine	1.00 2.00	Explodes with difficulty.	....do	......do	Nitro-glycerine almost absorbed by sugar.
Sugar, in lumps Nitro-glycerine	3.00 2.00	Explodes not at all.	......do	......do	Wholly absorbed.
Glycerine Nitro-glycerine	1.00 3.00	Explodes with difficulty.	Explodes badly	......do	These liquids separate in a short time.
Alcohol, methylic Nitro-glycerine	3.00 1.00	Explodes not at all.	......do	......do	Do not separate.
Oil Nitro-glycerine	3.00 3.00	Explodes only with difficulty.	Does not explode	......do	Forming an emulsion; separating in time.

Table of explosive mixtures, &c.—Continued.

Composition.			Beneath a weight of ten and one-half pounds avoirdupois, falling from a distance of—			Observations.
			65 inches.	40 inches.	20 inches.	
Nobel's powder.	Nitrate barytes.	0.70	Explodes well	Explodes	Requires several shocks.	Moist powder; soaks into paper.
	Resin	0.10				
	Nitro-glycerine	0.20				
Nobel's powder.	Nitrate barytes.	0.68	do	do	Explodes when compressed.	Do.
	Pitch	0.12				
	Nitro-glycerine	0.20				
Nitro-glycerine alone			Explodes	do	Explodes from 10-inch fall.	Liquid.

While the mixture of nitro-glycerine with inert matter may at times be useful, provided that a due distribution and not a loss of force is had, the adulteration by other explosives, as powder, picrates, &c., in order to make it stronger and act quicker, is entirely useless, and necessarily fails in its purpose.

Nitro-glycerine, being in itself the strongest and most rapid explosive used for blasting, cannot be aided by the addition of any of its older and slower rivals. Their action is so much behind that of nitro-glycerine that their force is wasted and consequently useless.

The comparative power of powder and nitro-glycerine has been variously estimated. Elwyn Waller (Chemical News) makes the following:

A measure containing 1 cubic foot will hold 796 ounces of blasting-powder and 997.1 ounces of water; *i. e.*, the sp. gr. of powder is about .8. The sp. gr. of nitro-glycerine is 1.6; therefore, bulk for bulk, supposing explosive power to be the same for same mass, nitro-glycerine is twice as strong as powder. In reality, the following vols. of gas are generated:

1 vol. most effective powder gives	221.4 vols. carbonic-acid gas.
	74.6 vols. nitrogen.
	296.0 vols. gas.

1 vol. of another, exploding at a lower temperature, gives—

	391 vols. carbon protoxide.
	66 vols. of nitrogen.
	457 vols. gas.

1 vol. of nitro-glycerine gives	469 vols. carbonic anhydride.
	554 vols. steam.
	39 vols. oxygen.
	236 vols. nitrogen.
	1298 vols. gas disengaged.

These vols. are at 0° C., except steam, 100° C.

For 1000° C., supposed temperature of exploding gunpowder, we have, using the formula $V' = V(1 + at)$,

For (1) powder, 1480 vols.

For (2) powder, 2285 vols.

The supposed temperature of exploding nitro-glycerine is 2000° C. By this same formula we have vol. of gas equals 10,607. Taking into account the specific gravities, we have for the nitro-glycerine 21,214 vols.; nearly ten times the amount of gas from the powder yielding the most gas.

M. Berthollet gives this table. The first column indicates heat furnished by one kilogram of the matter under consideration; the second, the volume of gas disengaged; the third, the resulting product of the two quantities, serving as an approximate estimate of the explosive power:

	Heat.	Vol. of gas.	Est. exp. force.
Blasting-powder	509 units,	0.173 liter,	88
Artillery-powder	608 units,	0.225 liter,	137
Sporting-powder	641 units,	0.216 liter,	139
Powder, nitrate of soda for base	764 units,	0.248 liter,	190
Powder, chlorate of potash for base	972 units,	0.318 liter,	309
Gun-cotton	590 units,	0.801 liter,	472
Picric acid	687 units,	0.780 liter,	536
Potassium picrate	578 units,	0.585 liter,	337
Gun-cotton mixed with chlorate of potash	1420 units,	0.484 liter,	680
Picric acid mixed with chlorate of potash	1424 units,	0.408 liter,	582
Picrate mixed with chlorate of potash	1422 units,	0.337 liter,	478
Nitro-glycerine	1320 units,	0.710 liter,	939

M. Papillon describes tri-nitro-glycerine as "the ideal of portable force: it burns completely, without residue, in fact gives an excess of oxygen; develops twice as much heat as powder, three and a half times more gas, and has seven times the explosive force, weight for weight, and, taken volume for volume, it possesses twelve times more energy."

M. Berthollet says: "Theoretically, there is but one substance which can surpass it—liquefied protoxide of nitrogen, whose energy is represented by 1000."

But this cannot be used; for the gases must be reduced to liquids, and hermetically sealed, in which form they must be mixed and fired to obtain the full force. But, in all these calculations, the consideration of rapidity, which must greatly heighten the effect, is not taken into account.

The extreme rapidity with which nitro-glycerine decomposes is the reason why it does not have to be confined. In the short time such decomposition takes place, the air, pressing down with a force of over a ton per square foot, cannot be raised, and consequently the body on which it rests must give way.

The many accidents which have occurred with nitro-glycerine have been generally due to ignorance or carelessness, and used properly it is safer than many other weaker explosives. Finally, the greatly superior power of nitro-glycerine, its freedom from noxious and offensive gases during combustion, the great rapidity of decomposition in explosion, and its safety when intelligently used, are destined to make it the important agent in all great public and national works where there is need of the strongest and most rapid blasting material.

CHLORATES.

By Cadet-Midshipman James H. Glennon, Third Class.

United States Naval Academy,

June 9, 1876.

Of the compounds of chlorine and oxygen, the most important is perhaps chloric acid, which gives rise to a series of compounds called chlorates. The chlorates are all soluble in water, although some are only so to a very slight extent. Mixtures containing them are very sensitive to friction and percussion, and the operation of mixing them is an extremely dangerous one. A characteristic of the class is that all the chlorates are decomposed by heat, giving off all or part of their oxygen. If potassium chlorate ($KClO_3$) be taken, it may be decomposed in accordance with the reaction,

$$KClO_3 = KCl + 3O.$$

In the case taken, however, the decomposition of potassium chlorate into potassium chloride and oxygen would be effected only at a very high temperature. But if potassium chlorate be mixed with black oxide of manganese (MnO_2), though the oxide will not be affected, the oxygen will be given off at a much lower temperature from the potassium chlorate. All the chlorates except one deflagrate when thrown on lighted charcoal. Thus, with ammonium chlorate, the following reaction takes place:

$$2(NH_4)ClO_3 + 3C = 2(NH_4)Cl + 3CO_2$$

All the chlorates give up their oxygen readily to combustible substances, especially when heated, combining with some, as phosphorus (P), sulphur (S), antimony (Sb), with sufficient violence to cause an explosion. On this account, they are much used for fireworks and colored fires; the metal with which they are combined imparting different colors to the flame.

The following are a few of the characteristic colors as imparted:

Substance.	Formula.	Color of flame.
Potassium chlorate,	$K Cl O_3$,	Violet.
Sodium chlorate,	$Na Cl O_3$,	Yellow.
Copper chlorate,	$Cu Cl_2 O_6$,	Blue.
Strontium chlorate,	$Sr Cl_2 O_6$,	Red.
Barium chlorate,	$Ba Cl_2 O_6$,	Green.

A mixture which detonates powerfully may be obtained by mixing powdered antimony tersulphide ($Sb_2 S_3$) and potassium chlorate ($K Cl O_3$) by means of a feather. Potassium chlorate is also used as the basis of many fuse-mixtures. Many are so liable to explosion as to be unfit for use. The following are taken from a treatise on explosives by Professor Hill, of the Torpedo Station at Newport:

CHLORATE MIXTURES.

Potassium chlorate, $K Cl O_3$, with rosin.

Potassium chlorate, $K Cl O_3$, with galls (Horsley's powder).

Potassium chlorate, $K Cl O_3$, with gambier (Oriental powder).

Potassium chlorate, $K Cl O_3$, with sugar (used in fuses).

Potassium chlorate, $K Cl O_3$, with potassium ferrocyanide, $K_4 Fe CN_6$.

Potassium chlorate, $K Cl O_3$, with tannin (Erhardt's powder).

Potassium chlorate, $K Cl O_3$, with sulphur (Pertuiset powder).

The mixture of potassium chlorate and potassium ferrocyanide is known as the "white or German gunpowder," and is used in the cartridges of the needle-gun. Pertuiset powder is used in explosive bullets.

Potassium chlorate ($K Cl O_3$) is composed of 31.89 parts by weight of potassium (K), 28.95 parts of chlorine (Cl), and 39.16 of oxygen (O). At the ordinary temperature it exists as white crystals, which are rhombic and tabular. It is soluble, according to Wagner, in 16 parts of water at 15.8°, in 8 parts at 35°, and in 1.6 parts at 100°. It is not altered by exposure to the air; from this fact it derives its advantage over sodium chlorate ($Na\,Cl\,O_3$), which, being hygroscopic, absorbs moisture when so exposed. Potassium chlorate, and, in fact, all the chlorates, may be prepared from chloric acid.

Chloric acid is itself prepared from barium chlorate ($Ba\,Cl_2\,O_6$) by the action of sulphuric acid ($H_2\,S\,O_4$),

$$Ba\,Cl_2\,O_6 + H_2\,S\,O_4 = 2\,H\,Cl\,O_3 + Ba\,S\,O_4$$

Any chlorate may be prepared by neutralizing chloric acid by means of the oxide or carbonate of the metal. Thus, for lead chlorate, taking lead oxide ($Pb\,O$),

$$Pb\,O + 2\,H\,Cl\,O_3 = Pb\,Cl_2\,O_6 + H_2\,O$$

and for potassium chlorate, taking potassium carbonate ($K_2\,C\,O_3$),

$$K_2\,C\,O_3 + 2\,H\,Cl\,O_3 = 2\,K\,Cl\,O_3 + H_2\,C\,O_3$$

Potassium chlorate may be better prepared as follows:

A current of chlorine (Cl) is passed into a saturated solution of potassium hydrate ($K\,H\,O$). Potassium chlorate is produced in accordance with the reaction,

$$6\,K\,H\,O + 6\,Cl = 5\,K\,Cl + K\,Cl\,O_3 + 3\,H_2\,O$$

This, however, is not economical in practice. It is therefore customary, on a large scale, to use calcium chlorate ($Ca\,Cl_2\,O_6$) instead of potassium hydrate ($K\,H\,O$). Calcium chlorate is itself prepared by passing chlorine (Cl) through a boiling solution of milk of lime ($Ca\,H_2\,O_2$). By the addition of potassium chloride ($K\,Cl$) to calcium chlorate, potassium chlorate is formed, which may be separated from the calcium chloride ($Ca\,Cl_2$), formed by crystallization,

$$Ca\,Cl_2\,O_6 + 2\,K\,Cl = 2\,K\,Cl\,O_3 + Ca\,Cl_2$$

In order that much energy may be brought into action on the explosion of substances, the volume occupied by the results of the explosion must be very great as compared with the original volume. It might be said, not taking into consideration the expansion of the gases formed by the heat produced, that the work done will be proportional to the resulting volumes as compared with the original.

Now, the products of the decomposition of ammonium chlorate ($(N\,H_4)\,Cl\,O_3$) are all gaseous.

Thus,

$$(N\,H_4)\,Cl\,O_3 = (N\,H_4)\,Cl + 3\,O$$

Ammonium chloride ($(N\,H_4)\,Cl$), at the ordinary temperature, is a solid; but, at the high temperature produced, it exists as ammonia ($N\,H_3$) and chlorhydric acid ($H\,Cl$), both of which are gaseous. If two molecules of potassium chlorate be taken from it, we may obtain three molecules of oxygen (O) and two molecules of potassium chloride. But the potassium chloride formed, being a solid, occupies but very little space. The three volumes of oxygen are, however, gaseous. In the case of ammonium chlorate, however, we obtain not only the three volumes of oxygen, but two other volumes of gas, or, in all, five volumes. Now, as a molecule of ammonium chlorate weighs only $\frac{100.5}{122.6}$ as much as a molecule of potassium chlorate, it can be seen that for equal weights of the two, nearly twice as great a volume of gas can be obtained from ammonium chlorate as from potassium chlorate.

Ammonium chlorate has another advantage over other chlorates. This is that no residue is left when it is decomposed. In the case of potassium chlorate, the potassium chloride is solid, and remains as a residue. Unfortunately, however, ammonium chlorate explodes even at ordinary temperatures from no apparent reason, so that it is very dangerous to use it. Consequently it has never gained the place that the less explosive potassium salt has. It has been found in pyrotechny that the perchlorate of potassium ($K\,Cl_2\,O_4$) is preferable to the chlorate, being less dangerous to manipulate, and, owing to the different arrangement of the atoms, it emits more light.

Barium chlorate is prepared by saturating aqueous chloric acid with barium hydrate or carbonate,

$$2\,H\,Cl\,O_3 + Ba\,H_2\,O_2 = Ba\,Cl_2\,O_6 + 2\,H_2\,O$$
$$2\,H\,Cl\,O_3 + Ba\,C\,O_3 = Ba\,Cl_2\,O_6 + H_2\,O + C\,O_2$$

It detonates powerfully with combustibles, producing a green flame when heated with sulphur (Duflos), and emitting a bright flashing light with sulphuric acid. According to Hutstein, it emits light on crystallizing.

Percentage composition.

Barium (Ba)	45.22
Oxygen (O)	31.68
Chlorine (Cl)	23.10
	100.00

Calcium chlorate is prepared like barium chlorate. With water, it forms deliquescent crystals. When heated, these first dissolve in their water of crystallization, and decompose at a higher temperature.

Percentage composition.

Calcium (Ca)	19.42
Oxygen (O)	46.60
Chlorine (Cl)	33.98
	100.00

Cupric chlorate ($Cu\ Cl_2\ O_6$) detonates on red-hot carbon, and is used in pyrotechny for the production of a green fire.

Percentage composition.

Copper (Cu)	27.64
Chlorine (Cl)	30.52
Oxygen (O)	41.84
	100.00

Magnesium chlorate ($Mg\ Cl_2\ O_6$) is easily soluble in alcohol. With water, it forms deliquescent crystals, which melt at 40°, and give off their water at 120°.

Percentage composition.

Magnesium (Mg)	12.63
Chlorine (Cl)	38.64
Oxygen (O)	50.53
	100.00

Uranium chlorate ($Ur\ Cl_2\ O_6$) decomposes spontaneously, evolving chlorine and oxygen.

Percentage composition.

Uranium (Ur)	41.96
Chlorine (Cl)	24.47
Oxygen (O)	33.57
	100.00

Manganese chlorate ($Mn\ Cl_2\ O_6$) is known only in solution.

Percentage composition.

Manganese (Mn)	24.89
Chlorine (Cl)	31.67
Oxygen (O)	43.44
	100.00

Mercuric chlorate ($Hg\ Cl_2\ O_6$) is obtained by dissolving mercuric oxide in warm chloric acid; mercuric chloride crystallizes out and mercuric chlorate remains in solution. Mercuric chlorate forms with water crystals which are deliquescent. It is resolved by heat into oxygen, mercurous chloride, and mercury. It does not deflagrate on red-hot charcoal.

Percentage composition.

Mercury (Hg)	54.64
Chlorine (Cl)	19.13
Oxygen (O)	26.23
	100.00

Silver chlorate ($Ag\ Cl\ O_3$) deflagrates on red-hot coals. When mixed with sulphur, it detonates violently on very slight pressure. Chlorhydric acid ($H\ Cl$), nitric acid ($H\ NO_3$), and acetic acid ($C_2\ H_4\ O_2$) convert it into the chloride.

Percentage composition.

Silver (Ag)	56.39
Chlorine (Cl)	18.54
Oxygen (O)	25.07
	100.00

Sodium chlorate ($Na\ Cl\ O_3$) is, next to potassium and ammonium chlorates, perhaps the most important of the chlorates. It would perhaps be used even more than the potassium chlorate, were it not for the fact that it is hygroscopic, and consequently cannot be kept in the air for any length of time without absorbing moisture. The gas resulting from the explosion of equal weights of the potassium and sodium chlorate is the greater in the case of the sodium chlorates.

Percentage composition.

Sodium (Na)	21.60
Chlorine (Cl)	33.33
Oxygen (O)	45.07
	100.00

Of the other chlorates, some are known only in solution; some, like the ammonium chlorate, decompose spontaneously; while others, like the potassium chlorate ($K\ Cl\ O_3$), are permanent, but all to some extent soluble in water except one.

The two following analyses are of the same sample of powder:

ANALYSIS OF GUNPOWDER.

BY CADET-MIDSHIPMAN HARRY P. HUSE, THIRD CLASS, U. S. N. A., 1876.

U. S. NAVAL ACADEMY LABORATORY,
May 30, 1876.

The following are the results of an analysis of gunpowder No. 2 made in this laboratory. The gunpowder was unglazed, and had a slightly brownish tinge. Some impurities were present, preventing any very accurate results:

I. NITER.

Weight of crystal + powder	10.5989
Weight of crystal	6.0019
Weight of powder	4.5970
Weight of evaporating-dish and niter	69.4857
Weight of evaporating-dish	66.0499
Weight of niter	3.4358

$$3.4358 \div 4.5970 = .7474$$

$$\therefore \varphi = 74.74\%$$

II. SULPHUR.

Weight of crystal + powder	9.1048
Weight of crystal	6.0026
Weight of powder	3.1022
Weight of Ba S O_4 + crucible × filter-ash	14.0707
Weight of crucible	11.5640
Weight of Ba S O_4 + filter-ash	2.5067
Weight of filter-ash	0.0003
Weight of Ba S O_4	2.5064

2.5064 grams Ba S O_4 = .3442 grams S, equivalent to 11.09%

$\therefore \varphi = 11.09\%$

III. CARBON.

Weight of crystal + powder	10.0551
Weight of crystal	6.0069
Weight of powder	4.0482
Weight of carbon + filter	1.1497
Weight of filter	0.4905
Weight of carbon	0.6592

$0.6592 \div 4.0482 = .1629$

$\therefore \varphi = 16.29\%$

IV. MOISTURE.

Weight of glass + powder	46.9350
Weight of glass	38.3407
Weight of powder	8.5943

Weight of glass + powder	46.9350
Weight of glass + powder (air-bath, 24 hours at 60° C)	46.8524
Loss of weight	.0826

$$.0826 \div 8.5943 = .0096$$
$$\therefore \varphi = .96\%$$

RESULTS.

Niter	74.74%
Sulphur	11.09%
Carbon	13.21%
Moisture	.96%
	100.00

The results in the case of the carbon not being accurate, owing to the fact that the ammonium sulphydrate did not dissolve all the sulphur, the percentage of carbon was determined by difference.

METHOD OF ANALYSIS.

The analysis was conducted in the following manner:

To determine the niter:

Weigh out from 4 to 5 grams of the powder, and place it in a beaker-glass, covering it with about 50 cm^3. of distilled water; then boil it for some time. When it has been heated for a sufficient length of time to dissolve the niter, filter the solution, and wash the residue with hot water until no signs of niter occur in the filtrate.

The filtrate is then poured into an evaporating-dish, the weight of which has been previously ascertained, and evaporated to dryness over a water-bath. The dish is then thoroughly dried by ignition, and, when cool, weighed. The difference in the weights of the dish before and after the experiment will give the weight of the niter.

To determine the amount of carbon:

Weigh out about 4 grams of the powder and place it in a beaker-flask, covering it with from 20 to 30 cm^3. of ammonium sulphydrate. This will dissolve out the sulphur. We then filter it through a filter-paper previously dried at 100° C. and weighed, washing out the niter by means of boiling water. Then dry the filter, first in an evaporating-dish, then in the air-bath at 100° C., and weigh it. This weight, minus the weight of the filter-paper, gives the weight of carbon.

To determine the sulphur:

Place from 3 to 4 grams of the powder in a beaker-flask, and cover it with a small amount of nitric acid (fuming). Heat gently over a water-bath, adding, from time to time, small quantities of potassium chlorate. The sulphur and carbon are oxidized to sulphuric acid and carbon dioxide; the latter going off as a gas, and the former uniting with the water resulting from the decomposition of the nitric acid, and with the potassium of the potassium chlorate. During the first part of the operation, nitrous fumes are given off, and, when these cease, the flask is filled with a greenish gas, chlorine and oxides of chlorine. When the oxidation is completed, the solution will be perfectly clear, and of a yellowish-brown color. It is now transferred to an evaporating-dish, and evaporated to dryness; when it has reached this state, hydrochloric acid is added until the solution is strongly acid. It is again evaporated to dryness, and very dilute chlorhydric acid added. The object of all this is to drive off the chloric acid by decomposing the excess of potassium chlorate by chlorhydric acid, forming potassium chloride and oxides of chlorine. The solution is then heated, and the sulphuric acid is precipitated with barium chloride, and the liquid portion filtered off. The precipitate is thoroughly washed with hot water, removing all the traces of barium and potassium chlorides. The filter-paper containing the residue is dried, placed in a porcelain capsule, and ignited. The weight of the capsule being known, as also that of the ash of the filter-paper, we may find the amount of barium sulphate, and from that the weight of the sulphur. The presence of traces of barium chloride in the precipitate would be shown by its grayish color.

To determine the moisture:

The powder is placed in a watch-glass, covered over with another glass, the two being held together by a spring. It is then placed in the air-bath for about twenty-four hours, and kept at a temperature of about 60°. It is taken out, weighed when cold, and the difference in weight before and after the heating ascertained. This difference is the weight of the moisture.

ANALYSIS OF GUNPOWDER No. 2.

BY CADET-MIDSHIPMAN H. KIMMEL, THIRD CLASS, 1876.

Gunpowder is a mechanical mixture of niter, charcoal, sulphur, and moisture.

NITER.

The separation of the niter from the other constituents depends upon the fact that it is soluble in water, while the sulphur and charcoal are not, and that it is much more soluble in hot water than in cold. The niter is then obtained, free from moisture, by evaporating the solution to dryness, and then igniting it.

I put a weighed quantity of powder in a beaker about half full of distilled water, and heated it upon an iron stand, being careful not to allow the water to boil, as, in that case, some of the niter might be lost. It was heated until the powder lost its granular condition, then allowed to settle, after which the solution was filtered. Hot water was added to the residue in the beaker, which was passed through the filter, and the charcoal and sulphur were washed with hot water, until the water passing through the filter showed no traces of potassium when tested in the flame. I then poured the filtrate into a perfectly clean evaporating-dish, previously weighed, and evaporated it to dryness over the water-bath, and then ignited it to incipient fusion to remove the last traces of moisture. I allowed the dish to cool, and then weighed it, and the difference between this weight and the weight of the dish was the weight of niter in the given weight of powder, from which the per cent. of nitre can be calculated.

The following was the result obtained:

Weight of glass and powder	12.8278
Weight of glass	6.0014
Weight of powder	6.8264
Weight of dish and niter	70.1358
Weight of dish	65.0745
Weight of niter	5.0613

$$\frac{5.0613}{6.8264} \times 100 = 74.14\ \%\ \text{of niter.}$$

SULPHUR.

A quantity of powder was weighed out in the same manner as for the determination of the niter, put into a beaker-flask, and covered with strong nitric acid. The flask was heated gently, and, from time to time, small pieces of potassium chlorate were added to aid in the oxidation of the sulphur and carbon; the former being oxidized to sulphuric acid and the latter to carbon dioxide. The potassium nitrate and chlorate were converted into potassium sulphate and potassium chloride, and there was also left an excess of potassium chlorate. It was then put into an evaporating-dish and evaporated about one-half, then treated with strong chlorhydric acid, which converted the remaining potassium chlorate into potassium chloride, and oxides of chlorine were given off. I heated the liquid until it was evaporated to dryness and the oxides of chlorine were all given off, and then added chlorhydric acid and distilled water, and heated until completely dissolved. It was then poured into a beaker, diluted with distilled water, heated gently, and a solution of barium chloride was added to it. The sulphuric acid acted upon the barium chloride, and barium sulphate was formed and deposited as a white precipitate. The barium sulphate was boiled with distilled water to dissolve all the potassium chloride, so that it could pass through the filter, and filtered through a filter the weight of whose ash was known. After allowing the filter to dry, it was placed with its contents in a porcelain crucible, which had been previously ignited and weighed. The crucible with its contents was ignited until the paper was reduced to a white ash. When cool, it was weighed, and the total weight, minus the weight of filter-ash and crucible, was equal to weight of barium sulphate, from which the weight, and therefore the per cent. of sulphur, can be obtained.

Weight of glass and powder	8.6144
Weight of glass	6.0043
Weight of powder	2.6101
Weight of dish and Ba S O_4	13.1262
Weight of dish and filter-ash (.0003)	10.9985
Weight of Ba S O_4	2.1277

$$2.1277 \times \frac{32}{233} = .2922 \text{ weight of sulphur.}$$

$$\frac{.2922}{2.6101} \times 100 = 11.20\,\% \text{ of sulphur.}$$

MOISTURE.

For this purpose, two watch-glasses, held together by a wire-spring, contain the powder. The apparatus is weighed, and a given weight of powder is then put between the glasses. The glasses are opened a little, so as to allow the moisture to escape, and then put into an air-bath, where they are kept twenty-four hours at a temperature of 60° C. They are then taken out, the glasses shut to keep out all moisture, and weighed: the difference between the weight before and after being placed in the bath is the weight of the moisture, and from this the per cent. of moisture can be obtained.

Weight of glasses, spring, and powder	42.8483
Weight of glasses and spring	32.3359
Weight of powder	10.5124
Weight with moisture	42.8483
Weight without moisture	42.7480
Weight of moisture	.1003

$$\frac{.1003}{10.5124} \times 100 = .95\% \text{ of moisture.}$$

CHARCOAL.

The separation of charcoal from the other constituents depends upon the solubility of niter in hot water and sulphur in ammonium sulphydrate. The weighed powder is placed in a beaker-flask and completely covered with ammonium sulphydrate and heated very gently over the water-bath. In a few moments the sulphur is dissolved, and the carbon and niter remain. The mixture is filtered through a weighed filter, and thoroughly washed with hot water to remove the niter. It is washed with water and sulphydrate until no traces of niter or sulphur remain in the filter. The filter is then placed in the air-bath, where it remains for twenty-four hours at 100° C., thus removing all moisture. At the end of that time it is removed and weighed; the weight, minus weight of filter, being weight of charcoal, from which per cent. of charcoal may be determined.

Weight of glass and powder	17.0269
Weight of glass	6.6093
Weight of powder	10.4176
Weight of filter and charcoal	2.059
Weight of filter	.3706
Weight of charcoal	1.6884

$$\frac{1.6884}{10.4176} \times 100 \times 16.20\% \text{ of charcoal.}$$

As there appears to be some inaccuracy in the work, and this is most likely to be in the charcoal, we will take the per cent. of this constituent by difference:

$$100\% - 86.29\% = 13.71\% \text{ of carbon.}$$

SUMMARY.

Niter	74.14
Sulphur	11.20
Carbon	13.71
Moisture	.95
	100.00

ANALYSIS OF GUNPOWDER, REGULATION No. 12.

CANNON-POWDER, MADE BY ORIENTAL POWDER COMPANY, SPECIFIC GRAVITY 1.754.

By Cadet-Midshipman F. C. Skinner, Third Class, 1876.

DETERMINATION OF NITER.

The separation of the niter from the other ingredients of the gunpowder depends upon the fact that it is soluble in hot water, while sulphur and carbon are not.

The manner of carrying on the analysis is as follows: A watch-glass is first weighed alone and afterward with a quantity of gunpowder: the difference in weight is the weight of the gunpowder. The powder is next put into a beaker, covered with distilled water, and heated until the water boils. By this process, the niter is dissolved by the water, and may be separated from the sulphur and carbon by filtration. An evaporating-dish is then weighed, after having been ignited and cooled, and the filtrate is evaporated to dryness in this dish over a water-bath. The dish with its contents is again ignited to incipient fusion to remove the last traces of moisture.

After the dish has been allowed to cool, it is again weighed, and the difference between its two weights is the weight of the niter.

Having the weight of powder taken, and the weight of the niter obtained from it, it is very easy to calculate what per cent. of niter the powder contains. In gunpowder No. 4, the following results were obtained:

Weight of watch-glass + powder	14.1453
Weight of watch-glass — powder	6.0026
Weight of powder taken	8.1427

Weight of evaporating-dish + KNO_3	56.4263
Weight of evaporating-dish − KNO_3	50.4798
Weight of KNO_3	5.9465

$$\frac{5.9465}{8.1427} \times 100 = 73.03\,\% \text{ of niter.}$$

DETERMINATION OF SULPHUR.

The gunpowder is weighed in the same manner as before, and is put into a beaker-flask and covered with strong nitric acid. The flask is then warmed and crystals of potassium chlorate are thrown in from time to time. The sulphur and carbon are oxidized, the former to H_2SO_4 and the latter to CO_2. The potassium nitrate and chlorate are converted into K_2SO_4 and potassium chloride, and there is also left an excess of potassium chlorate. The liquid is then put into an evaporating-dish and treated with chlorhydric acid, which converts the remaining potassium chlorate into potassium chloride, and oxides of chlorine are given off. Heat the liquid until it is evaporated to dryness, and the oxides of chlorine are all driven off. Dissolve the residue in chlorhydric acid and add distilled water. When the solution is complete, transfer the liquid to a beaker, dilute with distilled water, heat to gentle ebullition, and add a solution of barium chloride.

The sulphuric acid of the solution acts upon the barium chloride, and forms barium sulphate, which is precipitated as a white powder. The liquid is decanted after the precipitate has been allowed to settle, and the barium sulphate is then boiled with distilled water, which removes the potassium chloride, and we have left nothing but barium sulphate. The water with which the sulphate is mixed is then passed through a filter, the weight of whose ash is known. After being allowed to dry, the filter-paper with its contents is placed in a porcelain crucible, which has been previously ignited, cooled, and weighed. The crucible is then heated until the filter-paper is reduced to a white ash, when it is allowed to cool.

When entirely cooled, the crucible with its contents is weighed, and from this weight is subtracted the weight of the crucible and ash of the filter-paper: the remainder is the weight of barium sulphate.

The method of calculating the weight of sulphur in this weight of barium sulphate depends upon the law of definite proportions.

The atomic weight of sulphur is 32; the molecular weight of $BaSO_4$ is 233: therefore the weight of sulphur is $\frac{32}{233}$ of the weight of barium sulphate.

Now, having the weight of sulphur, we may calculate what proportion it bears to the weight of the powder taken:

Weight of watch-glass + powder................	7.5233
Weight of watch-glass — powder................	6.0019
Weight of powder taken......................	1.5214
Weight of crucible + $BaSO_4$ and ash of filter-paper.	11.8561
Weight of crucible — $BaSO_4$ and ash of filter-paper.	10.7704
	1.0857
Weight of ash of filter-paper....................	.0003
Weight of barium sulphate....................	1.0854

$$\frac{32}{233} \times 1.0854 = .14907$$

$$\frac{.14907}{1.5214} \times 100 = 9.798\,\% \text{ of sulphur.}$$

DETERMINATION OF MOISTURE.

For determining the moisture, two watch-glasses, held together by a wire-spring, are used. This apparatus is weighed, and then a quantity of powder is put between the glasses, and the whole is weighed: the difference in the weights is the weight of the powder.

The glasses are then opened a little, so as to allow the vapor to escape, and are put into an air-bath, where they are kept for twenty-four hours at a temperature of 60° C. They are then taken out, and the glasses are shut, and the whole is again weighed. The loss in weight is due to the loss in moisture. From this weight of moisture we calculate the per cent. of moisture which the powder contains:

Weight of glasses + powder	46.6900
Weight of glasses — powder	35.5172
Weight of powder taken	11.1728
Weight of glass + powder before heating	46.6900
Weight of glass + powder after heating	46.5470
Weight of moisture	.1430

$$\frac{.1430}{11.1728} \times 100 = 1.28\,\% \text{ of moisture.}$$

DETERMINATION OF CARBON.

The separation of the carbon from the other constituents of the gunpowder depends upon the solubility of sulphur in ammonium sulphydrate and of niter in hot water.

The powder, after having been weighed, is put into a beaker-flask and covered with ammonium sulphydrate and allowed to stand for a few moments. The sulphur is dissolved and the carbon and niter remain. The mixture is filtered on a weighed filter, and thoroughly washed with boiling water, which dissolves all the niter and leaves all the carbon on the filter.

The filter with the carbon is now put into an air-bath, and remains there twenty-four hours, thus taking away all the moisture.

Finally, the carbon and filter are weighed, and, subtracting the weight of the filter, we find that of the carbon. From this weight of carbon we calculate the per cent. of carbon in the powder:

Weight of watch-glass + powder	12.4373
Weight of watch-glass — powder	6.0025
Weight of powder taken......................	6.4348
Weight of filter-paper + carbon...............	1.5041
Weight of filter-paper — carbon	.5173
Weight of carbon	.9868

$$\frac{.9868}{6.4348} \times 100 = 15.34\% \text{ of carbon.}$$

SUMMARY.

Niter	73.03
Sulphur	9.80
Moisture	1.28
Carbon	15.34
	99.45%

ANALYSIS OF GUNPOWDER-CAKE.

By Cadet-Midshipman James H. Glennon, Third Class.

United States Naval Academy,
June 9, 1876.

Gunpowder is composed of three chief constituents, nitre (KNO_3), carbon (C), and sulphur (S). Besides these, there is generally another constituent in ordinary gunpowder. This constituent is moisture, which enters the powder when exposed. In analyzing gunpowder, the first thing necessary is to determine the niter and then the other three constituents.

DETERMINATION OF THE NITER.

From four to five grams of the powder are poured upon a watch-glass, the weight of which is known. The watch-glass must be free from dust and moisture; if any is present, it can be seen, and should be wiped off. The watch-glass and powder are weighed together. The weight of both, minus the weight of the glass, is the weight of the powder taken.

In order that we may be certain that no powder is lost, it is well to weigh the glass after the powder has been taken. In the case in question, gunpowder cake, some powder is almost certain to remain upon the glass, as the powder is unglazed. The powder is emptied from the watch-glass into a beaker, which has previously been cleaned, and rinsed with distilled water. About 50 cm^3. of distilled water is next added to the powder, and it is then boiled for a certain length of time. The object of this is to dissolve the niter. Care must be taken that the boiling is not too tumultuous, as niter may be lost mechanically. The liquid is next poured upon a filter. As neither sulphur nor carbon are dissolved by water, the filtrate contains only niter. But it is not certain that all the niter has been dissolved. Consequently, fresh portions of boiling water are added from time to time to the filter, until a drop of the filtrate, taken from the lower extremity of the funnel, no longer colors the flame violet. The filtrate is next placed in an evaporating-dish, the weight of which has been previously determined. In order to find the exact weight of the dish, it must be first cleaned and rinsed with distilled water, and then dried by ignition. The filtrate is evaporated in this dish over a water-bath. The reason for evaporating it this way is, that if the heat were too strong or too sudden, the niter might be decomposed. When evaporated to dryness, it is ignited to incipient fusion to free it completely from moisture. After having attained the temperature of the balance-room, the niter and dish are weighed. The weight of the dish and niter, minus the weight of the dish, is the weight of the niter. From this and the weight of the powder, the per cent. of niter may be determined:

	Grams.
Weight of watch-glass and powder.............	10.3425
Weight of watch-glass	6.0019
Weight of powder............................	4.3406
Weight of evaporating-dish and niter...........	65.3730
Weight of evaporating-dish	62.1875
Weight of niter	3.1855

$$\frac{3.1855\times 100}{4.3406}=73.38$$

Per cent. of niter, 73.38.

DETERMINATION OF THE MOISTURE.

A pair of watch-glasses of the same size are so placed as to be pressed together rather tightly by a clamp, so that when placed in position the two resemble a double convex lens. After having been heated for a certain length of time in an air-bath to drive off all the moisture, and then allowed to cool, they are weighed. From 7 to 8 grams of powder are next placed between the glasses, space being left at the edges to allow free access to the air. The whole is next placed in an air-bath, kept at a certain fixed temperature, and left for 24 hours. At the end of that time, it is supposed that all the moisture will be driven off, and, after cooling, it is weighed. The weight of the whole after heating, minus that before heating, is the weight of the moisture. From this and the weight of the powder, we compute the per cent. of moisture, as in the case of the niter:

	Grams.
Weight of watch-glass + gunpowder............	38.5833
Weight of watch-glass	31.3346
Weight of gunpowder........................	7.2487
Weight of watch-glass + gunpowder before heating......................................	38.5833
Weight of watch-glass + gunpowder heated 24 hours at 60°............................	38.5238
Weight of moisture	.0595

$$\frac{.0595}{7.2487} \times 100 = .809 \text{ per cent. of moisture.}$$

DETERMINATION OF THE CARBON.

The powder is weighed as in the preceding cases, and is placed in a beaker-flask. Enough ammonium sulphydrate ($(NH_4)HS$) is added to the powder to completely cover it. The whole is next very gently heated over a water-bath, and is then poured upon a weighed filter. The object of adding the ammonium sulphydrate is to dissolve the sulphur. In heating the liquid, care should be taken that the heating is not too strong, as the sulphur is apt to collect and sink to the bottom. Consequently, it is heated on a water-bath. In the first determination of the carbon, in the present instance, a result too large by 2 per cent. was obtained, perhaps owing to the fact that the collected sulphur was poured upon a filter, and remained with the carbon. The filter upon which the liquid is poured is one whose weight is known. Supposing all the sulphur to have been dissolved by the ammonium sulphydrate, the residue on the filter contains carbon and niter. Boiling water is therefore poured upon the filter until niter is known not to be present.

The filter is next dried, first in an evaporating-dish, and then for twenty-four hours in an air-bath at 100° C. At the end of that time it is allowed to cool, and is then weighed. The weight of the filter and carbon, minus the weight of the filter, is the weight of the carbon. From this and the weight of the powder, it is easy to compute the per cent. of carbon:

	Grams.
Weight of watch-glass + gunpowder	11.6648
Weight of watch-glass	6.0096
Weight of gunpowder	5.6552
Weight of carbon + filter	1.3140
Weight of filter	.4325
Weight of carbon	.8815

Per cent. of carbon, 15.5.

DETERMINATION OF THE SULPHUR.

Two or three grams of the powder are placed in a beaker-flask, and covered with a small quantity of fuming nitric acid. This is heated gently over a water-bath, and from time to time small quantities of potassium chlorate are added. Both nitric acid and potassium chlorate are powerful oxidizing agents, and through their joint agency all the carbon and sulphur are oxidized; the first to carbonic acid (CO_2), and the second to sulphuric acid (H_2SO_4). The carbon dioxide, being a gas, goes off, while the sulphuric acid combines with the potassium of the potassium chlorate and the water resulting from the decomposition of the nitric acid. During the first part of the operation nitrous fumes are given off, and when these cease the flask becomes filled with a greenish gas consisting of chlorine and the oxides thereof. When the oxidation has been completed, the solution is perfectly clear and of a yellowish-brown color. It is then transferred to an evaporating-dish, which is placed upon the water-bath, and chlorhydric acid is added. The object of this is to decompose the excess of potassium chlorate forming potassium chloride and the oxides of chlorine, which last, being gaseous, pass off. Fresh portions of the chlorhydric acid are added until these oxides are no longer formed, which is shown by the fact that there is no effervescence when the acid is added. The liquid is then evaporated to dryness, a fresh portion of chlorhydric acid is added, and to the solution is added barium chloride ($Ba\,Cl_2$). This acts upon the sulphuric acid and potassium sulphate, and barium sulphate is precipitated. This barium sulphate contains all the sulphur of the original powder. It is therefore separated from the liquid portion by filtering through a filter the weight of whose ash is known. The residue on the filter is thoroughly washed with water, in order to remove all traces of barium and potassium chlorides. The filter is next dried, placed in a small porcelain crucible, and ignited until the substance in the crucible exists as a white ash. The weight of this crucible is known. When the ignition is completed, the crucible is allowed to cool, and is then weighed. The weight of the crucible and ash, minus the weight of the crucible and filter-ash, is the weight of the barium sulphate.

	Grams.
Weight of watch-glass + gunpowder	8.6051
Weight of watch-glass	6.0024
Weight of gunpowder	2.6027
Weight of capsule, filter-ash, and $Ba\,S\,O_4$.........	12.7568
Weight of capsule	10.6465
Weight of filter-ash and $Ba\,S\,O_4$	2.1103
Weight of filter-ash	.0003
Weight of barium sulphate	2.1100

Weight of sulphur $= \frac{32}{233}$ weight of $Ba\,S\,O_4 = .28978$ grams.

Per cent. of sulphur, 11.1.

SUMMARY OF RESULTS.

Niter	73.38%
Moisture	.81
Carbon	15.50
Sulphur	11.10
Total	100.79%

The error is probably in the carbon, as some sulphur is almost certain to separate and remain on the filter with the carbon.

NOTE G.

Plan for a Naval School, as originally submitted by Commander Buchanan.

[From the Original Document in the Navy Department, at Washington.]

The Superintendent is to be appointed by the Secretary of the Navy from the list of captains or commanders. The Superintendent will have the immediate government of the institution, will be responsible for its management, direct all academic duties, and command all professors and others connected with the school. He will frame a code of rules and regulations for the internal government of the school, to be submitted to the Secretary of the Navy for his approval.

Professors and instructors are to be selected from the list of lieutenants, chaplains, professors, passed midshipmen, and teachers in the Navy.

Professors, under the orders of the Superintendent, will constitute a board for the transaction of business, will conduct the examinations during the course, decide on the merits of the midshipmen, report on the system of instruction, and suggest any improvements or alterations which experience may dictate.

Every applicant for admission to the school must be of good moral character, not less than thirteen nor more than sixteen years of age; be examined by the surgeon of the institution to ascertain if he be free from all deformity, deafness, nearness or other disease of sight, disease or infirmity of any kind which would disqualify him from performing the active and arduous duties of a sea-life. He must be able to read and write well, and be familiar with geography and arithmetic. The academic board will examine him on these branches and certify to his capacity for admission into the school.

When an acting midshipman receives his appointment he is to be attached to the naval school, subject to the exigencies of the service. At the expiration of one year, should his conduct and proficiency meet with the approbation of the Superintendent and Academic Board, he will be retained in service and sent to sea. After performing sea-duty for six months, and receiving a favorable report of his conduct during that time from his commander, he will be entitled to a warrant bearing the date of his acting appointment. Otherwise he will be dropped from the lists and returned to his friends.

A midshipman after serving three years at sea, as now required, and having received a short leave of absence, at the discretion of the Department, to visit his friends, will report, at its expiration, to the Naval School to pursue his course of studies preparatory to his final examination. All midshipmen on shore, not on leave, will be ordered to the Naval School.

The course of studies will include English grammar and composition, arithmetic, geography, and history, gunnery and the use of steam, Spanish and French languages, and such other branches desirable to the accomplishment of a naval officer as circumstances may render practicable.

The professors will be required to keep records of all the recitations, and report weekly to the Superintendent the progress and relative merit of the students. From these weekly reports the Superintendent will make quarterly reports to the Secretary of the Navy.

Classes will be arranged according to the acquirements and capacity of the midshipmen.

The final examination for promotion will embrace all the branches taught at the school.

All midshipmen at the Naval School must provide themselves with such books as are necessary to pursue their studies, a quadrant, their uniform, and bedding.

A sloop of war or brig may be connected with the institution as a school of practice in seamanship, evolutions, and gunnery.

The board annually appointed under the regulations of the Navy for the examination of midshipmen for promotion are to inspect generally the management of the institution, and report to the Secretary of the Navy on its condition and the means of improving it.

Note H.

Schedule of subjects represented by the books of the Library.

THEOLOGY.

1. Sacred writings, commentaries, criticism.
2. Natural theology and the evidences of Christianity.
3. Miscellaneous theological works.
4. Ecclesiastical history.

MENTAL AND MORAL PHILOSOPHY.

1. Mental philosophy and logic.
2. Moral philosophy and education.

HISTORY.

1. General treatises and lectures on history, universal history, chronology, &c.
2. Ancient history, antiquities, mythology, numismatics.
3. Continental Europe.
4. England, Ireland, Scotland.
5. Asia, Africa, Australia.
6. North and South America.
7. Naval and military history.

BIOGRAPHY.

1. Collective biography.
2. British biography.

3. American biography.
4. Miscellaneous biography.
5. Naval and military biography.

GEOGRAPHY AND TERRESTRIAL PHYSICS.

1. Universal, descriptive, and historical geography, ethnography, &c.
2. Physical geography, geology, and meteorology.
3. Voyages, travels, geographical exploration and surveys.
4. Atlases, maps, &c

MATHEMATICAL SCIENCE AND ARTS.

1. Mathematics in general, including collected works, histories, dictionaries, journals, &c.
2. Arithmetic and algebra.
3. Geometry, trigonometry, descriptive and analytical geometry, geometry of curves, &c.
4. Calculus of differential, integral, and other functions.
5. Mathematical tables and treatises on use of instruments.
6. Mensuration, surveying, engineering, &c.
7. Miscellaneous mathematical works.

ASTRONOMY AND GEODESY.

1. Histories and journals of astronomy.
2. General, physical, and practical astronomy.
3. Observations, observatories, and treatises on use of instruments.
4. Ephemerides, catalogues, maps, and tables.
5. Cometography.
6. Miscellaneous astronomical works.
7. Geodesy, geodical operations, and cartography.

PHYSICAL SCIENCE AND ARTS.

1. Natural philosophy in general.

2. Mechanics, (including statics, dynamics, &c.)
3. Optics, acoustics.
4. Light, heat, electricity, and magnetism.
5. Chemistry and chemical arts.
6. Miscellaneous works.

NATURAL HISTORY.

1. Natural history in general.
2. Zoology, anatomy, physiology, botany.
3. Geology, mineralogy.

MILITARY SCIENCE AND ARTS.

1. Artillery, small-arms, pyrotechny.
2. Infantry-tactics, &c.
3. Military engineering, science of war, &c.
4. Military organization, laws, courts, statistics, &c.
5. Military dictionaries, journals, and miscellanies.

NAVAL SCIENCE AND ARTS.

1. Navigation, nautical astronomy, nautical surveying, tables and treatises on use of instruments.
2. Maritime geography, hydrography.
3. Naval architecture, wood, iron, and composite ship-building, docks, and other constructions.
4. Seamanship, naval tactics, rigging, stowage, sail and mast making, &c.
5. Steam-navigation, steam-engineering.
6. Naval ordnance, naval gunnery, torpedoes, ammunition, &c.
7. Naval signals.
8. Naval organization, naval regulations, registers, laws courts, statistics, &c.
9. Nautical dictionaries, journals, and miscellanies.

ARTS AND MANUFACTURES.

1. General and miscellaneous works.
2. Steam-engine and other machinery.
3. Civil engineering.
4. Civil architecture, drawing, painting, and sculpture.

LAW AND POLITICS.

1. Constitutional and international law, maritime, military, and naval law, treatises on evidence, United States Supreme Court decisions, law dictionaries, United States Statutes at Large, United States Revised Statutes, British and American admiralty decisions in prize cases, &c.
2. Political economy.
3. Government documents, executive and congressional, reports, &c.
4. Miscellaneous works.

LITERATURE.

1. Grammar and language.
2. Dictionaries of language.
3. Rhetoric and criticism.
4. Poetry and drama.
5. Fiction.
6. General literature, histories of literature, &c.

POLYGRAPHY.

1. Encyclopedias, dictionaries of the arts and sciences, collected works, &c.
2. Proceedings, reports, and transactions of academies and societies.
3. Scientific, art, literary journals and magazines.

BIBLIOGRAPHY.

1. American and foreign bibliography.

NOTE I.

List of officers holding seats at the Academic Board.

SUPERINTENDENTS.

Assumed command.

Sept. 3, 1845. Commander Franklin Buchanan.
Mar. 15, 1847. Commander George P. Upshur.
July 1, 1850. Commander Cornelius K. Stribling.
Nov. 1, 1853. Commander Louis M. Goldsborough.
Sept. 15, 1857. Captain George S. Blake.
Sept. 9, 1865. Rear-Admiral David D. Porter.
Dec. 1, 1869. Commodore John L. Worden.
Sept. 22, 1874. Rear-Admiral C. R. P. Rodgers.

COMMANDANTS OF MIDSHIPMEN.

Reported for duty.

Oct. 1, 1845. Lieut. James Harman Ward.
Sept. 1, 1847. Lieut. Sidney Smith Lee.
July 1, 1850. Lieut. Thomas T. Craven.
May 28, 1855. Lieut. Joseph F. Green.
Mar. 22, 1858. Commander Thomas T. Craven.
Sept. 21, 1860. Lieut. C. R. P. Rodgers.
Sept. 22, 1861. Lieut. George W. Rodgers.
May 18, 1862. Lieut. Edward Simpson.
Aug. 3, 1863. Commander Thomas G. Corbin.
Sept. 23, 1863. Commander Donald McN. Fairfax.
Oct. 11, 1865. Lieutenant-Commander Stephen B. Luce.
Sept. 30, 1868. Capt. Napoleon B. Harrison.

Feb. 1, 1870. Capt. Samuel P. Carter.
June 5, 1873. Commander K. Randolph Breese.
Oct. 31, 1874. Commander Edward Terry.

EXECUTIVE DUTY.

Reported.		Detached, resigned, or transferred.
1863.	Lieutenant-Commander C. C. Carpenter	1864
1864.	Lieutenant-Commander Alfred Hopkins	1865
1865.	Lieutenant-Commander James A. Greer	1866
1866.	Lieutenant-Commander Oscar F. Stanton...	1867
1866.	Lieutenant-Commander Bushrod B. Taylor..	1867
1867.	Lieutenant-Commander Thomas O. Selfridge.	1868
1868.	Lieutenant-Commander Charles L. Franklin.	1870
1870.	Lieutenant-Commander Henry L. Howison.	1871

DEPARTMENT OF SEAMANSHIP.

1850.	Lieut. Thomas T. Craven, (commandant) ...	1855
1855.	Lieut. Joseph F. Green, (commandant)	1858
1858.	Commander Thomas T. Craven, (commandant	1860
1860.	Lieut. William H. Parker.................	1861
1861.	Lieutenant-Commander Joseph N. Miller ...	1862
1862.	Lieutenant-Commander Stephen B. Luce....	1863
1863.	Lieutenant-Commander Marshall C. Campbell	1865
1865.	Lieutenant-Commander Robert F. R. Lewis.	1866
1866.	Lieutenant-Commander Richard W. Meade.	1868
1868.	Commander Joseph S. Skerrett	1872
1870.	Lieutenant-Commander A. R. Yates........	1871
1872.	Commander Frederick V. McNair	1875
1875.	Commander Henry L. Howison.	

ORDNANCE, GUNNERY, AND STEAM.

1845.	Lieut. James H. Ward	1847

Reported.		Detached, resigned, or transferred.
	ORDNANCE, GUNNERY, NATURAL AND EXPERIMENTAL PHILOSOPHY.	
1847.	Prof. Henry H. Lockwood	1850.
	GUNNERY AND INFANTRY TACTICS.	
1850.	Prof. Henry H. Lockwood	1860.
	ORDNANCE AND GUNNERY.	
1860.	Lieut. Edward Simpson	1861
1861.	Lieutenant-Commander Stephen B. Luce	1862
1862.	Lieutenant-Commander E. O. Matthews	1864
1864.	Lieutenant-Commander C. C. Carpenter	1865
1865.	Lieutenant-Commander Francis M. Ramsay	1866
1866.	Lieutenant-Commander Montgomery Sicard	1867
1867.	Lieutenant-Commander E. O. Matthews	1869
1869.	Lieutenant-Commander Edward Terry	1870
1870.	Commander Augustus P. Cooke	1873
1873.	Commander Edward Terry	1874
1874.	Commander John A. Howell	1875
1875.	Commander James O'Kane.	
	MATHEMATICS AND NAVIGATION.	
1845.	Prof. William Chauvenet	1853
	MATHEMATICS.	
1853.	Prof. John H. C. Coffin	1859
1859.	Prof. Joseph Winlock	1861
1861.	Prof. John H. C. Coffin	1864
1864.	Prof. William Henry Willcox	1870
1870.	Prof. Richard Somers Smith	1873
1873.	Prof. William Woodbury Hendrickson.	

Reported.		Detached, resigned, or transferred.
	STEAM-ENGINEERING.	
1865.	Chief Engineer William W. W. Wood	1867
1867.	Chief Engineer Thom Williamson	1869
1869.	Chief Engineer Henry L. Snyder	1873
1873.	Chief Engineer Charles Henry Baker.	
	NAVIGATION AND NAUTICAL ASTRONOMY.	
1853.	Prof. William Chauvenet	1859
1859.	Prof. John H. C. Coffin..................	1865
	ASTRONOMY, NAVIGATION, AND SURVEYING.	
1865.	Lieutenant-Commander Robert L. Phythian.	1870
1870.	Lieutenant-Commander John A. Howell....	1871
1871.	Lieutenant-Commander S. Dana Greene....	1873
1873.	Lieutenant-Commander Alexander H. McCormick	1875
1875.	Commander John A. Howell.	
	NATURAL AND EXPERIMENTAL PHILOSOPHY.	
1845.	Prof. Henry H. Lockwood................	1850
1850.	Prof. William Fenn Hopkins	1859
1859.	Prof. Augustus W. Smith..................	1866
1866.	Prof. Henry H. Lockwood................	1869
1869.	Lieutenant-Commander William T. Sampson.	1871
1871.	Lieutenant-Commander George P. Ryan....	1872
	PHYSICS AND CHEMISTRY.	
1872.	Lieutenant-Commander George P. Ryan....	1873
1873.	Prof. John M. Rice......................	1874
1875.	Commander William T. Sampson.	
	CHEMISTRY.	
1845.	Surgeon John A. Lockwood	1850

Reported.		Detached, resigned, or transferred.
	APPLIED MATHEMATICS AND MECHANICS.	
1876.	Prof. John M. Rice.	
	ENGLISH STUDIES.	
1845.	Chaplain George Jones....................	1850
	ETHICS AND ENGLISH STUDIES.	
1850.	Prof. Joseph E. Nourse..................	1865
1865.	Lieutenant-Commander Joseph N. Miller ...	1867
1867.	Lieutenant-Commander John S. Barnes.....	1868
1868.	Lieutenant-Commander F. B. Blake........	1869
1869.	Lieutenant-Commander Thomas L. Swann ..	1871
1871.	Lieutenant-Commander A. R. Yates........	1873
	ENGLISH STUDIES, HISTORY, AND LAW.	
1873.	Prof. James R. Soley.	
	MODERN LANGUAGES.	
1845.	Prof. A. N. Girault......................	1853
1873.	Commander W. S. Schley..................	1876
1876.	Prof. Lucien F. Prud'homme.	
	FRENCH.	
1853.	Prof. A. N. Girault......................	1866
1866.	Prof. L. V. Dovilliers....................	1871
1871.	Commander E. Y. McCauley	1873
	SPANISH.	
1853.	Prof. E. A. Roget.......................	1873
	DRAWING.	
1853.	Prof. E. Seager.........................	1867
1867.	Lieutenant-Commander Montgomery Sicard .	1868

Reported.		Detached, resigned, or transferred.
1868.	Lieutenant-Commander E. P. Lull	1871
1871.	Commander Frederick V. McNair..........	1872
1872.	Lieutenant-Commander Gouverneur K. Haswell	1873
1873.	Prof. Richard S. Smith.	

IN CHARGE OF SCHOOL-SHIPS.

1860.	Lieut. George W. Rodgers................	1861
1861.	Lieutenant-Commander E. P. Lull	1863
1862.	Lieutenant-Commander R. L. Phythian.....	1864
1863.	Lieut. Henry M. Blue	1864
1864.	Lieutenant-Commander P. C. Johnson......	1866
1867.	Lieutenant-Commander George Dewey.....	1870

NOTE J.

Supplementary notices.

Commander GEORGE P. UPSHUR, the second Superintendent of the Naval School, entered the service April 23, 1818. He was a native of Virginia. His administration of the school extended from March, 1847, to July, 1850, when he was relieved by Commander Stribling, at the re-organization of the institution. He had a large share in bringing about the change, being one of the members of the board of 1849 to which was intrusted the revision of the regulations. Commander Upshur went from the school to a command in the Mediterranean squadron. He died November 3, 1852, on board the sloop of war Levant, at Spezia.

Captain GEORGE W. RODGERS was a son of Captain George W. Rodgers, of Maryland, a distinguished naval officer of the war of 1812, and a nephew, through his mother, of Commodore Oliver H. Perry. He was attached to the Naval Academy in 1860–'62, at first in charge of the school-ship and afterward as commandant of midshipmen. The organization of the school-ship system, during the period when the quarters were insufficient for all the cadets, was mainly due to his judicious efforts. He commanded the Constitution when the war broke out, and brought her with the midshipmen to Newport. In 1862, he was detached from the Academy and entered into active service. During the attacks upon Charleston in 1863, he served as fleet-captain of Admiral Dahlgren's squadron, and later, in command of the monitor Catskill. It was while commanding this vessel, in a gallant attack on Fort Wagner, that he was killed, August 17, 1863. Admiral Dahlgren refers to his death in his report of the engagement: "The close and confidential relation which the duties of fleet-captain necessarily occasion, impressed me deeply with the loss of Captain Rodgers. Brave, intelligent, and highly capable, devoted to his duty and to the flag under which he passed his life, the country cannot afford to lose such men; of a kind and generous nature, he was always prompt to give relief when he could."

Lieut. SAMUEL MARCY was a son of Hon. William L. Marcy, of New York, Secretary of War under President Polk, and Secretary of State under President Pierce. He entered the Navy in 1838. In 1845 he was attached to the Naval School as assistant instructor in mathematics, being at that time a passed midshipman. He also assisted Lieutenant Ward in the performance of executive duty. He was detached in 1847, and between that time and 1861 he was twice connected with the Academy for considerable periods. He served with distinction during the first year of the war, and died January 29, 1862, from injuries received while firing a boat-howitzer at a blockade-runner in the Southeast Pass of the Mississippi River.

Prof. WILLIAM HENRY WILLCOX was born October 19, 1823. He entered the service as a midshipman January 30, 1841. He was ordered to the Academy as instructor under Commander Goldsborough, but resigned his commission as lieutenant June 19, 1857, and was soon afterward appointed an assistant professor of mathematics. He was commissioned professor of mathematics, June 3, 1858. In the summer of 1864, the department of mathematics, which had been since 1861 united with that of navigation, was made once more independent, and Professor Willcox was placed at the head. He remained in charge until the time of his death, August 20, 1870. He showed great skill in the management of his department, and devoted himself to the best interests of the Academy with a singleness of purpose seldom equaled.

He received the degree of A. M. from Yale College in 1870.

ERRATA.

Page 146, *line* 13. *For* "fire-bell," *read* "fire-bill."

Page 189, *after line* 23. *Insert:* "*Text-books of Cadet Midshipmen.*—Bourne's Handbook of the Steam-Engine; King's Practical Notes on the Steam-Engine."

Pages 189 *and* 190. NOTE.—In cases where practical instruction is given, in the Department of Steam-Engineering, part of the time otherwise devoted to study is occupied with practical exercises.

Page 190, *line* 8. *Insert:* "King's Practical Notes on the Steam-Engine; Willis's Principles of Mechanism; Zeuner's Valve Gear."

Page 331, *after line* 1. *Insert:*

"1867. Chief Engineer Eben Hoyt..1867."

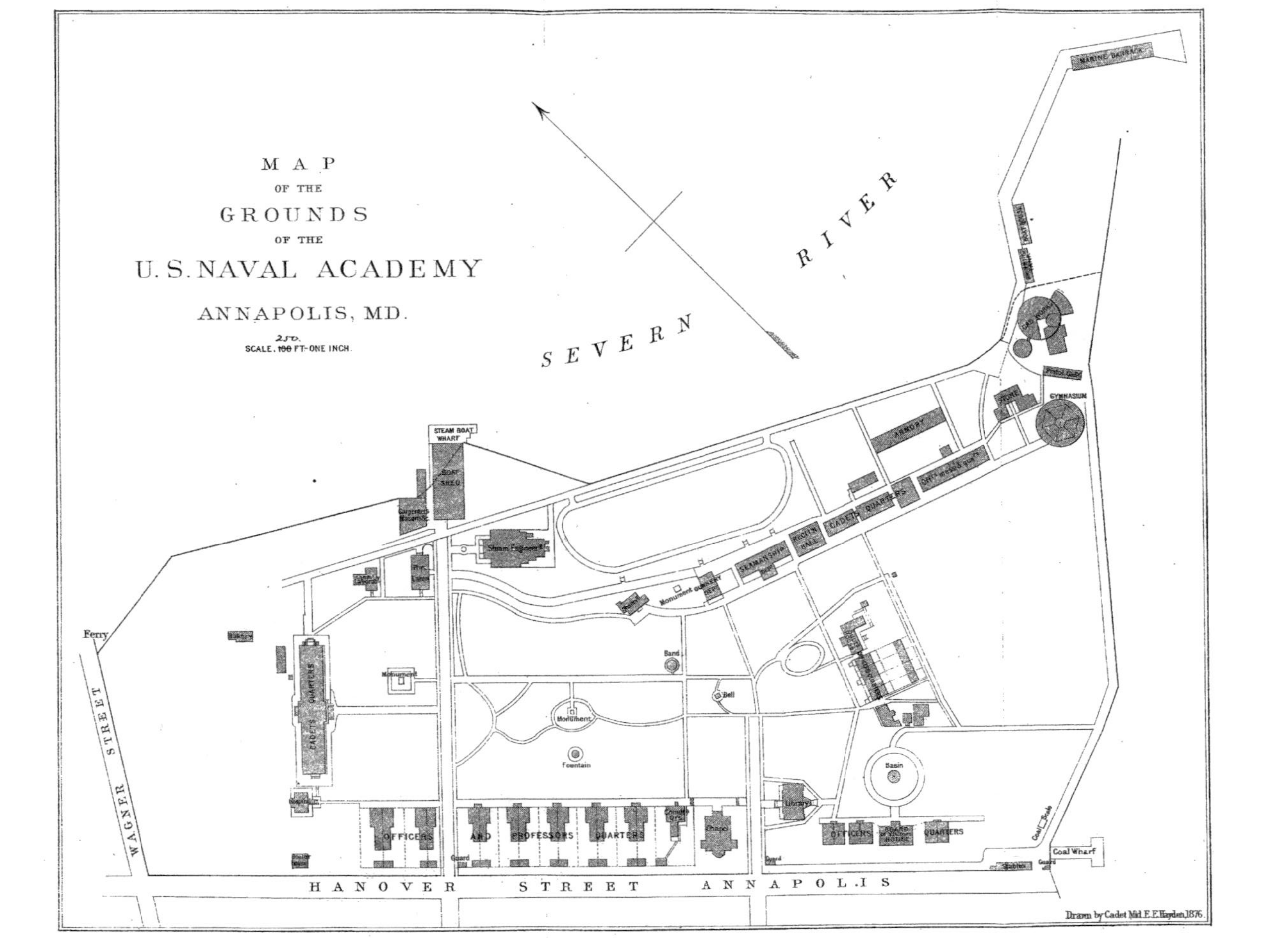
MAP
OF THE
GROUNDS
OF THE
U.S. NAVAL ACADEMY
ANNAPOLIS, MD.
SCALE. 250 FT-ONE INCH.
SEVERN
RIVER
MARINE BARRACK
GYMNASIUM
ARMORY
CADETS
QUARTERS
RECIT'N HALL
STEAM BOAT WHARF
BOAT SHED
Steam Engineer'g
Monument
Band
Bell
Fountain
Basin
Library
Chapel
OFFICERS
AND
PROFESSORS
QUARTERS
BOARD HOUSE
Guard
Stables
Coal Wharf
Ferry
CADETS QUARTERS
WAGNER STREET
HANOVER STREET ANNAPOLIS
Drawn by Cadet Mid. E. E. Hayden 1876.

INDEX.

A.

D.

G.

H.

I.

J.

O.

P.

U.

V.

W.

www.ingramcontent.com/pod-product-compliance
Lightning Source LLC
LaVergne TN
LVHW010159110826
845151LV00002B/552

9781425537562